PRACTICAL TRACKING

TRACKING

A Guide to Following Footprints and Finding Animals

Louis Liebenberg, Adriaan Louw,
and Mark Elbroch

STACKPOLE
BOOKS

Copyright © 2010 by Stackpole Books

Published by
STACKPOLE BOOKS
5067 Ritter Road
Mechanicsburg, PA 17055
www.stackpolebooks.com

Printed in Singapore

10 9 8 7 6 5 4 3 2 1

First edition

On the cover: Cougar by Mark Elbroch
Cover design by Wendy Reynolds
Photographs by the authors, as indicated
All drawings by Mark Elbroch

Library of Congress Cataloging-in-Publication Data

Elbroch, Mark.
    Practical tracking : a guide to following footprints and finding animals /
    Mark Elbroch, Adriaan Louw, and Louis Liebenberg. — 1st ed.
        p. cm.
    ISBN-13: 978-0-8117-3627-5
    ISBN-10: 0-8117-3627-X
    1. Animal tracks. 2. Tracking and trailing. I. Louw, Adriaan.
    II. Liebenberg, Louis. III. Title.

QL768.E43 2010
591.47'9—dc22
                                                                    2009028678

Contents

Introduction

Tracking skills are not magic; they are learned through patience and practice. Yet watching a master tracker work a trail can be magical, since we may not understand what they are doing, nor did we witness the years they invested in learning and acquiring their tracking skills. No one is born a tracker, and each of us has the potential to follow and find wildlife. This is a liberating revelation—anyone, regardless of background or race, can learn tracking skills.

Before we talk about the basics of tracking, we need to understand what tracking is. A common analogy is that the tracks of animals are like letters and words; tracking is like reading that text. When a child learns to read, the learning process starts with the identification of characters; in the western world, these are mainly the vowels and consonants of the alphabet. Characters are grouped together to form words, words are grouped together to form sentences, sentences to paragraphs, and so on. Eventually, it is the reader's ability to identify characters at speed, group them together, and interpret the context in which they appear that determines whether they learn to read or not. Reading is thus about identifying, following, and interpreting characters. To complete this analogy, tracking is identifying, following, and interpreting wildlife tracks and sign.

There are countless anecdotes about historic trackers who could follow their quarry across any terrain, or in total darkness, and who were able to reconstruct and age spoor with incomprehensible accuracy. But there are few truly accurate records of historic trackers or historic tracking skills. So we have turned to modern-day trackers in an attempt to better comprehend what was and what is possible in the field. We have been fortunate enough to meet amazing people and witness incredible tracking, and we are happy to report that everything we've seen in the field seems achievable given enough focus and practice.

Tracking was fundamental to hunting in early humans (Liebenberg 2006) and is still practiced today by hunter-gatherers, hunting guides, biologists, search-and-rescue teams, soldiers in war, and forensics investigators. Increasingly, people are also practicing wildlife tracking as a form of environmental education (Elbroch 2003) and to learn more about themselves (Young and Morgan 2006). This book is not about the why but rather about the how. Here we attempt to compile an inspirational and practical guide to learning to interpret tracks and sign, follow trails, and find wildlife.

What is shared in this book is the accumulated knowledge of the authors as well as all those they have been fortunate to meet through the growing community that participates in CyberTracker Conservation's Tracker Evaluations. The CyberTracker evaluation process

Animal tracks cover Newspaper Rock in southern Utah, a collection of petroglyphs estimated to be three thousand years old. ME

is divided into two parts: track and sign interpretation (identification and interpretation) and trailing (advanced interpretation, finding the animal). Track and sign interpretation is fundamental to competent tracking, but it is just the "letters" and "words" necessary to allow us to read. It is based upon the second component of CyberTracker tracker evaluations that this book is being developed: Here we will attempt to describe *all* the necessary components of competent tracking, and successfully finding quarry.

MODERN-DAY TRACKERS

*L*ouis tells a wonderful story about his first trip to LoneTree, a remote community in the Central Kalahari. Louis had been practicing tracking on his own in the hopes of developing the skills needed to pursue studies of tracking as used by Bushman communities. He was fortunate enough to meet a missionary who worked at LoneTree who assured him that he knew the top hunters there and that he could introduce them to Louis. One man, he told Louis, each week after Sunday mass, would recount all the animals he had successfully hunted during the previous week. And the preacher assured Louis they were always an impressive list.

So Louis successfully navigated the sandy roads deep into the bush to arrive at LoneTree. As promised, the preacher introduced Louis to an old Bushman hunter, who immediately began to assure Louis that he was among the very best. He proceeded to list all the animals that he had successfully killed in the recent past. Louis subsequently asked if the hunter would be willing to guide him on a hunt in the bush—to share what he knew with Louis. The hunter agreed, and then said that his great friend was also among the very best hunters, and he wanted to come along as well. Louis agreed, thrilled to have two potential master hunters instead of just one.

Overhearing the conversation, a young hunter named !Nate approached Louis and asked to join the expedition. He said that if the elders were going to teach him about tracking, he too would like to learn. Louis agreed, but only just in time for !Nate's friend to invite himself along on the trip as well. Feeling slightly overwhelmed, another old

Bushman came over and announced that he too would need to join the group. His name was !Nam!kabe, and he said that if the youngsters were to go along, he would need to join the group to make sure they didn't cause any trouble for Louis. And that was that; the group was assembled and with the addition of an interpreter they all set off the next morning into the wild bush east of the village.

Louis said that it was evident within the first day that the self-proclaimed top hunters were useless in the field but that !Nam!kabe was an indescribably gifted tracker and hunter. !Nate, !Nam!kabe's son, was also phenomenal. Louis said the same pattern repeated itself in every Bushman village in which he worked. He would ask who were the top hunters among them and then would approach those who did not speak out, who did not recount their prowess and success, and request that they guide him in the field.

—M. E.

GETTING STARTED

Each chapter in this book contributes a piece of the puzzle that is competent tracking. We start with a discussion of tracks and trails, then move on to other elements, including stealth and alertness. Then we attempt to put it all together and describe how these concepts are practiced in the field. Concepts and instruction are interlaced with stories that provide insight into tracking.

The authors are from both South Africa and North America. They have each tracked animals on both continents, and several others as well. Throughout the book, there are specific examples of diverse animals used to illustrate concepts relevant to developing tracking skills. Remember—tracking transcends location, and if you do not recognize the name of some animal, do not be distracted from the overall discussion. It doesn't matter what sort of animal you track, the concepts are all the same. Consider using Google images or other online or printed resources to look up animals unfamiliar to you. Visualizing each animal mentioned will be helpful, but do not allow unfamiliarity to become a distraction or hindrance in understanding what we are attempting to convey.

Enjoy!

1

Feet and Footprints

*I*t started out like so many days, except perhaps that the tracking
conditions were better than most. An inch of moist snow had fallen
during the night, and the crisp tracks of numerous animals interacted
with the roads. I had been charged by New Hampshire Audubon and the
state department of transportation with recording any animal tracks that
approached, entered, exited, or crossed two highways in northern New
Hampshire, just north of the Presidential Range. Our goal was to model
wildlife corridors and mitigate wildlife-automobile collisions by identifying locations for the construction of underpasses.

   I drove slowly along the road edge, searching for tracks, and my
assistant, Rose Graves, held the Garmin unit and recorded what we
found. Sunlight glittered like diamonds on the white snow, and, as the
morning waned, the day warmed enough so that the snow melted and
receded from the asphalt. We pulled into the Water Wheel Restaurant for
a rest, then to search the back of the parking lot for any animals that had
escaped our notice. Nothing. So we moved on. I stretched my neck backwards to look for traffic and began to pull out of the lot.

   "Wait!" Rose exclaimed. "There's something there." She paused.
"Oh, it's just a dog."

   I stopped anyway, just to be sure. I hopped out of the truck and
circled to the passenger side. The tracks were swollen and melting. They
were big, the nails were evident, and the tracks were splayed and skewed
as the animal raced up the shallow embankment to the cover of forest. But
something wasn't right for a dog. The toes and metacarpal pads were
strangely shaped. The behavior—crossing the road in such a rush—was

also off. And why were they there, where the forest edge snuck in close to the road, as if embracing it?

"What is it?" Rose asked from the passenger seat.

"Just a moment," I said. I was reluctant to say, because recognition was just dawning, and I couldn't believe it. I crossed the road and dropped off the embankment into a thicket of young fir trees to view the tracks in snow that hadn't yet begun to melt. The animal had twisted through the tight understory, forcing me to my knees to follow. Several yards into the thicket, the animal sat, as if assessing the road before crossing it. The behavior was unmistakable and the last confirmation I needed.

"Well?" Rose asked. She stood atop the crest of the road, peering down at me.

"Holy shit," I said, "this is a freakin' lynx!" I couldn't contain my excitement, but the tracks did not lie. Large footprints, muffled rather than distinct due to the copious fur on the underside of their feet. The animal walked rather than trotted and chose to move through the densest thicket it could find to approach the road, so typical of bobcats and lynx. I kept trying to talk myself out of it, but I couldn't. The evidence was plain. Rose was clearly skeptical.

"We need a camera," I said, mounting the road surface, electrified by our discovery. We raced back to town, retrieved my camera, and rushed back to the spot. The snow had now completely melted along the road edges—if we'd been an hour later, we'd have easily overlooked the tracks. I gave Rose another Garmin unit and sent her south to follow and record the trail. I went north, and we agreed to meet back at the vehicle in several hours.

It was a joy to follow the trail, picturing the lynx skirting the edges of fields and lingering where hare sign was plentiful. The cat moved steadily north, tightrope-walking fallen logs, trotting when exposed, and slowing when under the cover of forests. At regular intervals, I photographed the trail, including a ruler for scale. By mid-afternoon, Rose and I had each recorded several miles of trail, and, when we were finished, we immediately reported our discovery to our project coordinator.

Our report created an explosion of media attention and controversy. It was the second lynx to have been recorded in New Hampshire in sixty years. The first was an animal killed on a highway to the south of our

Tracks of a rare Canada lynx in northern New Hampshire tightrope-walking along a fallen tree. ME

*research site. In general, people were thrilled with the news, and news-
papers and radio recounted our tale throughout New England.*

*The United States Forest Service was not so easily convinced, how-
ever, and announced that they would not acknowledge the find without a
DNA sample to confirm the identification. Sadly, footprints alone are
often not considered scientific evidence for the record of a rare species, or
they are the sort of evidence easily contended and ignored. Every other
agency had accepted my photographs with rulers as sufficient documenta-
tion, and it frustrated me that the U.S.F.S. would be so stubborn.*

*When I met Rose two days later to return to our routine and begin
running our transect, I updated her on the chaos. "If we'd only found a
scat," I said, "we'd have our DNA sample."*

"I saw a scat," Rose said. What?! *After quizzing her to see if she
could remember the spot, we raced to the large field on a small dirt road
that she had crossed when back-tracking the lynx. Both the cat's and
Rose's footprints were still preserved in the snow layer. We nearly ran up
the hill and into the clear-cut above, zigzagging as we followed the lynx
(and Rose) and negotiated brush and debris. And then I came to the spot
Rose had described—the lynx had squatted atop a low stump, and defecated. I snatched it up, and, with the help of Jennifer Vashon at Maine
Fish and Game, we sent it to a genetics lab in Montana. They confirmed
it: The scat was from a purebred adult female Canada lynx,* Lynx
canadensis.

—M. E.

SPOOR IDENTIFICATION

While species may be identified by some general characteristics,
each individual animal's spoor (a footprint or track) differs in subtle
ways; it is, in principle, possible to identify an individual animal
from its spoor. Apart from the functional and environmental adaptations of the species, an individual animal's spoor may vary according to its age, mass, sex, condition, and the terrain, as well as random
variations. The animal might also have a unique way of walking or
a particular habit that distinguishes it from others. Kalahari San

trackers, for example, can distinguish the antelope they have shot from the rest of the herd and track down that individual.

While the spoor of most larger mammals and birds can be identified as belonging to a particular species, the spoor of smaller animals might be identified only as belonging to a genus, family, or order. The smaller the animal, the more difficult it becomes to distinguish its spoor from that of similar species, and while some mammal families consist of only a few species, insect families may contain many. Some antelope may have spoor typical of their species but variations may also occur that are similar to those of other species.

Steenbok spoor, for example, are usually sharply pointed with straight sides, while duiker spoor are normally more rounded. However, some steenbok may have spoor similar to typical duiker spoor, and vice versa. A small antelope spoor that has a typical steenbok shape could therefore only be identified as probably steenbok, but possibly also duiker, unless other evidence rules out either possibility. Even in soft sand, where the shape of the hoof is not clear, the species can be distinguished by the way they tread. Steenbok tread with their hoofs pointing down into the ground while duiker treads in a more flat-footed way. Furthermore, the presence of droppings may indicate the species, since steenbok normally bury their droppings while duikers do not.

The best footprints are usually found in damp, slightly muddy earth, wet sand, a thin layer of loose dust on firm substrate, or a thin layer of fresh snow. Ideal wet conditions are found along streams, rivers, waterholes, dams, wetlands, beaches, after rain, or in the morning when the sand is still damp from dew. Puddles that have just dried out, leaving a thin layer of silt over a firm substrate, are ideal for the tracks of small animals. Dirt roads and paths might have a thin layer of very fine dust on firm ground that can reveal the finest details of the spoor.

Usually, however, footprints are partially obliterated, and one should walk up and down the trail to find the best imprints. Even if no clear footprints can be found, one can collect bits of information

Front and hind steenbok tracks. ME

by studying several footprints and then piece them together to compile an image of the complete spoor.

When you study spoor in loose sand, try to visualize the shape of the footprint before the loose sand grains slid together to obliterate the well-defined features. As much information may be lost in loose sand, it is not always possible to distinguish the spoor of similar species. When loose wind-blown sand has accumulated in a footprint that was made in damp or wet sand, it is sometimes possible to carefully blow away the loose sand to reveal the features of the spoor underneath. Footprints in mud may in fact be preserved for quite a long time underneath a layer of loose sand. When blowing away the sand, however, great care must be taken to not destroy the footprint itself. When leaves are covering the spoor, or even when the animal has stepped on top of leaves, they can be carefully removed to reveal the spoor underneath. This is especially the case in a forest, where the wet or damp earth may be covered by a layer of leaves.

Footprints can be distorted owing to slipping and twisting of the feet on the ground. When an animal is

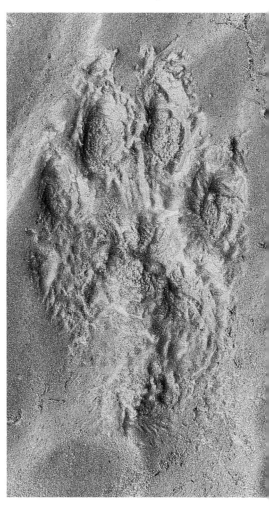

A perfect fisher track along a silty riverbank. ME

walking on a slope or running, its feet might slip, so the spoor may appear elongated or warped. If the fore and hind spoor are super-imposed, it may look like an elongated spoor, or the toes of the fore footprint may be confused with those of the hind. When an animal is trotting or running, its mass is supported mainly by the toes, and only part of the metacarpal/metatarsal pads may show. On hard ground, padded toes may not show and only claw marks may be seen.

If the spoor could be that of several possible species, known dis-tribution, habitat preference, and habits should be considered. Socia-bility and daily rhythm, as well as feeding signs and feces, should be included in your analysis to narrow down the range of possibilities.

The best way to learn how to recognize a track is to prepare an accurate sketch showing its exact dimensions. This compels one to note all the details of the footprint and therefore remember them

Louis Liebenberg drawing a gray wolf track in central Idaho. ME

better. Sketching also helps create an image of the tracks in your mind, which helps you recognize them in varied substrates.

Spoor identification requires not only a great deal of knowledge but also skill and experience. Although the inexperienced naturalist should, in principle, be able to use a field guide to identify near-perfect spoor in ideal conditions, the accurate identification of imperfect spoor, especially in loose sand or very hard ground, may be possible only after considerable experience.

ANATOMY OF FEET

Variations Between Species

Different species can be identified by variations in their respective morphologies. The most notable characteristics are usually determined by functional and environmental adaptations of the feet. Similar species may also be differentiated by subtle differences in the size and shape of the feet. Understanding characteristic features of spoor enables trackers to analyze fractional or partially obliterated spoor which may otherwise be difficult to identify and interpret.

Functional adaptations of feet might be for specific types of locomotion or for use as tools or as weapons. Feet adapted for speed will have only a small area in contact with the ground relative to the size of the animal; the exceptions to this general rule are animals adapted to northern climates, which have disproportionately larger feet to aid them in snow. The feet of predators have soft pads for stealth, and some have sharp claws to hold down their prey while others have short blunt claws that aid in traction. Some animals have claws that are well-developed digging tools and others that are adapted for grooming.

Feet can have specific environmental adaptations for different types of terrestrial, aquatic, or arboreal environments. Feet adapted for soft muddy ground require a large contact area for support. In soft sandy terrain, sharp pointed hooves can dig into the sand to obtain a firm grip, while on firm ground hooves need to be rounder. On hard rocky surfaces, small rounded hooves can find small footholds

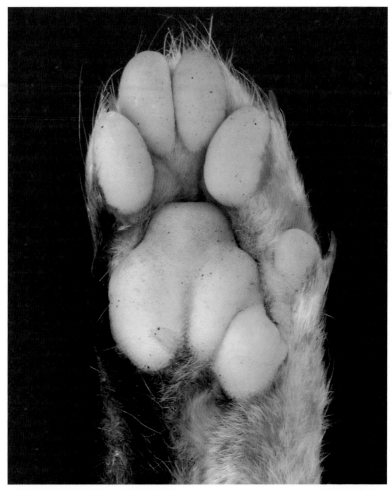

The delicate pads on the hind foot of a ringtail, an animal very much like the genet in Africa. ME

and indentations for swift agile movement. Some animals, such as otters, are adapted to semiaquatic environments and are able to move on dry ground and swim well. Other animals, such as seals, are mainly adapted to an aquatic environment. Animals adapted to swimming usually have webbed toes to increase the area of the feet and, therefore, the resistance with which to pull themselves through the water. Animals adapted to arboreal environments usually have sharp claws that dig into the bark of trees (such as squirrels) or they have opposable joints or toes that can grasp branches (examples with joints are fishers and martens; examples with toes are monkeys and birds). Some animals, such as cats, are terrestrial but also able to climb trees.

Apart from functional and environmental adaptations, feet might also have redundant features. The first toe of many species, for example, is reduced and has become redundant but may still show in the spoor.

Heavier animals usually have larger feet to support their mass, but the shape of the feet is also determined by the animal's body structure. A strongly built animal usually has broader feet and rounder toes while an animal with a slender body build has more narrow feet with slender toes. This can be seen when comparing the

The padded feet of a lioness. AL

broader spoor of the bat-eared fox with the more slender spoor of the Cape fox, or the broader spoor of the caracal with the slender spoor of the serval. It can also be seen in variations in the shape of hooves of ungulates.

The exact shape of an animal's foot need not have any specific function but might be an arbitrary shape determined by random variation. Antelope hooves might have straight, hollow, or rounded sides, with no apparent reason why one variation should be an advantage over another. Yet these features might be characteristic of a species.

Variations Within a Species
While species can be identified by characteristic features, there also exist individual variations within a species. These variations make it possible for an expert tracker to determine the sex as well as an approximate estimation of an animal's age, size, and mass. A tracker might also be able to identify a specific individual by its spoor. Stander (1997) tested these abilities in four Ju/'Hoan San trackers in Namibia, and they answered 557 of 569 questions correctly. The Ju/'Hoan trackers correctly identified the species of the spoor in 100 percent of the tests. They correctly identified the relative age of cheetahs and leopards (juvenile, cub, young adult, or adult) 100 percent of the time in 30 tests but the relative age of African lions only 34 out of 39 times (87 percent)—their mistakes were all in identifying a subadult animal as a full adult. They correctly identified the sex of lions in 100 percent of 39 tests, cheetahs in 12 of 13 tests, and leopards in 16 of 17 tests. They also correctly identified the individual lion, leopard, or cheetah by its tracks in 30 of 32 tests (96.4 percent).

The sexes are usually distinguished by the fact that the males in mammals are usually larger than the females, or by exceptions such as the spotted hyena and some of the smaller antelopes in which the females are larger than the males. Females of most predatory birds are also larger than males. The more massive body structures of the larger sex are evident in the fact that their forefeet are usually proportionately broader, as are their trails. While the spoor of adult males are usually larger than that of adult females, those of young males may be the same size as those of adult females, but young males' forefeet may be broader due to their more massive body structure. For example, in cougars, the tracks of young males are typically much larger than their mothers' by sixteen months of age. But the width of their trails is proportionately larger than their mothers' at an even younger age, a difference that becomes more pronounced as the males reach their full body mass.

The sexes can also be distinguished by association. The spoor of an adult in close association with a young is probably that of a female. Nursery herds can be identified by the presence of several young; the absence of young might indicate a bachelor herd. When a species is gregarious, a solitary individual will probably be an adult male. The sex can also be determined by the relative position of the urine to the back feet or feces, or by behaviors such as leg lifting and squatting (see chapter 3).

The age of an animal can be indicated by the size of the feet. The hooves of young antelope will also have sharper edges, while older individuals may have blunted hooves with chipped edges. In animals with padded feet, younger individuals might have more rounded pads. Some animals have specific breeding periods. If you know at what time of the year an animal is born and the relative growth rates for the species, you can often make an accurate estimate of a young animal's age.

The size of an animal is proportional to the size of the spoor while its mass may be indicated by the depth of the imprint. It should be noted that the depth of the imprint also depends on the firmness of the ground. Two animals might be the same size, in which case their spoor will be about the same size, but one might be more massive and therefore make deeper imprints. A small animal might have the same mass as a larger animal but have smaller feet that will consequently leave deeper imprints. A larger animal must be proportionally more massive than a smaller animal to leave the same depth of imprints. The depth of the imprint is determined by the pressure exerted: The pressure is equal to the weight of the

Right front track　　　　　　Right hind track

FEMALE LEOPARD

Right front track　　　　　　Right hind track

MALE LEOPARD

cm
Reduced

Male and female leopard tracks. LL

animal divided by the area in contact with the ground at any one time. The weight, or gravitational force, is equal to the mass of the animal multiplied by the acceleration due to gravity at the earth's surface. The depth of the imprint is also determined by the pressure exerted due to the acceleration of the animal. When running or jumping, an animal will leave deeper imprints than when it's walking slowly.

Apart from features characteristic of a species there also exist random variations within a species that can vary from individual to individual. The exact shapes of the feet of every individual are unique; it is therefore in principle possible to identify an individual animal by its tracks. In practice, this requires considerable skill and experience and is usually possible only with large animals. With elephant and rhinoceros, it is easy to identify an individual by the random pattern of cracks underneath the feet.

The shape of feet can also be altered by environmental factors. In hard rocky terrain, hooves of ungulates might be blunted by

Individual elephants can be identified by expert trackers by the distinctive patterns of cracks on their feet. AL

excessive wear; in soft sandy terrain, ungulates might develop elongated hooves due to the lack of natural wear. Similarly, animals such as jackals might develop elongated claws in soft terrain, or their claws might be worn down in hard terrain. Accidental alteration can also occur. A claw or even a toe can be broken or lost. Hooves can be chipped or broken. Mammals are injured in contests, survival, or in escaping human traps, and these injuries and peculiarities are particularly useful in identifying individuals in the field.

Variation of an Individual's Spoor

The shape of a footprint can vary considerably depending on the substrate. In very soft ground, an antelope's toes splay out, and the feet sink and appear larger because the dew claws also show in the spoor. On hard dusty ground, the dew claws may not show and the spoor appears shorter. The toes of padded feet are rounded in soft ground but will spread out on firm ground to appear larger and different in shape. On very hard ground, only the tips or edges of hooves might show, or only the claws of padded feet might show. In soft loose sand a spoor loses definition, and it requires considerable experience to identify and interpret it.

Movement and activities also change the shape of spoor. The feet might have slipped to create the impression of elongated toes. Twisting and dragging of the feet might partially obliterate some features. The forefeet and hind feet might be superimposed so the toes of one foot might be confused with those of another. When an animal is moving slowly, its toes might be together; they might splay out when the animal is running. Some species have tremendous control over how much they spread their feet. Cats walking in soft mud or wet snow, for instance, splay their feet and leave tracks nearly twice the dimensions as those on firm ground. The spoor also indicates whether the animal was lying, sitting, standing, walking, trotting, running, or jumping. Different activities might be evident, such as digging, scratching, eating, drinking, mating, or fighting. The condition of the animal might also be evident in the spoor. The spoor can also indicate whether the animal is still fresh, tired, or injured.

STRUCTURE OF FEET

Primitive mammals had five clawed toes on each foot, and they were plantigrade, that is, they trod on all the bones making up the foot (Hildebrand and Goslow 2001). This primitive type of foot is found today in some insectivorous small mammals and rodents. In animals with five well-developed toes, they are numbered from one to five, beginning with the inner toe, which corresponds to the human thumb. The third toe in most mammals is the longest, followed in order by the fourth, second, fifth, and first. If all five toes show in the footprint, the inner toe is the shortest. In many cases the first toe only makes a weak impression, sometimes none at all, and the footprint will show four toes, with the outer toe the shortest. If all five toes are showing and the shortest toe is on the left side of the footprint, the track was made by the right foot. If only four toes are showing and the shortest toe is on the right side of the footprint, then the track was also made by the right foot (Bang and Dahlstrom 1972).

The undersides of the feet are protected by pads—thick elastic masses of connective tissue covered by a strong, flexible, horny layer. The secretion of sweat glands in the pads is transferred to the footprint, giving it a scent. The pads themselves are naked, but, in most animals, the skin between them is covered with hair. There is a toe pad beneath the tip of each toe (this is also known as the digital pad). Behind the toe pads is a further row of pads, called the metacarpal pads on the front feet and the metatarsal pads on the hind feet; these correspond to the respective bones they protect (Elbroch 2003). These pads on the forefeet are also known as the "palmar pads"; on the hind feet, they're known as the "plantar pads." In many animals, the metacarpal/metatarsal pads are fused to form a single large pad. As well, some animals have one or two additional pads to the posterior. The larger is the carpal pad, which covers the carpal bone. When there is a second, it is another metacarpal pad linked with a reduced and sometimes redundant inner digit. Carpal pads are found only on the forefeet of mammals.

The skeletal structure of the forefoot comprises the carpal bones, metacarpal bones, and phalanges while that of the hind foot comprises the tarsal bones, metatarsal bones, and phalanges. While the

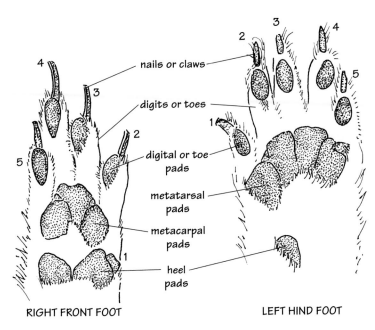

nails or claws

digits or toes

digital or toe
pads

metatarsal
pads

metacarpal
pads

heel
pads

RIGHT FRONT FOOT

LEFT HIND FOOT

Gray squirrel (numbers refer to digital formula).

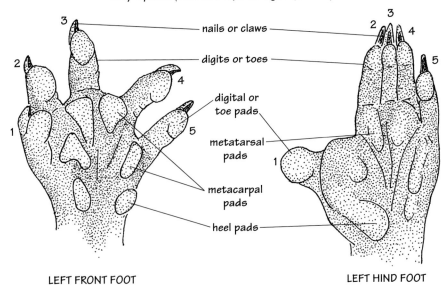

nails or claws

digits or toes

digital or
toe pads

metatarsal
pads

metacarpal
pads

heel pads

LEFT FRONT FOOT

LEFT HIND FOOT

Opossum

first toe consists of two phalanges, the other toes each consist of three. Each toe of the forefoot articulates (forms a joint) with a metacarpal bone, which in turn articulates with a distal carpal bone. The toes of the hind foot articulate with the metatarsal bones, which in turn articulate with the distal tarsal bones.

Primates, including humans, support their weight on the whole foot. Most mammals support their weight on the distal ends, or heads, of the metacarpal bones and the phalanges of the forefeet and the distal ends of the metatarsal and phalanges of the hind feet. Most ungulates support their weight only on the tips of the distal phalanges of the third and fourth toes.

Plantigrade animals have relatively short limbs and normally move at a steady pace because the construction of their feet is not well adapted for jumping or running any distance. An animal that runs fast over long distances must have long limbs, and the area of foot in contact with the ground must be as small as possible (except in snowy climates, where they are disproportionately larger). In order to obtain a firm grip, the foot must exert the greatest possible pressure to dig into the ground. Pressure is equal to force per area: For any given force, which depends on the mass of the animal and its acceleration, the contact area must be as small as possible to ensure the greatest possible pressure. Animals whose survival depends on their ability to run very fast do so on their toes or the tips of their toes. By elongation of the limb bones, they have developed long slender legs, and at the same time there has been a reduction in the number of toes. The toes on which they support their weight also have become very powerfully developed. The most common reduction involves the first toe, which might disappear completely so that the animal becomes four-toed. The second and fifth toe may be reduced, as in antelope, to form dew claws, while the weight is supported on the third and fourth toes. In the equids, the third toe is fully developed and ends in a hoof, and only the vestiges of the second and fourth, the splint bones, are present (Hildebrand and Goslow 2001).

In most mammals, the prints of the forefeet are larger and broader than those of the hind feet. The toes of the forefeet are

Female kudu exemplify the cervid and antelope form—long legs and small feet. NIKE ALBERTS/ISTOCKPHOTO.COM

usually also more splayed than those of the hind feet. This is because the forefeet need to cover a larger area to support the head, chest cavity, and forequarters of the body, which are usually heavier than the hindquarters. Some mammals, such as rodents and otters, have larger hind feet because the hindquarters are more massive than the head and forequarters. The forefeet are rounder in shape than the narrower hind feet because the forelegs are almost perpendicular to the ground while the hind legs are at an angle to the ground. A cylinder that is perpendicular to a plane has a circular cross-section; a cylinder that meets a plane at an angle has a larger elliptical cross-section.

TYPES OF FEET

The feet of most insectivorous small mammals and rodents are protected by small round pads, and the thin sharp claws are an adaptation for climbing and digging. Squirrels, for example, are able to climb up a vertical tree trunk by digging their sharp claws into the bark of the tree. Hedgehogs and porcupines have larger pads to support their more massive bodies. While the claws of the forefeet of the African porcupine, skunks, badgers, canerats, and spring hares are well adapted for digging, the broad pointed claws of the hind feet of the spring-hare are adapted for throwing the loosened soil clear of excavations.

All predators have well-developed pads adapted for stealth. They also have well-developed carpal pads to give them support on soft muddy ground, or when they are running or gripping prey. This can be seen in some of the mongooses, such as the large gray mongoose and the water mongoose. Mongooses adapted to drier or more arid conditions, such as the yellow mongoose, show only four toes and metacarpal/metatarsal pads, like canid or felid tracks in miniature. Otters have not only well-developed carpal pads to give them support on soft muddy ground but also webs between the toes for swimming.

While some mongooses, such as the slender mongoose, and American martens and fishers have thin sharp claws for climbing trees, many mongooses, as well as the suricate, striped polecat, striped skunks, badgers, and bat-eared fox, have long strong claws on the forefeet adapted for digging. Some predators, such as wolves, wild dogs, and cheetahs, which hunt in open terrain and rely on speed to capture their prey, have short blunt claws that act like spikes to prevent slipping. Some, such as the cheetah and caracal,

An eastern fox squirrel clings to a tree. Note the hind feet, which can point straight backwards to allow head-first descents, and the nimble toes tipped in sharp claws. ME have ridges under the metacarpal/metatarsal pads to give them additional traction. Most of the cats rely on stealth to stalk their prey in terrain that provides adequate cover. Even though the claws might be protracted to prevent slipping while charging, they cannot maintain high speeds, so they embrace their prey and hold it with their sharp claws to stop it from getting away while they deliver a killing bite. When not in use, their claws are retracted into sheaths to protect them from wearing down. The claws therefore do not show in the spoor, except when the animal is charging or slipping. The claws are protractile rather than retractable since their normal position, with the muscles at rest, is retracted within the sheaths; they are extended by the ligaments when required.

The padded feet of the rock dassie allow it to negotiate steep and often smooth rocky surfaces. The soles of the feet are naked, the skin thick and padded with glandular tissue that keeps the surface permanently moist.

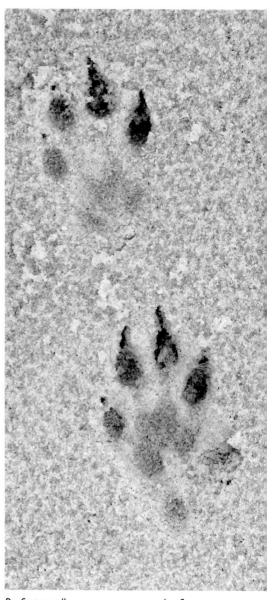

Perfect small gray mongoose tracks, front below, hind above, in beach dunes near Cape Town, South Africa. ME

Perfect rock dassie tracks can be sometimes difficult to find, given their prefer-
ences for rock jumbles and cliff sides. Note the grooming claws on the inside of
each hind foot (at the top of the photo). ME

The toes are short, ending in hooflike nails. The inner toe of the hind foot has a curved grooming claw (Smithers 1983).

Rabbits and hares lack pads. Instead, they have a tight springy layer of strong stiff hairs (Bang and Dahlstrom 1972). While the claws prevent slipping, the hairs muffle the sound of the feet as the animals run. The dense growth of the hair in the sole of the foot tends to obliterate the characteristics of the footprint.

The hands and feet of primates are adapted to grasping branches and ideally suited for an arboreal way of life. Bushbabies have grooming claws on the second toes of their hind feet (Smithers 1983). Antbears and pangolins have well-developed strong claws for breaking open and digging into termite nests, and North American porcupines have similar claws for climbing trees and digging up truffles.

The feet of elephants, rhinoceroses, and hippopotamuses are adapted mainly to support their massive bodies. Rhinoceroses and hippopotamuses have large broad toes to increase the area in contact with the ground. Elephants have springy feet that consist of a mass of soft muscles and ligaments, which enable them to move very silently (Lyell 1929).

Equids have only one toe, the third, on each leg and only tread on the outermost toe joint, which has a well-developed hoof. A hoof is a modified claw, and the wall of the hoof usually extends a short distance beyond the sole. In soft sand, the toe pad, or "frog," shows clearly in the spoor. In tracks on very hard substrates, only the edge of the hoof might appear in the footprint, as is also the case with animals with cloven hooves. Hooves are an adaptation for speed, which is essential for the survival of an ungulate.

Ungulates with cloven hooves have four toes, the first toe being absent, but they only tread on the tips of the third and fourth, which are well developed. The second and fifth toes, the dew claws, are much smaller and are at the rear of the foot. They are usually positioned so high up on the leg that they do not touch the ground, except when the animal treads in soft mud or is running at full speed. The hoof consists of the wall, which encloses the sole, and the toe pad behind the sole. In very distinct tracks, the toe pad can

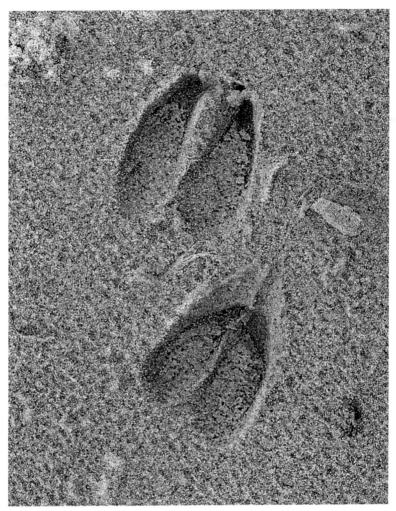

Tracks of a white-tailed deer illustrate a versatile heart-shaped morphology. ME

appear as a round depression. In some cases, it extends to the tip of the hoof. The impressions of the two halves of the hoof are usually almost mirror images of each other. The track made by the forefoot is larger and more splayed than that of the hind foot. When the animal is moving fast, the front hooves splay even more.

Apart from random variations, the shapes of hooves are adapted for different conditions. The more massive ungulates, such as American bison, Cape buffalo, and eland, have broad round hooves, while lighter antelope and deer have slender narrow hooves. Very sharp pointed hooves are an adaptation for speed, especially in soft sandy substrate, and act like spikes to prevent slipping. Pronghorn, steenbok, oribi, and springbok, which prefer open terrain, have to rely on speed to escape capture and have sharp pointed hooves. Larger antelope, such as gemsbok, which prefer open country, have hooves that are broad to support their massive bodies and pointed for speed, especially in soft sand. On the other extreme, the klipspringer has small rounded hooves that are adapted for agility on rocky terrain. The small rounded hooves ensure not only a firm foothold on rocky surfaces but also enable the klipspringer to change direction abruptly as it leaps from rock to rock.

Hooves can vary widely, from sharply pointed to rounded. While specialization, such as adaptation for speed in open terrain or agility in rocky terrain, has advantages, it also has disadvantages, for as more efficient performance is gained for a given function, efficiency in performance of alternative or complementary functions is lost. In contrast, a generalized form preserves a more-or-less versatile balance in performing various functions, although less efficiently in each case. For example, the heart-shaped hoof, such as that of North American deer, duiker, bushbuck, and kudu, is not as specialized but more versatile. These animals rely more on cover to escape detection, and, when detected, rely on a combination of speed and agility to swiftly find their way among bushes and other obstacles. For smaller duikers, sharply pointed hooves might be a disadvantage as they tend to fork up leaves in a forest habitat. In contrast, hooves that are too round might slip on leaves.

Another specialized adaptation is the long, slender, widely splayed hooves of the sitatunga, which are adapted to soft muddy substrate, papyrus, and other floating vegetation. Because of surface tension, toes that are splayed out distribute weight over a larger area. The toes of the reedbuck may be closer together on firm substrate but splay out in soft mud.

2

Gaits and Track Patterns

I hadn't been in Africa but a week before I was evaluated for the first
time. And if I were not nervous enough about having my tracking
skills tested by Louis Liebenberg, I was also being evaluated by a
stern-looking man called Vet Piet, who had been introduced as the indis-
putable top tracker in the entire southern Kalahari region of southern
Africa. There had been documentaries made about this man; he was the
stuff of legend.

We drove two Land Rovers over red sand dunes into the heart of the
Kgalagadi Transfrontier Park, a joint national park straddling the boundaries of Botswana and South Africa. It was also Vet Piet's homeland. The
vehicles were weighed down with supplies to camp for a week and all the
people involved: ten evaluation participants and several cooks from the
San community at the park's southern entrance, two evaluators, and several visitors, including myself. Vet Piet rode in the forward vehicle and I
in the second.

Suddenly, we came to a halt. Vet Piet exited the first vehicle and
walked ahead, studying the ground. Louis joined him, and I could see
them forming questions. They announced that the evaluation was to
begin. Louis called me to the front of the queue, telling me that he wanted
me to go first so I could watch the process while the others in turn were
asked the same questions.

There were four questions to start. Vet Piet used the horn of a gemsbok antelope to point to a footprint. He spoke in Afrikaans, and Louis
interpreted. "One: What animal made this track? Two: Is it a male or a
female? Three: How was the animal moving from here to there?" He

pointed with his gemsbok horn to a spot perhaps ten yards away. "Four: Why did the animal change the way it was moving?"

There was nothing for me to do but dive in. I stared at the first track. I recognized it—it looked like the footprint of a cougar. Leopard, I thought, and the shape made me think it was the track of a female. I followed her trail to see what she was doing. She walked for about five yards and stopped, placing her front feet together, then moved off at a trot in a southwestern direction. I relayed this information to my evaluators. Their faces remained impassive. They waited patiently for my response to the fourth question.

I cannot describe the speed with which my mind raced through the possibilities of why this animal might have stopped and then sped off in a new direction. I was in the presence of one of the top trackers in the world—what could he see in this trail? What could he interpret about what this leopard was doing that I could not? Round and round my mind went, but in the end I decided to play it safe. I stuck to what I was sure had occurred, stopping short of making up an elaborate tale I could not substantiate.

"She heard something," I pointed to where she stopped, "and she's going to check it out. It's something she's interested in." Louis recorded my answers. Neither Louis nor Vet Piet so much as wrinkled their noses. Both would be excellent at poker. Then, one by one, the other participants went through the same set of questions. Truthfully, I could only learn so much watching them, as no one spoke English. When the last had answered, we gathered around Vet Piet, who told us what he thought about the tracks.

"It is a leopard. It is a female. She was moving like this." Vet Piet did not use words to describe her gaits, but instead acted them out. He mimicked her rolling walk and how she stopped and raised her head. He then mimicked her faster trotting gait, pointing with his horn into the distance. Then he paused. I was near bursting with expectation, dying to know how he would interpret the trail. Others appeared just as eager, and the group seemed to hold its breath.

"She has heard something," and again he pointed to the spot where she paused. "She has heard either a male leopard calling or something she might like to hunt." He looked in the direction she had traveled. "There is

Front and hind tracks of a female leopard—my first evaluation question in the southern Kalahari. ME

only one way to be sure. We must follow her." So off we went, Vet Piet pointing out her trail, and our entire group following behind. The leopard had covered the open terrain quickly, but as she climbed and approached a view of the next valley, she began zigzagging from shrub to shrub. Near one shrub, she sat down, and we could see where she arched her neck and body to look beyond it. Using what available cover she had, the leopard moved on.

Vet Piet turned back to the vehicles. "You see, she is hunting."

She had clearly heard some potential prey. This leopard behaved like any hunting bobcat or mountain lion I had tracked in North America. The tracks told the story, and Vet Piet and I had found a common language.

—M. E.

Competent trackers complete two tasks in interpreting a series of animal tracks. First, they analyze the pattern of tracks on the ground in order to visualize how the animal was moving. Second, they interpret the behavior—the meaning in what they are seeing. The first task is more systematic and scientific; the second more speculative. Let's take each in turn.

The trail of a Cape clawless otter along a beach in South Africa. ME

WHAT IS A GAIT?

A gait describes the way in which an animal is moving; it is not a description of a specific track pattern. There will be numerous track patterns for each gait, depending on the speed and behavior of the animal as well as the anatomy and morphology of the species.

We must also be aware of the complications caused by language. Trackers around the globe use different words to describe the same thing. Some people prefer words that describe track patterns on the ground; others prefer terminology that describes the way an animal was moving (the gait). This book presents the vocabulary most widely accepted by trackers across the globe, and that which was used by Eadweard Muybridge (1957) in his pictorial presentation *Animal Locomotion.* This vocabulary provides visual information about how an animal is moving—which is crucial to envisioning and becoming that animal in advanced levels of tracking (Liebenberg 1990). But understand: No one terminology is better than another. What's important when communicating with others about gaits and trails is that you are envisioning the same motions in your imagination. Consider Vet Piet: He preferred to act out animal movements rather than use words.

Gaits can be separated into three categories: 1) Walks, trots, and pacing, in which the front feet fall at consistent rhythmic distances

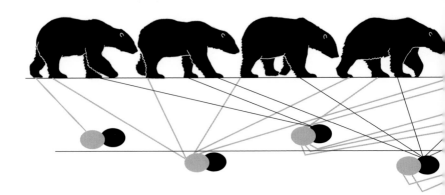

from each other (created by keeping the spine straight and allowing the momentum to be driven by motion in the legs); 2) lopes, gallops, hops, and bounds, in which the front feet land in alternating short and long distances from each other (created by stretching and contracting the spine in addition to moving the legs); and 3) bipedal gaits, in which animals move on only their hind legs. (Note: In these descriptions, we focus on the front feet, but the very same is true for the hind feet as well.)

Walks, Trots, and Pacing

Walking. Walking is a slow gait in which each foot moves independently, and at no point during a cycle of footfalls does the animal lose contact with the ground. We shall arbitrarily begin with the right hind foot in our example. The right hind leg moves forward, and, just before it touches down, the right front lifts up and moves forward. For a moment, two feet are off the ground, and then the right hind touches down. The right front continues forward and then touches down. The left hind moves forward, and, just before it touches down, the left front picks up and moves forward. For a second time in the cycle of footfalls, there are only two feet in contact with the ground, and then the left hind touches down. The left front continues forward and then touches down. Immediately the cycle

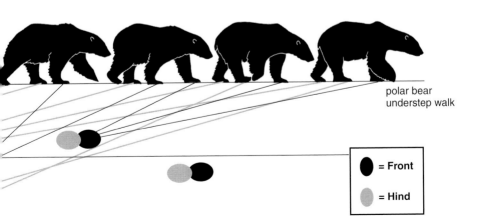

polar bear
understep walk

● = Front

● = Hind

*Walking trail of an
American badger.*

begins again, and the right hind picks up and moves forward. Musically, this would sound like 1, 2, 3, 4, 1, 2, 3, 4, 1, 2, 3, 4, where each number is an independent footfall. Note that the rhythm is continuous, without breaks or pauses.

In a walk, the hind foot might land in any relation to the front track. Remember, the right front foot picks up before the right hind touches down. For this reason, the hind foot might land exactly where the front had been placed, called a direct register, or even touch down beyond the front track, called an overstep.

A good portion of time during each cycle of footfalls only one leg is lifted from the ground, which allows for three feet to support the animal while it's in motion. These three legs act like the legs of a tripod, a sturdy arrangement that efficiently balances heavy objects, including wide animals with short legs.

Walking is common among almost all the animals. For many wide-bodied animals, such as beavers, porcupines, and bears, it is the most common method of moving. It is also the common gait for deer, moose, antelope, African civets, and all members of the cat family. Other species walk when exploring or while traveling in deep substrates, like snow, to save energy.

A variation of the walk is the stalk. In the stalk, only one limb moves at a time, but the order in which the feet move is the same as for the walk. The right hind foot moves forward and touches down.

The beautiful tracks of a bobcat in an overstep walk. ME

The right front foot moves forward and touches down. Then the left hind foot, followed by the left front foot. The resulting trail is an understep walk—the hind tracks in each pair register behind the front tracks.

There are numerous variables to consider when interpreting speed from a series of tracks in a trail, but a general rule holds true for walking gaits. As an animal walks faster, its hind track will move over and beyond the front track in each pair. Therefore an understep, where the hind track lies behind the front track, is probably a slower gait than a direct registering walk, where the hind lies on top of the front, and both are likely slower than an overstep walk, where the hind registers beyond the front track. A fast walk is also called an amble. Remember, there are other variables to consider as well, such as the depth of substrate and the anatomy and morphology of the specific animal you are tracking. But as a general rule, the speed can be inferred, up to a point, by considering the placement of the hind track in relation to the front, for an animal can only walk so fast before it must change gaits to increase speed.

Trotting. Faster trots are easily differentiated from slower walks. They are characterized by a front and hind leg on opposing sides moving together, as if joined by a cable. Rather than each foot moving independently, two legs move simultaneously, and there is a moment during each cycle of footfalls when the animal becomes airborne, completely losing contact with the ground. This vertical

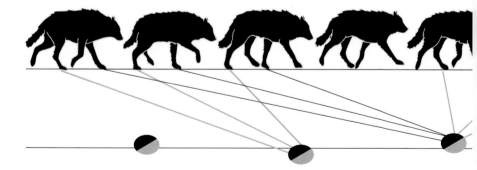

component is easily seen in any canid, from foxes to domestic dogs—there is a little bounce in their common gait. This means that as the right hind foot shifts forward in the air, so does the left front foot. Just before the right hind foot and left front foot are placed down, the right front and left hind feet push off, maintaining forward momentum. Then, just before the right front foot and left hind foot touch down, the animal pushes off with the right hind foot and left front foot. The cycle begins all over again. Musically, the beat is a continuous 1, 2, 1, 2, 1, 2, where each number represents two diagonally placed feet landing simultaneously.

The common gait of canids, numerous mongooses, many voles, and short-tailed shrews is the trot. Many other species also use trots as a travel gait, including badgers, woodchucks, black bears, and members of the cat family. Bighorn sheep tend to trot on flat ground, where they are at greater risk of predation.

Direct register trots, in which hind tracks are superimposed on front tracks on the same side of the animal, are common in many species. Hind tracks land exactly upon the recently made front prints, as the front foot and opposite hind pick up just before the alternate pair touches down. The forward momentum of the animal carries the hind foot directly above the front track.

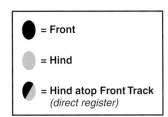

= Front

= Hind

= Hind atop Front Track
(direct register)

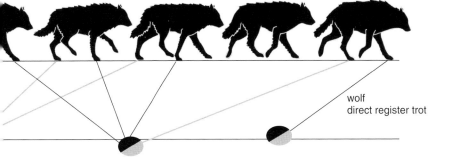

wolf
direct register trot

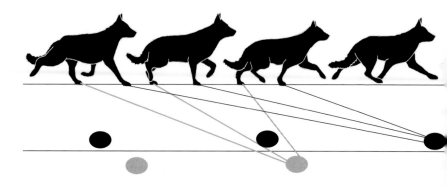

As with walking, speed estimates can be inferred by the position of the hind foot in relation to the front track. Direct register trots are theoretically slower than overstep trots, in which hind tracks in a given pair register beyond the fronts. Overstep trots are achieved by species in different ways. The hind foot can only move forward so far before it collides with the front foot of the same side. Animals typically overcome this obstacle in two ways. Canids tend to use the side trot, or crab, and trot with their entire body at an angle; they kick out their rear ends to one side. In this way, the hind feet pass to one side

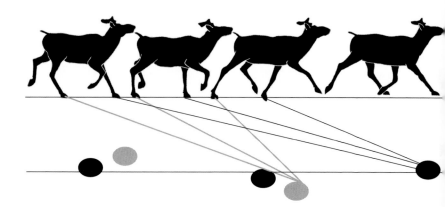

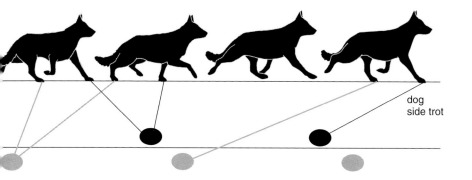

dog
side trot

of the front feet in order to move at a faster pace. When an animal is using a side trot, all the front tracks appear on one side of the trail, and all the hinds on the other side; the hind tracks are also slightly forward of each front track in each pairing. This unique gait and track pattern is easy to find along jackal, coyote, wolf, and red fox trails; gray foxes very rarely side trot.

Another option is to kick each hind leg out to either side of the fronts, and this is called a straddle trot. All canines use this gait, but it tends to be for

● = Front

● = Hind

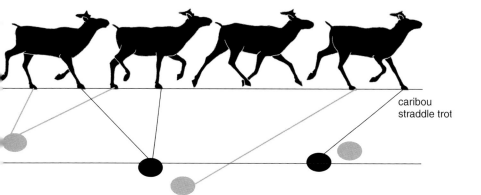

caribou
straddle trot

The straight trail of a coyote in a direct register trot in several inches of snow. ME

short sections of a trail and most often is a transition from a direct register trot to a side trot. However, gray foxes use this gait very often, as do caribou, moose, mule deer, and several shrew species. The final option to successfully make an overstep trot involves a longer air time, allowing the hind feet to glide over the front tracks with forward momentum, as seen in lizards and occasionally other animals. This last option is rare in mammals but is sometimes incorporated into dominance displays and aggressive interactions.

Some lizards (and running crocodiles, too) can trot in the technical sense and achieve high speeds, while other reptiles and amphibians use a gait that simultaneously exhibits characteristics of both trotting and walking. Most turtles and tortoises are so wide and heavy that they move each foot independently, as described for walking, so as to benefit from tripod support. Others, including crocodiles and salamanders, walk with their opposing (diagonal) front and hind limbs in synch, as described for trotting. However, unlike trotting animals, these creatures never leave the ground when moving in this manner, and their movements often appear exaggerated as they curve their spines side to side to increase speed. Note that this is why it is impossible for a salamander to completely direct register—the right front foot is still on the ground when the right hind comes in behind and therefore blocks the hind foot from moving any further forward. For this slower gait, we suggest the term diagonal walk to differentiate it from trotting. In a diagonal walk, the animal remains in contact with the ground yet is propelled forward by diagonal limbs moving simultaneously.

Trail of a red fox in a side trot.

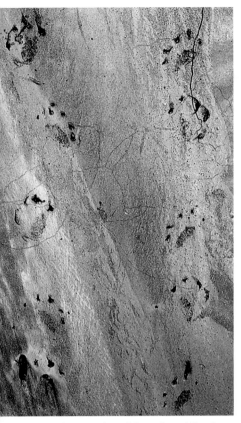

A painted turtle's trail, each hind foot registering behind the corresponding fronts on the same side of the body. ME

Pacing. Pacing is an uncommon gait in mammals, but characteristic of camels and several other species. Pacing is generally a fast gait, similar in speed to a trot, but is distinctive because legs on the same side of the body move in synch. Just as in trots, two legs move simultaneously, and there is a moment during each cycle of footfalls when the animal becomes airborne, completely losing contact with the ground. As the right hind foot shifts foward in the air, so does the right front foot. Then, just before the right hind and front feet touch down, the left front and hind feet push off, maintaining forward momentum. And just before the left front and hind feet reconnect with the ground, the animal pushes off with both feet on the right side to begin the cycle all over again. Musically, the beat is a continuous 1, 2, 1, 2, 1, 2, where each number represents two feet on the same side of the body landing simultaneously.

It is also possible to pace at a walking speed, in which the movements are just the same as described, but the animal never loses contact with the ground. Often what appears to be pacing in the field is actually walking, because the individual feet on one side of the body are placed down one after the other rather than exactly at the same time. Domestic dogs, springbok, blesbok, and giraffes may exhibit pacing, however.

Lopes, Gallops, Hops, and Bounds

Loping and Galloping. Lopes and gallops are very similar gaits and the fastest for mammals. During lopes and gallops, each foot lands independently of the others but in rapid succession. During both gaits, the animal becomes momentarily airborne just after pushing off with the front legs. But during gallops, there is a second point at which the animal is in the air, just after pushing off with the hind legs. It is difficult to see this second short flight when watching an animal move, and it's difficult to decipher between lopes and gallops when interpreting track patterns on the ground.

The order in which the feet touch the ground during lopes and gallops can be in one of two ways. If they land in a circular fashion—left front, right front, right hind, left hind—it is called a rotary lope or gallop. If the order does not circle the body but rather cuts across the body—left front, right front, left hind, right hind—then it is called a transverse lope or gallop. Musically, there are four beats for both gaits, followed by a pause: 1, 2, 3, 4, pause, 1, 2, 3, 4, pause, 1, 2, 3, 4, pause . . . This is not a continuous rhythm, as is found in walks and trots.

When looking at track patterns on the ground, one notices that a lope typically becomes a gallop when both hind feet land beyond both front feet, but this is not always the case. If the order of tracks on the ground in a single set of four prints is front, hind, front, hind, then it is a lope. If the order is front, front, hind, hind, then it is more likely a gallop.

As in walks and trots, the placement of the hind tracks in relation to the front tracks betrays speed. As the pair of hind tracks moves beyond the pair of front tracks, this indicates a faster lope or gallop. Also note the distance between the groups of four tracks. In general, the longer the distance spanned by four tracks in a series, and the shorter the length in between groups of four tracks, called the stride, the faster the animal is moving. At all-out speeds, some mammals will leave track patterns that at first glance look like trots—tracks are placed regularly and in a straight line. But each mark is a single track, rather than two.

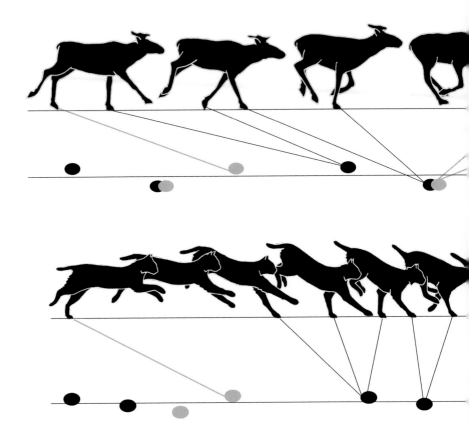

Two particular lopes are characteristic of the weasel family. They are the 3x4 lope and 2x2 lope. The 3x4 lope is a rotary lope, in which a front and hind on the same side of the body land in the same space, giving the impression of only three tracks in a set, rather than four. Hildebrand and Goslow (2001) show that weasels still have a front foot on the ground when the first hind foot touches down; therefore, this gait is a true lope.

The 2x2 lope is a transverse lope, although other than the order of footfalls, it is very similar in body mechanics to the 3x4 lope. The same fluid arcing motion is used for both gaits. What is unique about

caribou
rotary lope

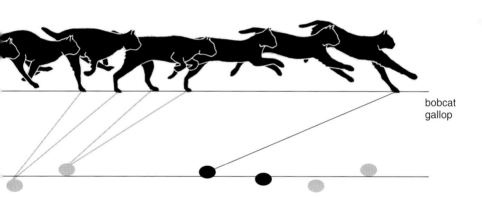

bobcat
gallop

| ● = Front |
| ◗ = Hind |

the 2x2 lope is that the front feet pick up and the hind feet land directly upon the front tracks—creating a trail of paired tracks, where each set of two prints is actually a set of four, the fronts registering first and the hind feet registering directly on top of them. Meadow voles and smaller shrews also use this gait in deep snows. Based upon Hildebrand's research on the 3x4 lope, we assume that a front foot is still in contact with the ground when the first hind touches down. Should we be wrong, then this gait would technically be a gallop.

Hopping and Bounding. The hopping and bounding gaits of rabbits and many rodents are differentiated from lopes and gallops in that the hind feet land and push off simultaneously, or nearly so. This is evident in the trail, as the hind tracks appear parallel to each other. Any local park should present ample opportunities to study squirrels using these gaits. Hops are similar to lopes, in that there is one moment when the animal is airborne during each cycle of footfalls, just after the hind feet push off. Bounds parallel gallops in that there are two times when the animal is airborne during each cycle of footfalls, first after the front feet push off, and again after the hind feet push off.

The difference between the track patterns of hops and bounds is found in the relationship between hind tracks and front. When hopping, the front feet of an animal land in front of the hind feet. Hopping is less common than bounding but can be observed in short-tailed shrews, large voles, muskrats, southern flying squirrels, toads, and frogs.

Hopping and bounding begin in the same way: The front feet either land as a pair (next to each other) or one after the other (one in front of the other) but in bounds the hind feet move forward beyond and to either side of the front feet. The front feet pick up as the hind feet pass to the outside, and there is a moment where the animal loses contact with the ground before the hinds come down and push off again. This push-off is followed by a second moment in the air before the front feet touches down and the cycle begins again. Numerous species, including squirrels, the small grey mongoose, chipmunks, and rabbits, bound.

Trail of a galloping kit fox.

The trail left by a male fisher moving in a 3x4 lope. ME

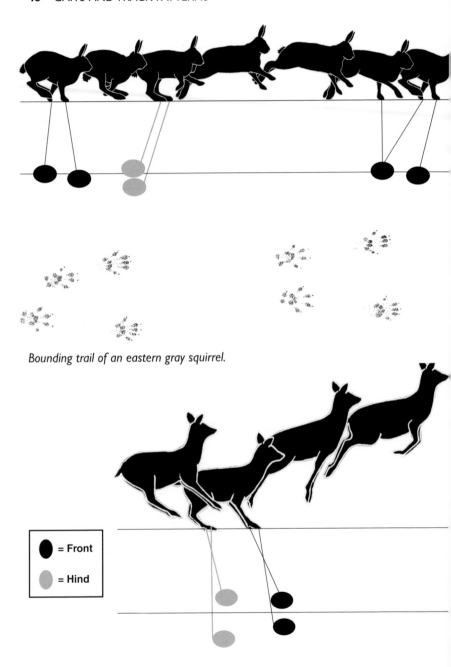

Bounding trail of an eastern gray squirrel.

● = Front

● = Hind

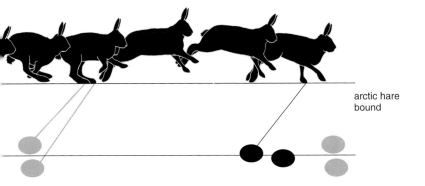

arctic hare
bound

Stott or Pronk

An unusual gait used by elk, mule deer, several African antelope, pronghorn, and occasionally other mammals is the stott. In this bouncing gait, an animal pushes off with all four feet at the same time and then lands upon all four feet simultaneously, or nearly so. Mammals moving in this way appear to be using pogo sticks.

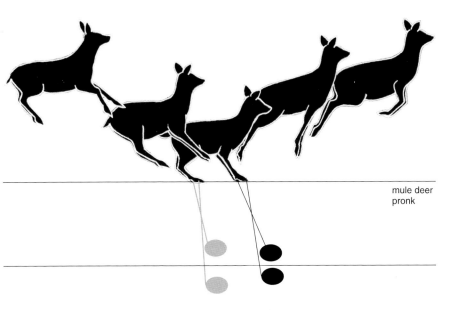

mule deer
pronk

Although not as fast as the gallop, the stott is better suited to traveling quickly over broken terrain. It also allows an animal to respond to external stimuli more quickly and change direction when it hits the ground.

GAITS ON TWO LEGS

Bipedal Hopping

Both hopping and skipping are saltorial motions that involve track patterns in which hind footprints are paired. In hopping trails, paired hind tracks appear right next to each other, or nearly so, and the gait is the typical kangaroo-style hop. This pattern is possible because both hind feet hit the ground simultaneously. Technically, feet would only truly hit simultaneously if the feet were placed exactly next to each other, or if the animal were coming straight

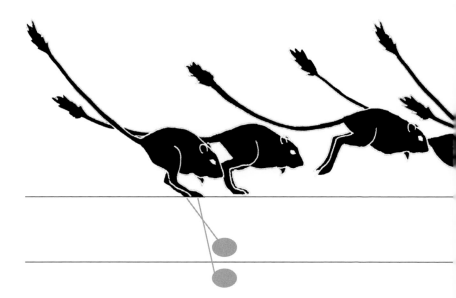

down. However, for our purposes we'll use the word "simultaneously" to mean at the same time, or nearly so.

Bipedal Skipping
In skipping trails, tracks are also paired, but each hind foot lands completely independently of the other. Looking at the trail pattern, a hop becomes a skip when one hind foot registers completely in front of the other hind track. When a kangaroo rat skips, it stays very low to the ground and takes very long strides. Its hind feet rotate forward, one striking down before the other, and, as the body moves forward over this foot, the second foot touches down. The animal's momentum continues, propelling its body forward over the second foot. As the body continues forward, the first foot to touch down lifts up behind the animal. Continuing forward, the second foot joins the first behind the animal, then the animal lifts off, and together the hind feet rotate forward to begin another cycle. Momentum is more horizontal than vertical, and very little energy is wasted in rise.

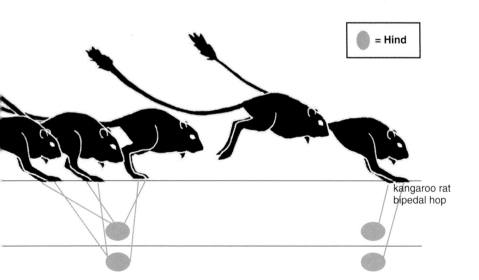

= Hind

kangaroo rat
bipedal hop

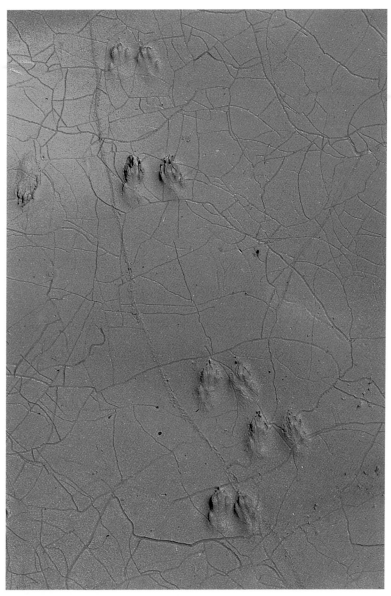

Look for the paired hind tracks in the bipedal trails of these Heerman's kangaroo rats. ME

INTERPRETING PATTERNS

> *"To interpret tracks and signs trackers must project themselves into the position of the animal in order to create a hypothetical explanation of what the animal was doing. Tracking is not strictly empirical, since it also involves the tracker's imagination."*
>
> —Liebenberg, 1990

Until now, we have discussed how an animal is moving in the technical sense of what limbs are moving when and in what order limbs make contact with the ground. Next, we leap into speculative interpretation based upon our initial understanding of how an animal is moving and ask ourselves why an animal is moving in a particular way. Since we can never know what an animal was thinking, nor exactly what an animal was doing at a particular moment (unless we actually witnessed the event), we speculate on its behavior, making our best guess. As in all aspects of tracking, we build a working hypothesis and test it as we continue to follow the animal. As we gather more information, we either toss out our original hypothesis and create a new one, or continue to refine and support it.

Natural Rhythms and Energy Efficiency

Gaits and their associated track patterns are reflective of energy conservation, substrate, and behavior. Energy efficiency is a tremendously important variable in interpreting trails, as well as in predicting how a given animal will move in a given depth of substrate. It is certainly true that the slower an animal moves the less energy it expends; however, it's more complicated than this. Every species reflects an anatomy, locomotion and behaviors that improve its fitness. Fitness is quite simply the quality of success experienced by an animal. In ecology, fitness is measured by how well an animal reproduces and perpetuates its genetic lineage. An animal has high fitness when it produces numerous offspring that themselves produce numerous offspring. Think of the measure of success as the number of grandchildren an animal has, since having grandchildren indicates successful production of offspring that were, in turn, able to survive and reproduce.

To simplify things further, let's focus on energy input and output. Each species balances its energy intake, meaning food collection, and energy output, which includes the ground covered to locate and pursue food. Weasels and mongooses have high metabolisms, insatiable appetites to meet their energy requirements, and gait preferences that propel them quickly over long distances. A weasel that too often walks might save energy in the short term but is denying that which makes it a weasel and will die of starvation in the long term because it does not gather enough food to meet its energetic requirements. In other words, a slow weasel will save energy but have low fitness. The balance point between energy intake and output influences the ways animals move, and the common gait that an animal has adapted for traveling is called its natural rhythm (Elbroch 2003).

Let's compare bobcats and caracals with coyotes and jackals. Each species has a body structure and biology that balance its individual energy intake and energy expenditure. In this way, each animal species also has a natural rhythm that best expresses the harmony between energy intake and output for their particular niche. Bobcats and caracals walk. Cats move through the forest slowly and stealthily, sitting and pausing frequently to study their environment, hoping to see or sense potential prey before they themselves are noticed. They may even lie low and wait for prey and do not generally cover long distances while hunting. When a potential quarry is selected, they stalk in and, when close enough, explode with enough speed to catch their intended victim before it is aware of them, or before it can escape. They grip their prey with their claws and deliver a killing bite to the head or neck.

Coyotes and jackals trot through the bush, hoping to catch smell, sound, or sight of potential prey, or to startle something and flush it out. Of course, coyotes and jackals do occasionally stalk, but, in general, coyotes and jackals cruise longer distances than medium-sized cats, allowing scents and sounds to betray the presence of prey species. When opportunities present themselves, they run down

Bobcat. ME

Coyote. ME

their intended prey, gripping and subduing it with their teeth. Their claws, which are never sheathed, project straight out from their toes and aid in traction while running.

Can coyotes and jackals walk? Of course. Can bobcats and caracals trot? Yes. Every animal is capable of a variety of gaits and speeds—but each animal will have one or two gaits that are the most energy efficient for it, and it uses these most of the time. Their common gaits are their natural rhythms.

Understanding the natural rhythms of animals is important because it gives us a place to start. Think of an animal's natural rhythm as its normal speed or middle ground. Each time an animal shifts from its normal speed, there is a reason and thus an opportunity to speculate why. Consider yourself as a starting point to better grasp how one might approach trail interpretation. You have your typical walking gait, speed, and track pattern. Should you be late for work or very focused on a specific destination, your pace and track pattern will change. If you are hungry and stand between five great restaurants, you will likely wander a bit, then move with determination once you have decided where to dine. You jump if you are scared and run when your life is threatened. The list of possibilities goes on and on. All these sorts of changes are also apparent in wild animal trails.

Certain gaits are associated with specific environmental conditions (substrates), while others betray behaviors, or intentions. From a series of footprints you can determine whether an animal feels exposed and potentially uncomfortable, or whether it is hunting. And if you really become familiar with an area and its inhabitants, the way an animal behaves and moves may betray that it is out of its usual territory, or allow you to identify a transient or trespasser.

Interpretation of track patterns is advanced tracking and only comes with experience and lots of mistakes. The more natural history information you have about a species and the more time you spend trailing a particular animal, the better armed you are for this process. Regardless of experience, there will always be trails that will perplex you. Accept the fact that tracking is not a perfect science but a lifetime of learning.

Beginning Interpretation

With experience, interpretation can be highly detailed, and we discuss advanced aspects of interpretation in later chapters. In the meantime, we encourage you to begin by interpreting the way an animal is moving as one of three categories: slow, normal (natural rhythm), or fast.

1. Slow is a speed slower than an animal's normal gait (natural rhythm) that might indicate foraging, stalking away from danger, hunting, scent marking, exploring another animal's scent post, or numerous other potential behaviors.
2. Normal is an animal's natural rhythm, the common gait in which an animal moves. It is exhibiting little or no undue stress and is not reacting to any strong stimuli in the environment. You might say that the animal is acting "casual."
3. Fast is a speed faster than normal that might indicate that an animal is chasing prey, being chased by a predator, or startled by something in the environment. It might also be exposed and/or uncomfortable in its surroundings.

Each of these categories is associated with some general interpretations. The key to applying this to an animal you are tracking is knowing its normal gait and associated natural rhythm. You can acquire this knowledge through experience in the field, watching animals in videos, or reading guides to tracking and animal behavior. The normal gait for caracals and bobcats is a walk, but the normal gait for jackals, coyotes, and wolves is a trot. The normal gait for a squirrel is a bound, and for spring hares and kangaroo rats, a bipedal hop.

Consider the desert kangaroo rat, an animal we've only ever seen use three gaits and speeds: slow, normal, and fast. When moving slowly, desert kangaroo rats bound on all four feet, like a squirrel, and drag their tails on the ground behind them. They move in this way when they are foraging and scent marking, or when they are exploring the scents of other kangaroo rats. The normal gait of desert kangaroo rats is a bipedal hop, which they use to travel between their burrows, foraging areas, and areas where they leave territorial scent marks. The bipedal hop is generally a sign of com-

A desert kangaroo rat in southern California. ME

fort, that everything is normal. Desert kangaroo rats skip to evade predators (it is a sign of fear) and during territorial chases with other kangaroo rats, including courtship rituals that precede mating. Thus, we have three clear categories of movement, three speed categories, and three distinct categories of behavior associated with these gaits and track patterns. This, of course, can be done for any and every animal you follow.

In mammals that use more than three gaits, consider splitting each of the three categories into three subcategories; thus you have nine potential speeds and interpretations. For example, the African lion and the cougar both use an overstep walk, or amble, as their normal gait. They speed up into a trot when exposed and crossing open ground, traveling to a known destination with some agenda in mind, and confronting conspecifics in territorial encounters (stiff-legged trots communicate dominance in many mammals). They gallop when pursuing prey or when startled and lope when slowing down should they recognize that an initial threat is not as dangerous as

The foraging trails of desert kangaroo rats. Note the lines created by the tail dragging along the ground. ME

they first thought or is remaining stationary. There are three versions of "fast," each with different potential interpretations. But start with just three categories, then add more as you feel more comfortable with the basics.

The Effects of Substrate

Substrate is a catchall word for what an animal has stepped in, whether it be sand, mud, snow, or grass. The depth of substrate, which is reflected in the depth of the print, has an enormous influence on the appearance, size, and shape of the spoor, as well as on how the animal moves. In shallow substrates, like moist hard sand, animals move easily and therefore tend toward their normal gaits. In deep or slippery substrates, animals tend to slow down. The conditions of different substrates in which an animal might step are infinite and thus create great challenges for the tracker.

Use yourself as an example. Compare the trails you leave while walking in an inch of snow with those you leave in two feet of snow, or on firm ground and in deep dry sand. It is likely that the length between your tracks decreases in deeper snow (or in deeper sand) and that the width of the entire trail pattern increases. This is a wonderful lesson in the effects of the depth of substrate upon trail characteristics.

Now, let's add another variable: speed. When looking at trail characteristics in relation to depth of substrate, it might be more accurate to discuss energy output rather than speed. In the two trails in the snow, for example, if you were to use the same amount of energy to make each one, you would move slower in the deeper conditions. If you wanted to move at the same speed in both trails, it would take a higher degree of energy output to maintain that speed in two feet of snow. Consider running in the two snow conditions. Could you run at the same speed in two feet of snow as you could in one inch of snow? Would the energy output be equivalent while maintaining a run in these two very different conditions?

Just as we adapt to changing conditions, so do other animals. In fact, as you track across varied substrates, you will begin to notice that animals change the way they are moving in ways that reflect an awareness of energy efficiency. Trotting in deep snow is intensively difficult if not impossible, and so coyotes are often found walking or bounding for short distances in these conditions. With this knowledge, we must then be flexible in our interpretations—the "normal" speed for a coyote in several feet of snow is a walk, not a trot. The bound would then be its "fast" gait, and its "slow" gait would be a slower walking gait than its normal walk. Fishers, which tend toward a 3x4, or rotary lope, change tendencies to a 2x2 or transverse lope in deep soft conditions and often walk longer distances as well.

Recognizing Patterns for Interpretation

There are also specific track patterns you will want to familiarize yourself with so you can quickly interpret them in the field. With practice, you will quickly be able to surmise what an animal was

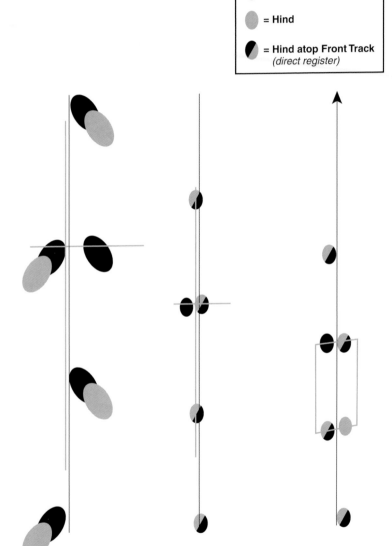

= Front

= Hind

= Hind atop Front Track
(direct register)

T-Trails

Box Stop

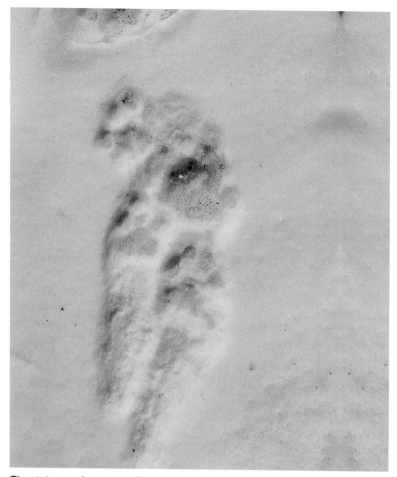

The sitting track pattern of a cougar kitten. Note the lines sticking out the back of the hind tracks, which are technically the heels of the hind feet. ME

doing from a peculiar series of tracks—sniffing something, pausing, urinating, feeding, and so on. Deer "point" to food with a single hoof; many mammals "T-up" when they pause; and bobcats kick out a hind leg when passing an object they intend to spray with urine.

3

Determining Spoor Age and Reconstructing Activities

*I*t was just getting light when I arrived at Bateleur Eco Safaris' camp in the Timbavati. The first cold front of the winter had arrived, and a strong south-easter had been blowing for the last day and a half. While having coffee and warming up at the campfire, our clients came to greet me in groups of twos and threes. All of them were businessmen, adventurers from Italy, and had been in the camp for the last few days, taking part in an antipoaching and game-capture course. This was their last morning, and we decided to do a bit of track and sign interpretation.

The bite of the wind made my eyes water as we drove out of camp. As the road took us through a sodic site between some natural pans, I saw an opportunity and signaled to Andreas to stop. The large number of animals visiting the pans had turned the clayish soils into a thick layer of fine dust. I slipped down from my vantage point in the tracker seat and immediately circled a block around one yard wide by five yards long. Keen to learn, the guests climbed off the Land Rovers and formed a circle around the block.

"You might be more interested in tracking humans when you are involved with antipoaching," I said, "but let me explain why it is also important to be able to identify animal tracks."

With Davide Bomben, the leader of the group, translating, I pointed at the human tracks in the block. "I can see that you walked here yesterday, and it looks like it was in the late afternoon, possibly while there was still sun shining here," I said.

The group moved to the western side of the block to allow the early morning sunlight onto the tracks. I pointed out the francolin track on top of a human track and said, "This is from yesterday, and not from this morning. Can you see how the wind had rounded off the edges of the track in the same way as your shoe print? It is also of the same coloration as your prints. But this small toad track, and that thick-knee [a ploverlike bird] track is still darker in color, and the edges are still sharp and crisp."

"Ah, and there the frog track is crossing our tracks!" one of them said, "but why is the color different?"

"Is it because of the moisture in the soil during the night, that it holds it better?" asked Davide.

"Yes, the sun had not yet bleached it, and the little bit of moisture has preserved it better. A track made during the night when the soil is cold will normally last longer than a track made during the day when the sun has warmed the soil and burned away the dampness. These elephants came to drink during the night, probably in the early evening. The soil had cooled down by the time they visited, as their tracks are still crisp, but all the nocturnal animal tracks are on top of it. There is a scrub hare track on the elephant track, and that is a larger toad. See, here is the thick-knee's track also on top."

"But that antlion trap on the footprint, when was that made?" asked one of the other participants.

"If the antlion had moved there during the night, we would have seen its trail, but there is no trail," I said.

"So it came first, and then we walked over it, and now it had only rebuilt the trap."

"Correct. And remember, the antlion will start rebuilding its trap within minutes after it is damaged."

"Of course, they need to eat," he said.

"This elephant was obviously in a hurry to get to the water—can you see how far the hind foot has stepped beyond the front foot? This is typical elephant, always in a hurry when they go to water." The edge of the pan was just fifteen or so yards to the north.

"Why do you think this track is so unclear and that one is showing all the cracks under the elephant's foot? You see, the one going to the water in a hurry is very clear, but this one is showing none of the cracks."

"Maybe he was dragging his foot?" said one, "like this," and he dragged his foot.

A foraging elephant. AL

"Does it look the same?"

"No. Then the edges will not be clear like that. But what is it then?"

"Which way was this animal moving?" I asked.

"To the water," most of them said.

"Look again. Can you see that this is the heel and that the toe of the hind foot? The elephant is walking away from the water, not in a hurry like the other one. And the pattern under that foot is not showing because of the mud sticking to the underside of it." I pointed at the front foot's track.

"Ah, it was standing in the water with the front feet while drinking, but the hind feet were not in the water!"

"Correct. But look, this one also looks like it stood in mud, maybe over there." I pointed to the pans south of us. "You see, this one is also still on its way to the water, but it is also not showing any cracks."

"There is no mud there anymore; it is all dried up," said Andreas, the owner of Bateleur.

"Maybe it is grass stuck under its feet. Look at those scrape marks behind the heel," said Davide.

Andreas pointed at a ball of dry elephant dung, and Neville, camp manager and resident guide, kicked down hard on the dung and dragged his foot forward. The marks it left on the ground were almost identical to that in the track. I looked around, and a few yards down the trail I saw a piece of flattened dry elephant dung. I got up and placed my foot in the same soft thick dust as the elephant track and lifted my foot fast. The suction effect left an undefined patch of dust in the middle, with the edges clear.

"Can local knowledge of the area and the resent history help you in interpreting sign?" I asked.

"You mean like what animals occur in the area?" asked Davide.

"That as well, but I am thinking more in terms of recent weather, where water occurs, and so on."

"Not sure I follow you."

"Let me explain by using this example. I started by saying that you had walked here late yesterday afternoon. I could say that because your tracks had not been obliterated by the diurnal animals coming in to drink. I also said it was possibly while there was still sun shining here. I said 'possibly' because the tracks were dull in color, as if bleached by the sun, but I know the wind was blowing yesterday, and the wind can also make it look dull. Looking at that elephant, when I was here a month ago, the pans to the south still had water. It was therefore easy for me to make the assumption that this last elephant track coming from the south also had mud under its front feet. It looks almost the same as that one leaving to the northeast. Because Andreas knew there is no water or mud left to the south, his mind immediately searched for an alternative answer. By experimenting with the elephant dung, and putting my foot in the soft dust, we could get to the correct interpretation."

—A. L.

AGE CATEGORIES

One of the most difficult aspects of spoor interpretation is determining the age of spoor. Only very experienced trackers can determine the age of tracks with reasonable accuracy—absolute accuracy is often not possible.

The distance an animal may be from trackers does not only depend on how old the tracks are, but also on how fast the animal had been moving or what it was doing. If an alarmed animal was fleeing, even a reasonably fresh spoor may not be worth pursuing, since the trackers may never catch up with the animal. On the other hand, a spoor may be old, but the animal may have lain down to rest not too far away and may still be in the near vicinity. A fresh spoor of an animal that has been browsing, moving slowly from bush to bush, would be the ideal animal to track down.

When estimating the age of tracks and the speed at which an animal was moving, it is important to decide whether or not the animal might be close enough for you to pursue, or for it to see, hear, or smell you. If the animal is too far ahead, a lot of energy will be wasted in fruitless pursuit. Old spoor is also more difficult to track, since it can be confused with old spoor made by other animals. Fresh spoor is much easier to track because it is easier to distinguish. If the animal is close enough to pursue, but not close enough for it to detect the trackers, the trackers do not have to worry about moving stealthily and can move ahead as quickly as possible. At this stage, moving stealthily will only waste time. If the animal is very close, however, the trackers must move stealthily, communicate with each other using hand signals, and look ahead so they will see the animal before it sees them. Although a reasonable estimate of the age of tracks is important, absolute accuracy is not necessary, since trackers can make allowances for any inaccuracy.

Spoor can generally be divided into three key categories: 1) old spoor that is too old to follow up (generally made more than twenty-four hours ago), 2) fresh spoor that is fresh enough to follow up but not too close to the animal (generally made within twelve hours), and 3) very fresh spoor that is so fresh that the animal may be able to see, smell, or hear the tracker (generally made within the past three hours).

TYPES OF ESTIMATES

When making an estimate of the age of the tracks, it is important to determine the different types of estimates that can be made. Depending on the type of evidence, the tracker can make an absolute estimate, probable estimate, relative estimate, or intuitive estimate.

Absolute Estimate

An absolute estimate gives the actual time the tracks were made. A reasonably accurate way of determining an absolute estimate of the age of tracks is possible when an animal has been resting in the shade of a tree. The position of the marks on the ground where the animal was lying or standing indicate where the shade was and, therefore, what the position of the sun was, so it is possible to estimate from the movement of the sun when the animal rested (Grainger 1967).

During the hottest hours, animals usually stand in the shade. Some, such as the blesbok and bontebok, might stand in groups facing the sun. On cold mornings, some animals, such as the Cape Mountain zebra, stand with their bodies at right angles to the sun's rays; during heavy rainstorms, they stand with their backs to the rain. At night, animals stand or lie in the open without being oriented any particular way. The various positions and situations in which the tracks of a standing animal might be found can indicate when the animal was standing there. If the tracks of a moving animal go under the west side of a stand of trees, the animal might have caught the morning shade. If tracks go under the east side, it might have caught the afternoon shade. If tracks go on either side of different trees, the animal might have been moving at midday (Lee 1979).

Probable Estimate

The activities of an animal might allow a probable estimate of the age of spoor if its habits are known. If an animal is either diurnal or nocturnal, the tracks will have been made either in the day or night. During the midday heat, an animal might rest in a dense thicket, or at night, it might sleep in the open. Animals might go to water holes or pans at specific times of the day and move to their favored feeding grounds according to a set routine.

Relative Estimate

An estimate of the age of tracks can be made relative to known events, such as dew, mist, rain, and snow. If dew has developed on top of spoor, the spoor was made during the night or the previous day; spoor on top of dew would have been made earlier that same day. Signs of dew can sometimes be very subtle, forming a thin crust on top of the spoor as sand grains stick together, even after the sand has dried. A light touch of the inside of the track reveals the distinctive feel of dried crust compared to the softness of loose sand that's apparent if the animal stepped on top of the dew. Dew dripping from branches can also form pockmarks in spoor made during the night or early morning. Spoor through long grass, made before dew or rain, will be covered with drops. If the spoor were made after dew or rain, the drops will be shed, often leaving a distinctive darker-colored trail through the grass. If rain or mist has fallen since the track was made, there will be pockmarks inside the tracks. Conversely, if the track was made after rain or mist, there will be pockmarks around but not inside the tracks. Heavy ground fog will smooth spoor and leave pockmarks under leafy branches (Grainger 1967).

Fresh tracks made after a thin layer of snow has fallen may have sharp crisp edges. As the snow thaws, the edges become rounded, and the size of the track increases. When temperatures remain below freezing, fresh tracks develop a thin crust within an hour. Touch the inside of the track, where snow beneath the surface is revealed, to determine the strength of such a crust. In deep snow, footprints can be obscured as snow crumbles into the deep holes. The track might also be rounded and fill in as more snow falls, gradually becoming indistinct hollows before being obliterated. Temperature changes or changes in the snow are also recorded in tracks. If temperatures

Fresh lion tracks show clearly after a brief rain. AL

started warmer and the snows were wetter, then temperatures dropped and snows became fluffier and lighter, the buried tracks will be distinct, well formed, and thickly crusted. Carefully remove layers of snow within tracks to determine changes in precipitation.

The estimate might also be relative to a probable estimate. With a detailed knowledge of the habits and movements of other animals, a tracker might be able to determine the relative age of spoor using superimposed animal spoor. The age of the superimposed spoor would be a probable estimate. If the spoor of a nocturnal animal is superimposed on the quarry's spoor, the quarry's spoor was probably made during the night or the previous day. Furthermore, if the quarry is diurnal, then its spoor would have been made the previous day. If the quarry's spoor is superimposed on a nocturnal animal's spoor, then the quarry's spoor was probably made during the night or earlier that same day, and if the quarry is diurnal, it would have been made that same day.

While tracking a quarry, a tracker might find the spoor of several animals superimposed on the quarry's spoor or the quarry's spoor superimposed on the spoor of other animals. In both cases, an upper and lower limit for the age of the quarry's spoor can be determined. Several relative estimates combined allow the tracker to bracket the possible age between events. For example: The spoor was made after dew was formed but before the tracks of a small bird feeding in the morning superimposed on top of it—the animal therefore passed early in the morning. The quarry's spoor might be superimposed on footprints of animals going toward a water hole, but the footprints of animals going away from the water hole might be superimposed on the quarry's spoor, indicating that the quarry's spoor was made at about the time the animals went to the water hole (Grainger 1967). If the pit of an antlion larva is stepped on, the creature will reconstruct it. If the pit inside the footprint is still being reconstructed, it may give an accurate indication of how old the spoor is. Spoor that are most commonly superimposed on footprints are usually those of mice and insects (which may be either diurnal or nocturnal) and small birds (which are diurnal, often feeding on the ground early in the morning). It is therefore possible to narrow down the range of possible estimates.

The age of a quarry's spoor relative to its own tracks might be determined if it circled back over its own trail. In this case, the fresher tracks can be followed. Alternatively, such a situation can indicate the age of spoor relative to an alternative quarry. For example, while tracking down a gemsbok, traditional hunters may find the spoor of a wildebeest superimposed on that of the gemsbok; they may then decide to follow the fresher wildebeest spoor. (Or if a tracker needs to find a lion for tourist clients, he might follow a fresher lion track, since it does not matter which lion he finds.)

Intuitive Estimate
When studying the aging processes that result in the gradual erosion of spoor, a tracker can only make an intuitive estimate of the age of tracks. In some cases, where the aging process is relatively rapid, it is possible to make a reasonably accurate estimate of the age of the spoor. However, due to the complex factors involved, an accurate estimate is usually not possible, especially where aging processes

are slow and may vary considerably depending on circumstances. Intuitive estimates require extensive experience with tracks of varying ages under different environmental conditions. An intuitive estimate also becomes less and less accurate for older spoor.

An indication of the accuracy of intuitive estimates of spoor is illustrated by data from a test conducted with two expert !Xo trackers. Before the test, a series of footprints were marked over a period of time. The trackers had to make intuitive estimates based only on the rate the footprints lost definition due to weathering. There were, for example, no superimposed animal tracks to assist them in their estimates. The trackers on average provided estimates of age for footprints ten hours old that were five hours inaccurate, and for tracks twenty-four hours old, ten to fifteen hours inaccurate, depending on the wind (Liebenberg 1990).

Heat and humidity, which determine the rate at which moisture content is lost, can vary considerably depending on the time of day, prevailing weather conditions, and season. Spoor ages faster in the heat of the day than it does during the cooler part of the day or at night. On a hot dry day, spoor will age faster than on a cool humid day, so the rate of aging might vary considerably from one season to another. It also depends on the climate zone, whether arid desert, dry savanna woodland, or wet tropics.

Wind not only increases the rate at which moisture is lost but also has an eroding effect. The rate at which wind changes a spoor will depend not only on how strong the wind is blowing but also on how long the wind was blowing. A strong wind that drops after a short while might have the same effect as a slight breeze that blows for a long time. The rate might also be complicated by wind that has not been blowing constantly. Fresh footprints have sharp edges that are rounded off by the wind, and they lose definition as leaves, seeds, and loose sand gather in them. Leaf spoor, created by leaves rolling in the wind, may also be superimposed on animal tracks.

Tracks made in shade and sheltered areas will also be less affected by the sun and wind. Tracks on top of dunes are eroded more rapidly than tracks in the valleys between dunes. A track can be sheltered by a bush or a rock and remain fresh-looking for a long time, while a nearby track in an exposed area may be obliterated in a short time. Vegetation can create microclimates that affect tracks in different ways. Tracks might be more sheltered in woodland than in grassland, and tracks in thicker grass might be more sheltered than on ground covered sparsely with grass.

The rate at which wind erodes tracks can also depend on the soil hardness. Spoor in hard compacted soil or clay are eroded more slowly than spoor in soft sand. Spoor in fine sand might erode faster than spoor in coarse sand. Barren sand with no vegetation will be looser, and tracks in it will erode more quickly. Sandy soil with vegetation will be held together by grass roots, and tracks in it will erode more slowly.

On hard rocky ground, a pebble or stone kicked over by the animal will be dislodged from its crater, which was originally formed by dust settling around the pebble or stone, or when loose topsoil was eroded by wind or rain. When the track is still fresh, the edge of the crater might still be sharp. As the spoor gets older, the edge of the crater will be rounded, and eventually the crater will disappear.

The most accurate indications of spoor age are provided by signs that involve rapid moisture loss, since these signs change relatively rapidly in the early stages. Examples of such signs are saliva on the leaves or the ground where an animal has been feeding or licking for salt, fresh urine and droppings, and water that has been splashed on the ground next to water holes or rivers.

A damp patch of urine, which might contain white foam when very fresh, dries into a hard crust of sand. Droppings, which are covered with mucus when very fresh, will still be sticky when reasonably fresh and dry from the outside as they get older. In the case of large animals, such as elephants, fresh droppings will also be warm and might stay warm inside (apparent when broken open) for awhile (Grainger 1967). Color changes in droppings might depend on the animal's diet and could vary from one animal to another. Droppings also shrink when they dry out. The time it takes for droppings to dry out depends on the initial moisture content, which will be greater when the animal has been eating green grass than when it

Old spotted hyena tracks baked into a road surface. ME

has been eating dry grass (the droppings might be smaller as well in the dry season than in the rainy season). The drying rate will also depend on the heat, humidity, and wind. Urine and droppings will take longer to dry out in the shade or a sheltered spot. While the rate of change is relatively rapid in the early stages, once droppings have dried out, the aging processes are much slower and therefore more difficult to estimate. Eventually, the hard crust of sand formed by urine will start to crumble, and dried-out droppings will slowly pulverize.

Because dung surveys are a common method used to determine animal densities in varied species (Lehmkuhl et al. 1994, Massei et al. 1998, Prugh and Krebs 2004), considerable research has been compiled on the decay rates of ungulate and hare pellets. Seasonal temperature and moisture variation have been shown to radically influence the persistence of pellet groups on the landscape, and observers are often unable to differentiate scats several days old from those much older. In Gabon, Africa, dung beetles were shown to be the primary factor in determining the persistence of duiker scats (van Vliet et al. 2009). During the rainy season, beetles would completely dismantle and remove scats within an average of 17 hours. During the dry season, beetles averaged 3.4 days to accomplish the same task.

Another sign that changes rapidly in the early stages is created when an animal walks through a river or a puddle of water or steps into the water when drinking. As the animal steps out of the water, its wet feet will leave wet footprints and splash marks that might dry out very rapidly, depending on the heat, humidity, and wind. In direct sunlight, water can evaporate in minutes. Where the animal has stepped into the water, silt might be stirred up that can take quite a while to settle (Robbins 1977). In muddy ground, tracks might dry out in a very short time or remain wet for a long time, depending on the moisture content of the ground and weather conditions. Usually, the elevated edges of the footprints dry out first while the deepest hollows of the track remain moist the longest. In very moist ground, water may run down and collect in the deepest part of the track, where it may remain for a very long time. Wet ground can also cause spoor to remain visible and look fresh for a considerable time, which can mislead the tracker. Once dried out, footprints might retain their fresh sharp appearance for a very long time, so it will be very difficult to make an accurate estimate of their age (Grainger 1967).

The rate of spoor discoloration is also difficult to estimate, since changes can be very subtle, and the rate of change might be very slow. Fresh footprints expose the darker color of the ground beneath the surface, which will gradually change to the color of the ground on top as it is exposed to the sun. When stones and leaves are overturned, their darker undersides will be exposed, which will also gradually become lighter in color. Stones might also become darker, depending on the mineral content. Broken vegetation will discolor at the break, and the rate of change might differ for different types of vegetation or weather conditions. To get an indication of the color change, a new break may be made and compared with the old break. Leaves might be knocked down by a moving animal or dropped by a feeding animal. These leaves might still be green when they have been dropped and will discolor as they dry. The amount of springback of a flattened tuft of grass can also indicate when it was stepped on (Robbins 1977).

Although superimposed animal spoor, dew, mist, rain, snow, or intuitive estimates do not indicate the actual age of the spoor, they can indicate the chronological sequence of a series of events. As more information is gathered, trackers can revise their hypotheses to create a more detailed sequence, combining information on the animal's activities with information on when these occurred relative to other activities or specific events. As the tracker homes in on the quarry, the estimate of the spoor age may become better and better until the tracks become very fresh. At this point, it is important for the tracker to know when to slow down and move stealthily.

RECONSTRUCTING ACTIVITIES

To reconstruct an animal's activities, specific actions and movements must be seen in the context of the animal's whole environment at specific times and places. Where an animal is moving at a steady pace in a specific direction, or following the easiest route along a well-defined path, and the tracker knows there is a water hole ahead, it can be predicted that the animal is going to that hole. A browsing antelope will move slowly from bush to bush, usually in an upwind direction, so a tracker who knows the animal's favorite food will be able to anticipate where the antelope will go next.

Reconstructions of activities are always hypothetical, however, and predictions could turn out to be wrong. For example, an antelope on its way to a water hole might have scented lions and changed direction to go to another hole. In this case, new evidence might be found, and the tracker might have to revise the initial hypothesis. Or the feeding antelope might not go to the bush the tracker predicted it would but instead select another bush, possibly a species the tracker did not know the animal ate. In this way, the tracker's hypotheses need to be revised by the addition of new knowledge about the antelope's feeding behavior.

An animal's relationship with other animals also influences its actions and reactions. If a walking or trotting animal stops to look at something, this will be indicated by the forefeet being turned in the direction the animal was looking. There might be signs of a confrontation between a territorial male antelope and an intruder showing pawing marks and the horning of shrubbery by one animal, and signs of flight by the other—or signs of fighting between two serious competitors. Signs of a sudden stampede might indicate that animals were fleeing from danger, and the tracks of a predator might be found close by. Conversely, signs that antelope did not react to a predator might indicate that the predator tracks were made at a different time. Or tracks might show where a predator stalked its prey then rushed up to bring it down. The fleeing animal might have crashed through bushes, and its remains might be surrounded by signs of its struggle as well as signs of feeding predators, with spoor of scavengers superimposed.

A family of lynx composed of a female and three kittens, followed by a male suitor. The interpretation was based upon knowledge of lynx mating seasons and behaviors in addition to the sign on the ground. ME

Since tracks can be partly obliterated or difficult to see, they might exhibit only fractional evidence, so the reconstruction of these animals' activities will have to be based on creative hypotheses. To interpret the spoor, trackers must use their imaginations to visualize what the animal was doing to create such markings. Such a reconstruction will contain more information than is evident from the spoor and will therefore be partly factual and partly hypothetical. As new factual information is gathered in the process of tracking, hypotheses might have to be revised or replaced by better ones.

A detailed knowledge of an animal's habits, which might be based partly on hypothetical spoor interpretation, as well as knowledge of the environment, can enable trackers to extrapolate from incomplete evidence and recreate a complete account of an animal's activities. Spoor interpretation can be based not only on evidence from the spoor itself but also on activities that might be indicated by the spoor in the context of the environment and in light of the tracker's knowledge of the animal's behavior. A hypothetical reconstruction of the animal's activities can enable trackers to anticipate and predict the animal's movements. These predictions provide ongoing testing of the hypotheses.

The reconstructions made by trackers can be incredibly accurate. Stander (1997) and colleagues observed a zebra dying of anthrax (blood sampling confirmed the cause), and, over the next several days, a lion pride, hyenas, and vultures feeding and disassembling the carcass. A team of four Ju/'Huan trackers was brought to the area three days after the zebra died and asked to reconstruct what had happened. They investigated the area for two hours, then correctly pointed out the spoor of the zebra and said that the animal was sick and had died from that sickness. They correctly identified all the scavengers and the order in which they fed. They also correctly estimated the relative age of events, including the death of the zebra.

4

Spoor Recognition

The city dweller might find it difficult to appreciate the subtlety and refinement of the tracker's perception of signs. In cities, "signs" (such as advertising, clothing, noise, and so on) all compete with each other for one's attention in an artificial environment. This results in a blunting of the senses, so people lose their sensitivity to their environment. In contrast, many animals in nature have evolved to be inconspicuous, and tracks and signs are all very subtle, so the tracker must develop a sensitivity to the environment. The tracker's ability to recognize and interpret natural signs might therefore seem uncanny to the uninitiated city dweller.

To be able to recognize signs, the tracker must know *what* to look for and *where* to look for it. Someone who's not familiar with spoor might not recognize them even when looking straight at them. It might seem as though no signs were there at all. When tracking through grass, for example, trackers will look for trampled grass, or, if the ground is covered with pebbles, they will look for pebbles displaced from their sockets. To recognize a specific animal's spoor, trackers will look for signs characteristic of that animal within that particular environment and terrain.

To recognize slight disturbances in nature, trackers must know the pattern of undisturbed nature. They must be familiar with the terrain, ground, and vegetation in its natural state. Only when they are familiar with all these aspects will they be able to recognize very subtle disturbances. For example, a disturbance might be revealed by the color differences of overturned pebbles, stones, and leaves,

Look closely to see an adult female cougar's track in this leaf litter. The arrow indicates the direction of travel and the smaller parallel lines define the front and hind edges of the track. ME

whose undersides are usually darker than their sun-bleached tops. Or a dark patch of soil might be revealed as the sun-bleached top layer is disturbed.

To recognize a specific sign, trackers can use a preconceived image of a typical sign, which could be defined by certain characteristics that enable trackers to recognize specific patterns in signs that have corresponding characteristics. Without such preconceived images, many signs can be overlooked—but with a preconceived image of a specific animal's spoor in mind, trackers can "recognize" spoor in markings that might be made by another animal. Of course, their minds will be prejudiced to see what they want to see, so in order to avoid making errors, they must be careful not to make a decision too soon. Decisions made after a quick glance are often erroneous: Trackers need to take time to study new signs in detail when they are first encountered.

While preconceived images might help trackers recognize signs, trackers need to avoid the preconditioned tendency to look for one set of signs in the environment to the exclusion of all others. Naturalists who have trained themselves to detect the smallest signs of a particular specialty, for example, sometimes miss almost everything else. Bird-watchers might recognize the smallest bird in the undergrowth but not see small mammals, plants, or tracks and signs. Botanists might recognize a multitude of plant species but not notice animals hidden in the bushes. One of the authors was once hiking with an archaeologist and, while talking about an unrelated subject, noticed a variety of tracks and signs but did not see any archaeological artifacts. The archaeologist, however, saw numerous stone flakes scattered along the way but did not notice any animal tracks. The two specialists were looking at the same stretch of ground, but they perceived completely different realities. Trackers need to be open to seeing new things in nature and avoid becoming too focused.

The same principle applies to spotting animals. Animals that are well camouflaged will not be easy to see with an untrained eye. Only if trackers know what to look for, and where to look for it, will they recognize the animal. The shape of the animal is defined by the shadows that contrast with highlighted parts. Animals' body shapes are often broken up by contrasting colors to make them inconspicuous. A puff adder has a chevron pattern on its body consisting of dark brown, medium brown, and very light yellow-brown. The dark brown seems to recede like shadow while the lighter color stands out like a highlight. The pattern on the snake is therefore perceived to be at different distances, effectively breaking up the shape of the body. Only when you recognize the distinctive chevron pattern as belonging to a puff adder will the body of the snake come into focus.

In dappled shade, the body of an animal is also broken up into dark shadows and light sunlit patches so it blends in with the leaves of the bush. It's natural to look at dense cover, but a tracker should make an effort to look *through* the cover to recognize the animal behind it.

Trackers will always try to positively identify an animal's trail by some distinguishing mark or mannerism in order not to lose it in any similar spoor. They look for such features in the footprints as well as in an individual's manner of walking. Often the hooves of antelope are broken, have chipped edges, or leave a characteristic scuff mark. The experienced tracker will memorize a spoor and be able to distinguish that individual animal's spoor from another's. When following a spoor, many trackers walk next to it, not on it, taking care not to spoil the trail so that it can easily be found again if the spoor is lost. Others walk atop the spoor because they have trained their minds to precisely recall what they have already seen.

Shadows cast by ridges in the spoor show up best if the spoor is kept between the tracker and the sun. When the sun casts its light from a position ahead of the spoor, the shadow cast by the small ridges and indentations in the spoor will be clearly visible. When the sun casts its light from a position behind the tracker, however, these shadows will be hidden by the ridges that cast them. Tracking is also easiest in the morning and late afternoon, since the shadows cast by the ridges in the spoor are longer and stand out better than at or near midday. As the sun moves higher, shadows grow shorter. At midday, spoor might cast no shadows at all, making them difficult to see in the glare of the sunlight (Grainger 1967).

Julius Mathebula exhibits excellent form—head up and eyes well ahead—while tracking a white rhino in the Garonga, Makalali Private Game Reserve Conservancy, South Africa. AL

Trackers never look down at their feet if they can help it, since this slows them down. By looking up, well ahead of themselves (about fifteen to thirty feet, and sometimes much further, depending on the terrain), they are able to track much faster and at a constant speed. Unless they need to study the spoor more closely, they do not examine every sign. If they see a sign ten yards ahead, they can ignore the intervening signs and continue to look for spoor beyond it.

Depending on the terrain, trackers look a distance ahead that allows them to move at a steady pace. Looking too far ahead and trying to move too quickly, however, can make them lose the spoor, resulting in a stop-start pace. Trackers often vary their pace, depending on how difficult the terrain is, to maintain a smooth steady walk. To do this, they must roll their vision gradually from about five yards ahead out to the farthest sign that can be seen. After scanning the distant terrain, trackers head toward the farthest sign. When they are about five to ten yards from it, their vision once again rolls ahead to look for new signs.

Trackers must be careful not to miss a sudden change in direction the trail might take. For example, a predator could have detected potential prey and abruptly altered its course. Over difficult terrain, it might not be possible to see signs well ahead, so trackers will look at the ground in front of them and move more slowly. Alternatively, trackers can move quickly across a difficult patch to look for signs in easier terrain further ahead. Trackers must also avoid concentrating all their attention on the tracks, thereby ignoring potential danger.

Factors that determine the degree of skill required to recognize, identify, and interpret spoor are: 1) the information content of signs, 2) the sparseness of signs, and 3) the number of proximate signs.

The information content of a sign can be defined as the amount of information that can be derived from it. Well-defined footprints in damp soft ground can provide detailed information on the identity, sex, size, mass, age, condition, and activities of an animal; a barely perceptible scuff mark on hard substrate might offer nothing more than the fact that some disturbance has occurred. Factors limiting the information content of signs include the relative hardness of the substrate, presence of loose sand, density of vegetative cover, and action of wind, rain, and snow. The quality of the substrate can provide valuable information even in the faintest scuff mark. For example, a small white scuff mark on a sandstone rock was probably made by a hoofed animal, since a predator with padded feet would have left no mark at all. Or an indistinct scuff mark on hard muddy soil might have been made by the rounded pads of a predator, since the hard edge of a hoof would have left more distinct scratch marks. Even the most indistinct markings can give an indication of the type of animal that made them. Several indistinct markings together might provide more complete information. Each marking might provide different information. Taken together, their positions relative to each other might indicate the size and gait of an animal. A group of four indistinct scuff marks can be distinctive of a hare; three claw marks can be distinctive of the striped skunk or honey badger. Given the context of the trail of the animal being followed, a fresh scuff mark can confirm that the animal probably passed that way, and a more distinct sign further ahead might confirm its identity. So even if an indistinct scuff mark on its own might not have enough information content to confirm the identity of an animal, the context within which the sign is found could.

It is also important for trackers to recognize when there are no signs at all. When the terrain is very hard, trackers need to be able to tell if the animal would have left some signs if it did in fact pass that way. This is important since trackers need to know when they are no longer on the trail. For example, an animal might have followed two potential routes at a fork in the trail. If the tracker can see that there are no signs where there should have been signs, then the animal probably followed the other route.

The sparseness of signs depends on the substrate, vegetation, and weather conditions. On soft barren substrate, every footprint might be clearly defined, and it would not require much skill to simply follow the trail. On harder substrate, footprints might not be well defined, while on very hard substrate, or on a rocky surface, spoor might be almost imperceptible. While footprints are more difficult to see on ground covered with vegetation than on relatively barren ground, signs in the vegetation itself can indicate the animal's route. The thickness and type of vegetation could determine the sparseness of signs. While it may be easy to distinguish an animal's trail through long grass, it could be very difficult to recognize signs in some types of scrubs. The trail created in long grass might also be distinctive of the animal. Antelope, with long and thin legs, might leave a barely perceptible trail in tall grass while a porcupine, lion, or human might leave a very clear one. In rocky terrain, an animal might leave hardly any signs at all, but it might still be possible to imagine its route by following the contours in between obstacles and finding signs along the route to confirm the trail. The sparseness of signs also depends on the extent to which signs have been obliterated by wind, rain, or snow.

Proximate signs can be defined as signs made by other animals in the vicinity of the spoor being followed. These signs might have

been made before, at the same time, or after the spoor of the animal being followed; if superimposed on each other, they could indicate the age of the spoor being followed. While the tracker may benefit from superimposed spoor, too many proximate signs can sometimes make tracking more difficult. On substrate where footprints are not well defined or where the ground is densely covered with vegetation, the spoor being followed may be confused with similar proximate signs. In difficult terrain with high animal densities, it might be very difficult to distinguish the spoor being followed from proximate signs.

TYPES OF SIGNS

In the narrowest sense of the word, "spoor" simply means "footprint," but in tracking it has a much wider meaning; it refers to all signs found on the ground or indicated by disturbed vegetation. The art of tracking involves each and every sign of animal presence that can be found in nature: scent, feeding signs, urine, feces, saliva, pellets, territorial signs, paths, shelters, vocal and other auditory signs, visual signs, incidental signs, circumstantial signs, and skeletal signs. Spoor are not only left by living creatures. Leaves and twigs rolling in the wind, long grass sweeping the ground, and dislodged stones rolling down a steep slope each leave their distinctive signs. As well, markings left by implements, weapons, or other objects can indicate the activities of humans who used them.

Spoor

Signs of spoor can vary considerably with terrain, weather conditions, season, time of day, and age. Fresh footprints usually show up slightly darker in color than the surrounding ground. On hard ground where there might be no definite indentations, footprints can show up as shiny patches of dirt. Scuff marks in the shape of scraped patches usually stand out as a different shade than the surface

A white rhino trail in tall grass, moving away from the photographer. AL around it. These may occur with accidental scuffing or abrupt turning of the foot to create pivot marks on the ground. When an animal walks across ground and then steps on rocks, some dirt might be transferred onto the rocks.

Wind and rain building up soil deposits around a pebble will form a little crater that becomes visible when the pebble is dislodged from its socket. If a pebble has been kicked out, it can also give an indication of the direction of movement. A freshly turned pebble or stone will generally appear different in colour, usually darker, from surrounding stones. A pebble that has been stepped on will be embedded in the ground, leaving a small gap between the pebble and the original surface of the ground. If a small twig or a dry branch is stepped on, a depression in the ground directly beneath it might be visible. Dead twigs and branches on the ground might be broken or cracked. To determine if the fracture is recent or old, similar twigs can be broken and compared. In contrast to a fresh break, an old break will appear dull and weathered.

A freshly turned dry leaf will appear darker in color as the shaded part is exposed, compared to the sun-bleached surrounding leaves. Some mud may also cling to the side that

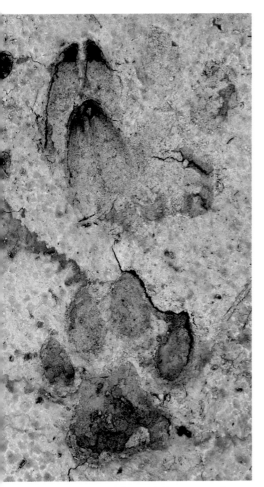

Predator and prey. Old mountain lion tracks stepped on by a mule deer. ME

was underneath. When the ground is covered with dry leaves, a trail of crushed leaves might be left behind. Where leaves lie thick, it might be possible to scrape them aside to examine the earth underneath. On a wet forest floor, clear footprints can be formed in the mud underneath a layer of leaves. Where moss is present, there can be signs of it having been scraped off trees, exposed roots, or rocks. It might be in the form of a scuff mark or bruise, or the moss might be completely scraped off.

Although it provides less information than ground spoor, disturbed vegetation might provide a quicker means of tracking. A very distinct path can be made as tall grass or similar vegetation is bent in the direction of travel. Grass trampled or flattened presents a shiny surface to the sun that can be seen from a considerable distance and makes the route appear lighter in color than the surrounding grass. The easiest spoor to follow are those made through patches of tall grass where other animals have not recently traveled. However, if many animals have been moving through the area, the trail could be confused with those of other animals. When the grass is green and the wind has obliterated other trails, it is easier. But when the grass is dry, old trails can remain for a long time. It is also more difficult to distinguish a fresh trail in dry grass. Tall straight grass is easier to track in than shorter curly grass. When an animal moves through dense bush or reeds, branches or reeds are pulled in the direction of travel, and some interlacing can occur when they are released. Leaves turned upward will also be lighter in color. Soft green vegetation might be bruised or cut, and branches or twigs might be bent or broken. Displaced at an angle, bent or broken vegetation might exhibit reflective properties that differ from unbent plants. Bark might also be scratched or chipped. Leaves might have fallen to the ground. Freshly fallen leaves might still be green compared to old dry leaves.

Where dew or frost occur, or after rain, the uniform distribution of droplets or ice will present a shiny surface. An animal will leave a distinct path that will show up as a dark line where the drops or ice have been shed. When an animal crossing a stream has to step into the water, water or wet mud may be displaced from the stream. The direction of travel is indicated by the wet marks on the ground where the animal left the stream. The presence of an animal that spends most of its time in the water, such as an otter, might be detected by splash marks or even wet paw marks on rocks. Since these signs are soon lost as water is evaporated by the sun or wind, they usually indicate that the animal is still in the near vicinity. If the river bottom can be seen, disturbed mud or overturned rocks or stones might be visible. Close to the water's edge, soft mud might also leave clear impressions.

Broken cobwebs can indicate that an animal moved through an opening between bushes; conversely, cobwebs across an opening or path indicate that an animal did not move through it. Unoccupied and unused holes in the ground are usually indicated by cobwebs in the opening, while occupied holes will be clean.

Scent

Animals produce secretions that leave a trail perceptible to the sense of smell. Many species have special glands that produce a secretion with a scent that is not only specific to the species but also to the individual animal. These glands might be concentrated in special scent organs on an animal's feet, from which scent is transferred to the animal's tracks. An animal might also have scent organs on its head or body, often around the tail region, that can be used to deposit scent at specific places by rubbing it on vegetation or the ground. Scent marking can also be accomplished with urine and feces.

Scent plays an important role in the lives of animals. During the breeding season, males are attracted to females by special odors. Many species also delineate their territories with scent marks. All animals that track follow scent, while humans, who do not have a good sense of smell, have to use dogs. Scent is influenced by temperature and weather conditions. Cool calm conditions help preserve scent while heat and wind erase scent trails. Conditions for following scent trails are better in the morning and evening than at midday, and better in winter than in summer. Wet ground is better than dry ground, but rain can obliterate scent. Scent also diminishes with time, so dogs must follow a relatively fresh trail.

When very close to animals, experienced trackers can sometimes smell and identify animals such as elephant, buffalo, wildebeest, zebra, waterbuck, giraffe, guanaco, and lion before they have seen them. After it has rained for a few days, when the air is very humid, a tracker might also be able to smell animals if the wind is right. Fresh droppings and urine also have a distinctive smell.

Urine and Feces

Fresh urine and feces, frequently indicated by flies and dung-beetles, often help identify spoor, especially if the ground is too hard to provide clear footprints. It can also give

An adult male yellow-bellied marmot scent-marks a rock with its oral glands, located at the corner of its mouth. ME

an indication of the age of spoor. It should be kept in mind that the feces of a single species can vary considerably from area to area, depending on the diet of the animal, its size and condition, time of year, and the age of the feces.

The position of the urine patch relative to the footprints can indicate the sex of the animal (Bang and Dahlstrom 1972). An antelope urinates with the hind legs straddled, which indicates where the animal was standing. The urine patch of the male will be between the tracks of the forefeet and the hind feet, whereas that left by the

A red fox pauses to lift a leg and urinate on a protruding bit of wood. ME

female will be between or behind the tracks of the hind feet. The relative position of a urine patch to feces deposited at the same time can also indicate the sex of the animal. Looking at the footprints to determine the direction, a urine patch in front of feces usually indicates a male, whereas a urine patch on top of or behind feces usually indicates a female.

A detailed examination of feces can provide much information on what the animal was eating. Feces consist of the indigestible parts of the food, such as hair, feathers, bone splinters, pieces of chitin from insects, undigested plant matter, and mucus. The shape and size of mammal droppings are usually characteristic of a species. The size will also depend on the animal's age—the droppings of young animals are smaller than those of adults. The shape may also depend on the composition of the food. In herbivores, lush grass might produce soft, sometimes liquid feces whereas dry grass may produce hard dry droppings. An animal's summer and winter droppings can also exhibit a difference due to not only the composition of the food but also the liquid content. In the dry season, the liquid content will be less, and the droppings might be much smaller than in the wet season. Droppings also shrink as they dry out, so old droppings might be much smaller than fresh droppings.

The droppings of herbivores are generally small and round while those of carnivores are often cylindrical or sausage-shaped with a point at one end. Since plant food has a relatively poor nutritional value, herbivores must eat large quantities and therefore produce large amounts of feces, which usually betray their presence (Bang and Dahlstrom 1972). Meat, on the other hand, is easily digested and of high nutritional value; carnivores, therefore, produce much less feces.

While many animals deposit their feces at random, some use special latrines where large quantities can accumulate. Some, such as cats, might bury their feces. Others use their feces to scent-mark their territories, in which case feces might be deposited in an elevated position, such as on a tree stump, rock, or the top of a small bush so that the scent is effectively disseminated.

Saliva

Saliva can sometimes be seen on leaves where an animal has been feeding or on the ground at a salt lick. Fresh cuds can also be found on the ground. These signs might indicate that the spoor is very fresh, since it does not take long for saliva to evaporate, especially on a hot day.

Pellets

Many birds regurgitate the parts of their food they cannot digest in compressed pellets covered with mucus. These may contain fur, feathers, chitin from insects, bones, pieces of mollusk shell, and undigested plant material. The diameter and shape of the pellet vary according to the species. Some birds produce almost spherical pellets; others produce cylindrical pellets with one or both ends rounded or pointed. The consistency, which may be firm or so loose that the pellet easily falls apart, depends on what the bird has been eating. Since each species has certain food preferences, the contents of the pellet can help identify it (see Elbroch and Marks 2001, and Lees, Ferguson, and Lawrence 2003). The location of the pellets can also indicate the preferred habitat of the species, which might help narrow the possibilities. Pellets are usually found at the birds' roosting sites and nests, and sometimes in feeding areas.

Feeding Signs

A detailed knowledge of the diets of animals for a particular area and time of the year can help a tracker identify spoor from feeding signs. Diets are very complex, however, and more than one animal might eat the same food. The remains left by large carnivores are usually also eaten by smaller carnivores and scavengers. Conversely, if the identity of the animal is already known from its footprints, then feeding signs can indicate what that particular animal has been eating.

Feeding signs can also help when following spoor. Feeding browsers generally move into the wind to scent potential danger ahead. Fresh browsing might be indicated by green leaves dropped on the ground. Twigs with clean cuts can indicate black rhino, while

A log ripped open by a foraging black bear looking for grubs and insect pupae. ME

elephant would leave twigs with frayed ends. Feeding black bears or elephants might also leave a trail of broken branches. White rhino leave grazing signs in grass that indicate their broad mouths. Circling ravens or incoming vultures can also help locate feeding predators or a wounded animal. When vultures settle in a tree instead of on the ground, the predator might still be feeding (Lyell 1929).

Since herbivores have to feed often and in large amounts, they may have many feeding sites along a trail. Since carnivores need to eat only a relatively small amount, the trail of a carnivore must often be followed for a long distance before evidence of a kill site is found. For example, cougars typically kill one large mammal only once every seven to ten days (Elbroch, unpublished data). Many animals prefer to remain hidden when feeding and may take their food to a place where they can feed safely. Some animals might have feeding places out in the open. Some large carnivores, for example, have nothing to fear, while animals such as squirrels might position themselves so they can detect an approaching enemy as they eat (see Elbroch and Rinehart 2010, and Estes 1992).

A browse line created by intensive feeding by white-tailed deer. ME

Apart from their choice of food, evidence in the form of marks left by the teeth or beak and methods of handling the food can also give an indication of the animal involved. (For these and other feeding signs, see Elbroch 2003, Rezendes 1999, Bang and Dahlstrom 1972, and Stuart and Stuart 2003). Distinctive claw marks where the animal was digging for food, such as roots, bulbs, or insects, can indicate the species. Rodents often leave teeth marks, as do deer and moose feeding on barks. Antbears and true bears leave broad claw marks while spring hares leave marks formed by long thin claws. Canids dig very narrow holes, and badgers broader ones. Mongooses may leave small holes, while porcupine digging for bulbs leave correspondingly larger holes. Warthogs and feral pigs may dig up the ground with their snouts and tusks while kneeling down on their front legs. The location of the feeding site will also be an indication of the species. Some feeding signs, such as debarking of trees, can be identified even when they are a few years old, but most feeding signs are usually obliterated relatively quickly.

Vocal and Other Auditory Signs

Vocal signs such as alarm calls can warn either the trackers or their quarry of danger. Since an alarm call usually alerts all other animals in the vicinity, trackers must be careful not to let other animals betray their presence. In North America, red squirrels, jays, chipmunks, and ground squirrels are among those that betray our presence. The gray go-away bird, a great source of annoyance to African hunters, utters a loud drawn-out "go-away" call when disturbed and will often follow or fly ahead of intruders, thus alarming the quarry (Grainger 1967). Baboons may alert other animals by loud barks, monkeys may give their alarm calls when a leopard approaches, a kudu may give a short bark before running off.

To avoid dangerous situations, it is important for trackers to recognize the sounds made by lions when they are feeding or mating, or when they have cubs with them. The presence of rhino or buffalo might be indicated by chirping ox-peckers. A disturbance can also be indicated by the absence of vocal sounds, such as the sudden silence of chirping crickets. Bears are often surrounded by a bubble of

A coyote howling. Such sounds help trackers locate animals. ME

silence—no bird or small animal chatters as bears walk by. The presence of predators might also cause a sudden hush of prey animals. The overhead flight of a bird-hunting raptor is often announced by the sudden silencing of birds that were singing at the tops of the canopy.

Other auditory signs might include rustling grass or bushes, crunching leaves, breaking twigs and branches, stones and pebbles licked in flight, splashing water, and galloping hooves. Depending on the quality of the sound, it might be possible to distinguish between a light or heavy animal, or one that is moving slowly or swiftly. A soft rustling sound in the grass might indicate a hidden snake. A sudden rustling of bushes might indicate a fleeing animal, or a rhino charging through thick bush toward you. A slow heavy rustling of reeds at the water's edge might indicate a crocodile. Feeding elephants can be detected by the sound of breaking branches. In thick bush, black rhinos can be heard feeding as they bite through twigs. Cupping one's hands behind one's ears can help isolate and amplify particular sounds.

Visual Signs
Apart from the actual sighting of an animal itself, visual signs include all signs of movement when the animal is hidden from view. An animal's presence might be betrayed by moving bushes or long grass. A fleeing animal might be detected only by the sudden movement of branches. When the slow rustling sound of a crocodile in tall reeds is heard, its position might be indicated by the moving tips of the reeds. The presence of a crocodile or hippo underwater can be detected by small bubbles rising to the surface.

Incidental Signs
Incidental signs might not necessarily be associated with the spoor in question. Such signs can include tufts of hair, feathers, or porcupine quills. It should be noted that although tufts of hair or feathers might belong to the animal in question, they might also have been blown in by the wind. Similarly, porcupine quills found next to a spoor that is difficult to identify may not belong to that particular

animal, but may have been lying there for some time. Incidental signs can provide potential evidence, but it needs to be confirmed by additional evidence.

Circumstantial Signs

Circumstantial signs are any indirect signs in the immediate vicinity of an animal or person that might betray its presence. Such signs are usually seen in the behavior of other animals. Birds might betray the presence of trackers to animals. Ox-peckers are most frequently found near large ungulates, such as buffalo, eland, and kudu, upon which they clamber about looking for ticks and blood-sucking flies. When approached, they will fly up and about, thus alarming the animals. Animals may become restless when they sense danger. Pronghorn, African antelope, buffalo, and giraffe often stand and stare at intruders. The mobbing behavior of small birds can indicate the presence of snakes or dangerous animals such as leopard or lion (Grainger 1967). However, birds will also mob animals that are dangerous to them, but not dangerous to humans, such as small cats, weasels, or mongooses.

A red-billed ox-pecker atop a buffalo bull. AL

Blood Spoor

A wounded animal may leave blood spoor in the form of spots or drops of blood on the ground and vegetation. An indication of the height of the wound might be given by marks on surrounding shrubs. Blood can also identify where the animal is wounded: Blood from a flesh wound or vein will be dark while clear blood containing air bubbles will have come from the lungs. A wound in the abdomen or intestines will be indicated by blood that includes stomach contents. If the wound is only slight, blood spots will decrease when the bleeding slackens or stops, and the animal will continue running. If the animal's condition worsens, and it decreases the animal's speed, blood spots might be closer together and gathered in pools (Wynne-Jones 1980).

The anal scent mark of a brown hyena. AL

Skeletal Signs

Skeletal signs indicate the remains of animals and can be identified by the size and shape of the skull, teeth, and, if present, horns. Skeletal signs can also indicate the presence of carnivores (see Elbroch 2006).

Territorial Signs

Territorial boundaries might be scent-marked with urine, feces, or scent transferred to bushes or the ground from scent organs. Scent will usually not be perceptible to human trackers, but territorial signs can be visible in the form of latrines, scraping, or the horning of shrubbery. Some small antelope wipe their preorbital glands on the tips of grass or twigs, leaving a black tarry secretion (Smithers 1983). Mountain lions, bobcats, leopards, jaguars, and lions scrape the ground with their hind feet. White rhinos and guanacos create middens.

Paths

Most animals have a network of paths or runs they follow most of the time. Animals know these paths very well and can take flight along them when disturbed. At night, animals are guided by the scent created by continuous use. Paths always take the route that is easiest to follow, going around obstacles. Several animal species might use the same path or parts of it. Elephants create wide paths used by other animals. Animals may also use paths and roads made by humans, incorporating them into their own network. Lions often use roads to cover distance when hunting; bears and mountain lions use human hiking trails. Some paths are very distinctive: Hippo paths consist of two parallel paths, as opposed to the much smaller single-track runs made by vlei rats and meadow voles through thick grass. Paths are usually most distinct in areas where food or water is dependably found. In the immediate vicinity of a water hole, paths are most distinct as animal movement is concentrated, forming a clearing around the hole itself. Farther away from the hole, paths become less distinct as they radiate outwards, branching off into smaller paths. Where smaller paths join to form a larger path, or where small paths join up with a main path, the larger path usually points toward the water hole. In thick reed beds, heavily wooded areas, and forests, a network of paths is usually the only route animals can follow through the thick undergrowth (Bang and Dahlstrom 1972). Well-defined paths are also formed in hilly and mountainous terrain, where the slope of the ground forces animals to follow specific routes. When tracking in such terrain, the tracker can look at the contours and anticipate where tracks will be found in paths ahead.

Homes and Shelters

Most animals continually move their sleeping quarters and may have a fixed home only during the breeding season in order to protect their young. Some animals do not even have fixed homes during

The worn trail of traveling hippos. ME

the breeding season if the young are mobile soon after they are born. Young may also be transported by a parent to avoid dangerous situations or escape parasite infestations. Only a few animals have a permanent home they use throughout the year. Homes are usually inconspicuous and in sheltered or inaccessible places that are difficult to find. In the breeding season, they may be betrayed by the activities of adults bringing food to the young. They might also be detected by tracking the animal's trail until it eventually reaches the home or shelter.

The most common homes found are bird's nests. They are usually sheltered among the leaves of trees and bushes or in ground vegetation. Nests of different species are characterized by their position, size, structure, and the materials used; they vary considerably in appearance. To find the nest of an ostrich, Bushmen trackers use their knowledge of the bird's behavior. For example, if they have found signs of where an ostrich had taken a dust bath, it would be quicker to backtrack in order to determine where it had come from rather than tracking forward to determine where it was going. This is because an ostrich takes a dust bath directly after it has left the

An American badger's burrow. ME

The large nest of a big-eared woodrat. ME

nest; it then goes on to feed in the veld, returning to the nest later that day. The distance back to the nest is therefore much shorter than the distance covered after it had a bath.

Some small mammals build their homes in vegetation, and these can look very much like bird's nests. Squirrels build their drays in trees, usually close to the trunk. They are spherical and consist of loosely plaited twigs lined with grass or leaves. Harvest mice and rice rats create spherical balls of grass elevated in bushes and other vegetative structure.

Animals that don't construct homes or shelters and simply lie down to rest in a sheltered place often leave a depression that has distinct outlines of the animal's limbs and body. The size of the depression, together with other signs such as footprints and droppings, can indicate the animal that was resting there. Hares and jackrabbits create distinctive forms in sheltered places in long grass or next to bushes. The hare scrapes away the leaves then lies down in a shallow depression, making the animal very difficult to detect.

Even when rain has obliterated footprints, excavated depressions made by animals can still be identified. I was once asked to investigate a complaint from a farmer in the Ghanzi district in Botswana that wild dogs had killed his cattle. His farm workers took us to a den where they claimed the wild dogs were seen. There were fresh tracks of brown hyenas but no sign of wild dog. They then took us to some bushes they claimed the wild dogs were lying under. It had been raining for several days, and there were no footprints to identify the animals. But there were still depressions in the ground around the bushes where the animals had been lying close together. !Nam!kabe, one of the Bushmen trackers who came with me, pointed out that it was brown hyenas that were lying under the bushes. He explained that if it were wild dogs, there would not be any depressions after several days of rain because dogs do not excavate depressions before they lie down; they simply lie down on the ground. Furthermore, dogs would not lie close together around a bush but would lie down scattered over a larger area. Brown hyenas, on the other hand, do make depressions in the ground and lie closer together.

—L. L.

Many animals make their homes in the ground, often within a system of burrows. These could have a main entrance as well as an escape exit. Underground burrows might be revealed by heaps of excavated soil, such as those made by mole rats and pocket gophers. Homes might consist of an extended network of burrows and house a whole colony of animals, such as suricates or ground squirrels. Many burrowers, such as antbears and badgers, play an important ecological role because their unused holes are often taken over by other animals. Apart from their permanent burrows, antbears also dig temporary holes to sleep in. Dwarf mongooses dig their burrows into termite mounds. The occupant of a burrow might be identified by the size and shape of the entrance hole, its position, and the method used to remove excavated soil, as well as tracks and droppings in front of and inside the entrance. The trail of an animal might indicate which direction its burrow will be found. To find an African porcupine den, for example, it helps to know that the trail going away from the den follows a meandering route as the animal searches for food, while the trail going back to the den follows a straight line. As you get closer to the burrow, you will find more sets of porcupine tracks of various ages radiating out. An occupied burrow will show fresh signs of use. Some animals, such as the antbear, will close up the entrance from the inside. A disused burrow will have fallen leaves collected in the entrance and cobwebs spun across the opening, or it may be overgrown.

5

Anticipating Spoor and Making Predictions

The day was waning, and we couldn't find another lion trail to follow, so I followed an old rhino track for practice. Wilson watched from the rear, ever critical, and Johnson followed quietly, watching the bush intently. Given our direction and progress, Adriaan circled around to retrieve our vehicle, and the three of us moved slowly along the trail. I was having great difficulty finding sign and increasingly wandering rather than following the trail. Wilson didn't tolerate such nonsense. He snapped his fingers to grab my attention and signaled that I fall back and allow Johnson to take the lead.

Johnson is a senior tracker with Singita Lebombo, a private concession in the Kruger National Park. He paused momentarily over the last footprint I had found. Then he stood erect and gazed into the bush where the rhino had moved. Then he started walking. We flowed through the bush, without pause or frustration, winding through the vegetation and along intersecting game-paths. All the while, Johnson never once dipped his head. Not too fast, and certainly not slow, the three of us moved silently along as the sun sank lower and lower. We walked this way for about half an hour, then Johnson abruptly stopped and turned to us.

"I've lost the trail," he said, as if it were the most normal thing in the world.

"Let's head to the vehicle," said Wilson, without comment.

"Johnson," I asked, "how did you do that?" He looked at me as though he wasn't sure what I was asking him. "What were you thinking when you tracked the rhino? How did you move so well?"

Johnson Mhlanga with his senior tracker certificate. ME

Then Johnson looked pleased, as if no one had ever asked him to explain what he did so naturally. "When I start on a track, I look in the direction the animal is moving. And then I move like that animal would on the landscape." He looked at me.

"And then you see signs to confirm you are moving in the right direction?" I asked.

"Sometimes," he replied.

His explanation was simple but profound. It took me a year to feel I understood what he meant by "sometimes" and why he responded the way he did.

—M. E.

Although trackers can follow a trail simply by looking for one sign after the other, this can become so time consuming that they might never catch up with their quarry. Unless the animal is resting in the midday heat, it's likely moving at a steady pace, and the tracker must therefore progress at a much faster pace in order to overtake it. Instead of looking for one sign at a time, trackers can place themselves in the position of their quarry to anticipate the route it might have taken. They can then decide in advance where they expect to find signs instead of wasting time searching for them. Trackers can look for spoor in obvious places, such as openings between bushes. In thick bushes, they can look for the most accessible throughways. Where the spoor crosses an open clearing, they can look for access routes on the other side. If the animal has been moving from shade to shade, they can look for spoor in the shade ahead. If the animal was feeding, and it is known what food it prefers, the tracker can look ahead for places where the animal will most likely have been feeding.

Animals usually use a network of paths to move from one place to another. If it is clear that an animal has been using a particular path, that path can simply be followed up to a point where it forks into two or more paths, or where the animal has left it. Where one of several paths may have been used, the trackers must, of course, determine which path that specific animal followed. This might not always be easy, since many animals use the same paths. Animals also often leave a path to take a shortcut. Roads, for example, are often used by animals, but roads might not follow the best route for an animal. African lions often use roads, but when the road curves, the lion may cut across the curve to shorten its trip. Or when the road turns away from the direction the lion intends to go, the lion may leave it. Often they leave the road at a point where a game path was formed and follow the path to where it joins another road.

In areas with high animal densities that include much-used interlinking animal paths, it might seem impossible to follow tracks. The path might be very hard and compacted; other animals may have walked over the spoor to obliterate or confuse it; a multitude of old tracks might make newer spoor difficult to distinguish. Where there are many confusing tracks, it becomes critical to distinguish the relative ages of the various tracks to identify the tracks that are being followed. Once tracks have been located on a specific path, however, it is also possible to follow the path even though no further tracks can be seen. By looking to either side of the path, the trackers can establish if the animal has moved away from the path, and they can then follow the new trail (Williams 1976).

When a herd of antelope or a pride of lions is followed, it is not necessary to follow one specific animal. A herd or pride might use several paths running more or less parallel to one another. As long as any one of the animals is followed, the movement of the whole group can be determined. If the trackers lose the spoor of one, they can pick up the spoor of another.

The same principle applies when tracking an African porcupine to its den. When it moves back to its den, a porcupine will follow a more-or-less-straight course. As you get closer to the den, you may encounter old spoor of the same porcupine from previous days. Following the general direction, trackers can home in on the den by following either the fresh spoor or any of the older spoor pointing in the same general direction.

When trackers come to hard stony ground where tracks are virtually impossible to discern (apart from the odd pebble that has been overturned), they may move across the patch of hard ground in order to find spoor in softer ground ahead (Williams 1976). Should they lose the spoor, they might first search obvious places for signs, choosing several likely accessible routes through the bush in the general direction of movement. When several trackers work together, they can fan out and quarter the ground until one of them finds the spoor. Experienced trackers are able to anticipate more or less where the animal was going and will not waste time in one spot looking for signs but will instead look further ahead.

*C*onducting a tracker evaluation in the Klein Karoo, I needed to find *an animal suitable for a trailing test. The terrain was mountainous, with sandy floodplains in the valleys. In the plains, it is relatively easy to follow tracks, but as soon as you go up the slope onto the side of a steep hill or mountain, the terrain becomes very rocky, with barely any sand in which to leave tracks. I decided to trail an aardvark to see if it were possible to follow it over the rocky terrain. The aardvark has thick strong claws that make it easy to follow on sandy ground, but the claws also leave scuff marks on rocky surfaces, especially if there is a thin layer of wind-blown dust collecting in rocky crevices.*

Tracking the aardvark in the sandy floodplain made it possible to get a general direction as it headed up the side of the mountain, but as soon as it walked onto the rocky ground, its footprints disappeared. The aardvark has short legs and tends to avoid going over boulders, so I could visualize the most likely route it followed between the rocks. Following the easiest path in the general direction up the mountain slope, I could find pebbles that were freshly displaced and the occasional scuff mark on a flat rock. But at one point, I completely lost the trail. Looking up at the steep mountainside, I visualized a path going up to the top, and by following the imaginary path, found one displaced rock that could have been a sign of the aardvark, but I was not sure. But it was the only sign, so, working on the assumption that it was the aardvark, I headed up to the top of the mountain. As the ground started to flatten, I found fresh tracks where the aardvark had dug for termites. The trail went down the other side of the mountain and into the next valley, where footprints were once again easy to follow. Then it again headed up the next slope, where I lost the trail but was able to follow an imaginary path over the rocky mountainside.

Aardvark tracks. JUAN PINTO

On the top, where there was sandy soil, I again picked up the trail where the animal had dug for termites.

On flat ground, you invariably find more sandy soil, in which it is easier to track. On steep mountain slopes, sandy soils are usually washed away, leaving barren ground. But the contours of the mountainside, together with boulders that channel the movements of animals, make it easier to predict the path an animal would have followed. Nevertheless, when an animal changes direction in an unexpected way and there are no scuff marks or displaced pebbles to indicate the path it followed, it can simply become impossible to follow the trail. It then requires a lot of persistence to search all the possible routes the animal might have taken until you find fresh tracks.

—L. L.

Knowledge of the terrain and animal behavior allows trackers to save valuable time by predicting an animal's movements. Once a general direction of movement is established, and it is known that an animal path, river, or any other natural boundary lies ahead, trackers can leave the spoor and move to these places, cutting across the trail by sweeping back and forth across the predicted direction in order to pick up the tracks a considerable distance ahead (Williams 1976). If the animal has been moving in a straight line at a steady pace, and it is known that there is a water hole or pan further ahead, the tracker can leave the spoor to look for signs of it at the hole or pan. To predict the movements of an animal, trackers must know the animal and its environment to such an extent that they can identify with the animal. They must be able to visualize how the animal was moving and put themselves in its place.

Before going out on a hunt, traditional Bushmen trackers discuss all the information at their disposal and work out a strategy to maximize their chances of success. With a detailed knowledge of the country, they are able to identify areas regularly visited by animals, such as water holes, pans, and dense thickets and the animal paths that connect them. Their knowledge of animal habits also enables them to predict what the animals' movements might be and at what times they will visit certain areas. The hunters will discuss past hunts and apply the knowledge they have gained from them. Each hunt is therefore a continuation of previous hunts, taking advantage of experience gained over many years.

Interpretation of spoor on recent outings can also enable hunters to identify favored feeding grounds and resting places. These might be indicated by the signs of animals visiting the same place repeatedly. On each outing, the hunters will systematically take note of all signs of animal movement, identifying all spoor and making an estimate of the animal's size, sex, the age of the spoor, where it came from, how fast the animal was moving, and where it was going. All information on recent animal movements gained from their own or others' observations is taken into account when predicting the whereabouts of a quarry. They will also take note of tracks they may not follow immediately but which they might follow in the future.

For example, they might find the tracks of a large eland, but the spoor might be old. They will note the direction of travel and age of the spoor and will look out for the animal in case they find fresh spoor.

The trackers' ability to interpret spoor enables them to reconstruct the context of a particular animal's communication even when they hear it but don't see it. By estimating the distance and direction of a call, trackers can go to the place where the animal was and study its tracks to determine what it was doing. So, for example, Bushman hunters are able to interpret the nocturnal calls of jackals. When a jackal gives a long smooth howl that diminishes in loudness (*WHAaaa . . .*), it is simply maintaining contact with other jackals. If, on the other hand, it gives a shuddering howl, diminishing in loudness and ending in a soft cough (*WHA-ha-ha-ha . . . umph*), it is following the spoor of a scavenger or large predator. Bushman trackers explain that it "stutters" because it is afraid. If the jackal gives the shuddering howl only once, then it is following a hyena spoor. It has

A black-backed jackal. ME

abandoned the spoor after the first call because it will not get much meat by following a hyena. If, however, it repeats the shuddering howl several times, it is following the spoor of a leopard or lion. It continues to follow the spoor because it knows that it will lead to a lot of meat. Apart from warning the hunters of the danger of lions at night, jackal calls can indicate the recent movements of predators and scavengers, which can then be taken into account when planning a hunting strategy.

In selecting a quarry, hunters consider not only its size, and therefore the meat yield, but also the ease or difficulty with which it can be captured—that is, the amount of energy that will be expended to gain a certain amount of meat. When setting out, hunters might have several working leads based on recent tracks. Once in the field, however, they might change their initial strategy as new information is gathered.

Because signs might be fractional or partly obliterated, it is not always possible to make a complete reconstruction of an animal's movements and activities based on spoor evidence alone. Trackers might therefore have to create a working hypothesis in which spoor evidence is supplemented with assumptions based not only on knowledge of the animal's behavior but also on an ability to solve new problems and discover new information. The working hypothesis might be a reconstruction of what the animal was doing, how fast it was moving, when it was there, where it was going, and where it might be at that time. Such a hypothesis can enable the tracker to predict the animal's movements. As new information is gathered, the tracker can revise the hypothesis, creating a better reconstruction of the animal's activities. Anticipating and predicting an animal's movements, therefore, involves a continuous process of problem solving, creating new hypotheses, and discovering new information.

Interpreting an animal's activities and predicting its movements can be done using not only spoor evidence but also a knowledge of the animal's behavior and the environment. The gait of an animal is indicated by the relative positions of its footprints. The speed at which the animal is moving is indicated by the distances between the footprints, as well as the way the soil is kicked up. The way the animal moves might further imply activities not evident in the spoor itself. If, for example, the footprints of a fox indicate that it was moving very slowly, this could imply that is was hunting, moving slowly so as not to be seen while scenting for its prey. The hunting activity itself is not evident from the spoor—unless signs of a catch are found—but is indicated by the way the fox moves when hunting. (It should be noted that the signs of the fox moving very slowly do not necessarily mean that it *was* hunting, only that it *might have been* hunting, since it could have been moving slowly for a different reason.)

The context of the spoor—the environment and a knowledge of the animal's behavior—can enable trackers to extrapolate from the spoor evidence in order to predict the movements and activities of an animal. Discussing the spoor of two black-backed jackals that were trotting in the direction of a nearby pan, for example, Bushmen trackers !Nam!kabe, !Nate, Kayate, and Boroh//xao maintained that the jackals (a male and female, which they said were a mating pair) were going to scavenge for meat, possibly in the pan. The trackers then went on to say that after eating, the jackals would lie down during the midday heat and, in the late afternoon, go back for more meat, after which they would hunt for mice. A similar extrapolation was made from the spoor of a meerkat that was trotting away from a nearby pan. The trackers explained that it was coming from its warren in the hard ground in the pan and was on its way to look for scorpions where the ground is soft and sandy.

When you are tracking, your ability to extrapolate from spoor evidence is important to predict the possible whereabouts of an animal.

While tracking down a solitary wildebeest spoor of the previous evening, !Nam!kabe pointed out evidence of trampling that indicated that the animal had slept at that spot. He explained that the spoor leading away from the sleeping place had been made early that morning and was therefore relatively fresh. The fresh spoor followed a straight course, indicating that the animal was on its way to a specific destination. !Nam!kabe investigated several sets of footprints in a particular area. He pointed out that the prints all belonged to the same animal but were made during previous days. He explained that that particular area was the feeding ground of a particular wildebeest. Since it was by that time about midday, he expected that the wildebeest was resting in the vicinity. He then followed the fresh spoor, moving stealthily, until he spotted the animal in the shade of a tree not far from the area he had identified as its feeding ground. The interpretation of the spoor was based not on the evidence of the spoor alone, but also on his knowledge of the animal's behavior, the context of the spoor in the environment, and the time of day. All this enabled !Nam!kabe to create a reconstruction of the animal's activities that contained more information than was evident from the spoor itself.

Tracks of a lioness ME

Looking at some lion tracks, Karel Kleinman, a Bushman tracker who worked in the Kgalagadi Transfrontier National Park, pointed out that the lion (a male) that was lying in the shade of a dune, got up and trotted a short distance, stood still, then trotted off at a *steady pace in a specific direction. He explained that the lion had heard a female in the distance, got up, and trotted higher up on the dune, where he stood still to listen; he then trotted off to go and find the female. Kleinman drove his vehicle around some high dunes to find his way to where he predicted the lion had been going. He picked up the tracks and followed them to a spot where the lion had encountered two other lions, a male and a female. The tracks indicated that the two males had been fighting over the female, after which one of the males went off together with the female. The original set of tracks only indicated a male lion that got up, stopped, and continued at a trot. But the way it moved showed that it was not hunting, since it was not trying to move stealthily to stalk prey. Rather, it stopped to listen to something in the distance, and then moved off at a steady pace. The way it moved indicated that it was attracted to a female.*

—L. L.

Another example is illustrated by the reconstruction given by Ju/wasi trackers of the hunting conduct of a pair of lions (Blurton Jones and Konner 1976). The reconstruction describes how the lions approached together to a certain point and then split up. One lion continued a short distance then lay down to wait. The other lion circled the prey then pounced on it, whereupon the waiting lion rushed up to join the attack. While the paths taken by the two lions were clear from the spoor, the interpretation of the relative timing of the attacks was based on the way the animals moved. The subsequent tracks of the lion that lay down did not indicate that it was stalking or was about to leap, but they did indicate that it was running in an erect posture. It should be noted that the reconstruction of the relative timing of the attacks was only hypothetical—the waiting lion did not necessarily get up only after the other lion started the attack. It is possible that the waiting lion got up into an erect posture before the other lion attacked in order to chase the prey toward the lion that circled it. If this had been true, however, there would have been signs indicating that the prey was fleeing toward the lion that first pounced.

TYPES OF PREDICTIONS

Tracking involves different types of predictions that are based on different types of logic. These can be divided into three main types: random, systematic, and speculative.

Random Prediction

Random predictions are made when the tracker has lost the spoor and has no idea where to look for it—he is genuinely "clueless." In this case, he can simply give up or try any direction, which is better than nothing. If he is lucky, he might find the spoor again. Or he can make random predictions before starting to track.

Traditionally, some Bushmen hunters resorted to a form of random prediction when they used sets of disks, usually made of leather, for divination. The disks were believed to be capable of revealing recent or current events and foretelling the near future. Hunters would consult the disks before going on a hunt to determine in what direction to look for animals (Marshall 1976). Hunters might express different opinions. They insist that some can interpret the disks better than others and mock each other for ignorance in disk reading. The meaning of the message, which is determined from the position of dropped disks, is apparently not governed by fixed rules. The interpretations are products of the imaginations of the hunters, who are free to see in the disks whatever comes to mind. Hunters know so much about animal behavior and spoor that their intuitive interpretation is more likely to be right than wrong. They might also selectively remember the predictions that were coincidentally right while wrong predictions are forgotten. It is also possible that the effect of divining is to randomize the routes or areas searched. Hunters know that animals learn the habits of humans and adjust their behavior accordingly. To guard against the possibility of falling into a predictable routine, divining may introduce an unpredictable component to the hunter's strategies (Laughlin 1968).

Systematic Prediction

Systematic prediction is based on past experience. If the trail is following a well-defined path going toward a water hole, and the tracker knows from past experience that animals following this path usually end up at the hole, then the tracker can predict that the animal was going to the hole. This type of prediction is based on repeated learning by trial and error and does not require imagination.

Systematic prediction does not go beyond known evidence. On the other hand, when the spoor is lost, and there is no direct evidence to go by, then a systematic prediction would involve looking everywhere until the spoor is found, since it is known that the animal must have gone somewhere. This usually involves searching in a wide circle around the last known track, repeated in wider circles until the tracks are found.

Speculative Prediction

Speculative prediction involves creating a hypothesis to explain what the animal was doing and then predicting where the animal was going. This is fundamentally different from systematic prediction, since it goes beyond the available evidence. The tracker might use knowledge of animal behavior, look for indicators in the broader environmental context, then predict where the tracks will be found. This makes it possible for the tracker to make predictions in situations not experienced before. Sometimes a tracker can even make unusual predictions about animal behavior, resulting in new discoveries.

SYSTEMATIC VERSUS SPECULATIVE TRACKING

Systematic and speculative predictions involve fundamentally different ways of thinking and result in different ways of tracking. Systematic tracking involves the systematic gathering of information from signs until it provides a detailed indication of what the animal was doing and where it was going. To reconstruct the animal's activities, the tracker primarily gathers empirical evidence in the form of spoor and other signs. Speculative tracking involves the creation of a working hypothesis on the basis of initial interpretation of signs and knowledge of the animal's behavior and the terrain. With a hypothetical reconstruction of the animal's activities in mind, trackers then look for signs where they expect to find them. The emphasis is primarily on speculation, looking for signs only to confirm or refute expectations. When expectations are confirmed, hypothetical reconstructions are reinforced. When expectations prove to be incorrect, trackers must revise their working hypotheses and investigate alternatives.

In systematic tracking, trackers do not go beyond the evidence offered by signs, and they do not conjecture possibilities which they have not experienced before. Their anticipation and prediction of the spoor are based on repeated experience of similar situations—they do not predict anything new. Even when a prediction is based on experience, of course, it might not necessarily be correct in that particular instance.

In speculative tracking, trackers go beyond the evidence offered by signs. Anticipation and prediction are based on imaginative pre-

Tracker and ranger attempt to unravel a set of elephant trails so as to remain with the animal they were following. AL

conceptions. They conjecture possibilities that are either confirmed or refuted. Even when expectations are confirmed, however, this does not imply that hypotheses were correct; they might still prove to be incorrect. When expectations prove to be incorrect, a process of negative feedback takes place, in which the trackers modify their working hypotheses to correspond with new spoor evidence. Speculative tracking, therefore, involves a continuous process of conjecture and refutation.

Speculative tracking is a self-correcting process, involving both positive and negative feedback. When signs confirm expectations, positive feedback reinforces the belief that you are on the right track. When it is clear there are no tracks in an area where tracks would have been visible, negative feedback indicates that you have veered off the trail and need to correct yourself. You can get false positive feedback, however, if you incorrectly interpret a sign as positive feedback when in fact the sign was made by another animal. In this case, you will stray further off the trail. Or you can get false negative feedback when crossing hard ground where no tracks are visible. You might mistakenly conclude that the animal did not go that way, when in fact it did go that way, but the ground is too hard to leave visible signs. In this case, you might waste valuable time searching for the tracks elsewhere.

Systematic tracking involves a cautious approach. Since the trackers do not go beyond direct evidence, the chances of losing the spoor are small. Even anticipation and prediction do not involve a great risk of losing the spoor, since they are based on repeated experience. If the trackers can progress fast enough, they will eventually overtake their quarry. While systematic tracking can be very efficient in relatively easy terrain, it can prove time consuming in difficult terrain.

Speculative tracking, on the other hand, requires a bold approach. Anticipating the animal's movements by looking at the terrain ahead and identifying with the animal on the basis of knowledge of the animal's behavior, trackers can follow an imaginary route, saving much time by only looking for signs where they expect to find them. Trackers might visualize animals moving through the landscape and ask themselves what they would do if they were the animals, and where they would have gone. By predicting where animals might have been going, trackers can leave the spoor, take a shortcut, and look for the spoor further ahead. While speculative tracking may save much time, thereby increasing the chances of overtaking the animal, it nevertheless involves a much greater risk of losing the spoor and wasting time finding it again. Alternatively, systematic tracking can prove to be so time-consuming in difficult terrain that it may be more efficient to risk losing the spoor occasionally for the time that can be saved by speculative tracking.

Most beginning trackers tend to be very systematic and look for tracks in front of them on the ground. Speculative tracking requires a lot of experience. So most trackers start off as systematic trackers and only become speculative trackers once they have mastered the basic skills. In the beginning, it is also easier to gain experience through systematic tracking. As the learner gains experience, the increase in knowledge should make it easier to use speculative tracking. Making the transition from systematic to speculative tracking can be very difficult, however. The two methods are so fundamentally different that many trackers struggle to change their methods. And the longer they use only systematic tracking, the more difficult it will become to switch to speculative tracking.

Even though there is a fundamental difference between systematic and speculative tracking, in practice they are complementary. A tracker can use both, so there might not always be a clear distinction between the two. Ideally, a tracker should know to what extent either systematic or speculative tracking, or a combination of both, would be most efficient in particular circumstances. In very easy terrain, such as an open, sparsely vegetated, sandy region, systematic tracking can be so efficient that it might not be worth risking losing the spoor by speculation. In very difficult terrain, a tracker might not get very far with systematic tracking; speculative tracking might be the only way to overtake the quarry. In open flat terrain, it can be difficult to anticipate an animal's movements, so systematic tracking may be more efficient. In thick woodland, where paths might be formed through gaps in the bush, or in hilly terrain, where paths are formed by the contours, speculative tracking might be more efficient. Trackers can also alternate between systematic and speculative tracking as the terrain and vegetation change during the course of tracking. Tracking conditions will often vary between conditions that favor one type of tracking, requiring an optimal combination of both.

Systematic tracking is more appropriate when tracking small species, such as the grysbok, a tiny antelope, that have a small home range and often circle back over its own spoor many times. In the rainy season, when the sand is wet, and spoor may remain fresh looking for several days, fresh tracks could be confused with old tracks, making it difficult to use speculative tracking. When tracking a calf of an antelope, systematic tracking is also more efficient. Calves of a certain age tend to run around in circles when their mothers hide them in thickets, crossing back over their tracks many times in a small area. To find a calf therefore requires extremely systematic tracking. On the other hand, when tracking large animals that cover great distances, speculative tracking can be more efficient.

In Noordhoek, where I live, I had been tracking the grysbok, a small elusive antelope, in the dunes and wetlands. The sun was shining, with just a few clouds in the sky, and a cool breeze was blowing. It had rained the previous night, and the wet sand was ideal for tracking. All the old tracks had rain on them, and the fresh ones were crisp and clear, as close to perfect as you can get.

I found a fresh grysbok track and started following it. It was running away from something, and dog tracks nearby suggested a possible culprit. The running tracks dug into the wet sand, making them easy to see from quite a distance—almost too easy. They were running into the wind, so I could move at a reasonable pace without worrying that the grysbok would smell me. But as I got closer to the thickets where the animal usually hides, it got more difficult. The tracks were easy to follow, but now there were many tracks crisscrossing each other. It could be the same animal moving in circles as it fed through the night, or there could be several grysbok in the same area.

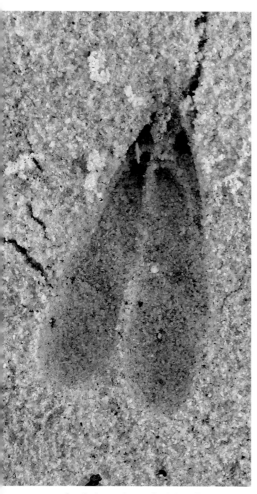

Grysbok tracks in the Noordhoek dunes. ME

Two sets of tracks going in opposite directions headed to the thicket in which I had once found my quarry. (I did not actually see her that time, but when I investigated some tracks going into the thicket, I heard a rustle. I did not want to flush her out, so I left.) This time, I studied the tracks carefully. It seemed as though there were two entry points into the thicket, little tunnels going into the bush about the size of a grysbok. But even though the tracks went right up to the entry points, I could not confirm whether she was just feeding, or whether she actually went into the bush. Inside the bush, the ground was covered with a thick layer of leaves, and I could not make out whether there were any tracks going in or not.

In case she was inside the thicket, I left the spot and explored another set of tracks leading away from the thicket. They went off toward the houses, going right up to them. It appeared that the animal was just browsing in the area.

I went back to the thicket and explored another set of tracks going in the other direction. Then I found some baby grysbok tracks. They seemed to be smaller than the young grysbok tracks I found the previous time. But I was not sure. Maybe there were two young grysbok in the same area.

I could see how the young grysbok was playing, running around in circles. They often do that to confuse predators that might be tracking them. There were also areas with a lot of tramping around on one spot, next to the adult: She must have been suckling. I followed the baby tracks to see where they went. I was moving into a stiff breeze, so the grysbok would not be able to smell me coming. But then an adult grysbok broke cover about fifty yards ahead of me and, in full sight, ran off to the safety of a bushy area. I was still quite far from her, so I did not actually flush her out. If I were just walking my dog, like all the other people who walk their dogs around Noordhoek beach, she would have remained hidden. Most people would just walk past and never see her. My border collie Cleo was lying quietly under a bush, so he did not flush her out. I taught Cleo to stay behind me when I am busy tracking, so whenever I start tracking, he can see from my body language that he must hang back and lie down when I stop to study tracks. The grysbok could not smell me; she must have been watching me.

This raised some interesting questions: Did she watch me track her baby? Did she actually realize that I was tracking them and not just walking my dog? Did she break cover to reveal herself and draw me away from where she was hiding her young? When other people walk through the area with their dogs, the grysbok simply sits tight. I was wondering whether this grysbok was getting to know me and Cleo and realized that I was following her tracks to where she was hiding.

I did not want to go over to the bush, in case her baby was still hiding there. Sometimes it is better to leave something as a mystery. Once she broke cover, I did not want to pursue her any further, since I didn't want to chase her from the area. When tracking animals, you should try to have as little impact on their behavior as possible.

—L. L.

Speculative tracking becomes more efficient when an experienced tracker knows a particular area very well. A detailed knowledge of the terrain and the animals in the area makes it easier to use speculative tracking. Trackers can also get to know individual animals and their particular habits, making it possible to predict where they will most likely be found. On the other hand, even expert trackers might not be able to do speculative tracking in an area they do not know and that contains species with which they are unfamiliar. When working in an unfamiliar area, even experienced speculative trackers might find it easier to use systematic tracking.

Speculative tracking is also important when tracking dangerous animals (or humans). When tracking a lion, rhino, or dangerous criminal, you cannot look at the ground in front of you, systematically following the trail. Your first priority is to look ahead for signs of danger. Secondly, you look ahead to anticipate and predict where the quarry was going. Only then do you look for tracks to confirm your predictions.

While systematic and speculative tracking are two complementary types of tracking, individual trackers can, under the same circumstances, tend to be either more systematic or more speculative. When they observe sparse spoor evidence, trackers might make interpretations that differ considerably. A group of four Bushmen trackers, for example, once gave different interpretations of dried-out droppings from a large antelope in a pan after the footprints had been obliterated by the wind. One tracker identified it as being that of a gemsbok, while another maintained that it was that of a hartebeest. A third tracker supported one interpretation, while a fourth supported the other. They could not reach a consensus. I did not have enough experience to know who was correct or if it was in fact possible under the circumstances to tell whether the dried-out droppings could be identified as being either from a gemsbok or hartebeest. One tracker then said that the antelope licked for salt, but that he did not know in which direction it went because he could not see the spoor. Another had a more creative approach. He proposed that the antelope came from the east and went off to the west to its feeding ground. He went on to say that it did not come back that morning but went to another pan. From that pan, it would have gone in the other direction to where the grass was green. Although the only sign of the animal was its dropping, the identity of which was disputed, he reconstructed the animal's movements on the basis of the estimated age of the droppings, the direction the wind was blowing at the time it was deposited, the fact that the antelope usually move into the wind (to scent danger from ahead), its daily feeding and salt-licking habits, and his knowledge of the environment. His hypothetical reconstruction went beyond the direct evidence of the signs but enabled him to make a prediction which, if followed up, would either be confirmed or refuted. Sometimes his speculative predictions would have been refuted, but sometimes they would have been correct. When they were, it would have given him a better chance of locating the animal than the more conservative systematic tracker, who would have no lead at all. While sparse spoor evidence will be of no use to the conservative systematic tracker, the more creative speculative tracker can make bold conjectures, enabling him to predict where the animal might have gone. This ability gives the speculative tracker a considerable advantage in difficult terrain, where footprints are not always clear.

The difference in approach by individual trackers might be the product of different types of scientific minds. Modern scientists can broadly be divided into two types: systematic and speculative (Beveridge 1950). (This classification is arbitrary, however, since the majority of scientists probably fall somewhere between the two extremes, combining characteristics of both types.) The systematic scientist works by gradual systematic steps, accumulating data until a generalization is obvious. Discovery of new facts is achieved by patient manual dexterity. Although systematic scientists might have a high intelligence that enables them to classify, reason, and deduce, they may not have much creative originality. In contrast, speculative scientists create a hypothesis first or early in the investigation and then test it by experiment. Making bold guesses, they work largely by intuition, going beyond the generalization of observed facts, and only calling on logic and reason to confirm the findings. While speculative scientists can be highly creative, they may not be storehouses of knowledge or highly intelligent in the usual sense. Both types of scientists are necessary, for they tend to have complementary roles in the advancement of scientific knowledge.

In the hunting process, systematic and speculative trackers can complement one another, too. When hunting in teams of two or more trackers, systematic and speculative trackers can be in constant dialogue so that some consensus is reached. Such a consensus might represent an optimal combination of the two extremes, but trackers do not always agree on their interpretations of spoor or the best strategy to adopt.

Systematic and speculative trackers might also have complementary roles in advancing and maintaining the shared pool of scientific knowledge of a hunter-gatherer band or alliance. Systematic trackers, on the one hand, might be able to accumulate and retain more knowledge, including knowledge gained from others. Speculative trackers, on the other hand, might be creative innovators, developing new knowledge, especially in changing circumstances, or rediscovering knowledge that may have been lost.

6

Staying Alert and Anticipating Danger

ow clouds had blown in from the southeast during the night, and
the early morning was gray and gusty. While driving around looking for a trail to follow, I listened to the chatter on the game-drive
radios. It was all about lions. It seemed two young males had finally been
pushed out of their natal pride by dominant males. The growling, fighting, and roaring were heard all over the reserve until early morning. The
youngsters were chased throughout the pride's territory until they were
finally spotted on the airstrip. They were skittish and mobile and clearly
wanted to put as much distance between themselves and the dominant
males as they could.

At nine o'clock, it was still cool, with low clouds and a strong wind.
We were evaluating Joe, a field guide at a commercial lodge in a provincial game reserve. When we arrived at the young lions' trail, it was less
than an hour old. Joe jumped off the vehicle, grabbed his rifle, and started
walking.

The soil was loose, and the game trail the lions had followed was free
of leaf litter and vegetation. This was the densest block on the reserve,
mainly sicklebush and low acacias, creating a maze of thorns about nine
feet high. In most places, visibility was only a few feet.

Both males had moved in a fast overstep walk. Joe moved well on the
trail, but every few yards he had to untangle himself from the claws of the
acacias. After a few hundred yards, he came to a halt. He recognized
the fresh tracks of a black rhino on top of the lion trail. The rhino had
walked in the opposite direction, but it seemed that Joe had suddenly realized he had been ignoring his environment and focusing only on the trail.

Immediately, he stopped plowing through the bush and instead tried to find the least-obstructed route. It was still cool, but within minutes, Joe's shirt was wet with perspiration. He changed his grip on his rifle every thirty seconds or so to wipe his palms on the seat of his pants.

Deeper in we went, and the smell of buffalo dung came floating in on the wind. A few paces on, Joe saw that the buffalo had walked out the way we came in, and the fact that the lion track was inside the fresh buffalo dung helped calm his nerves. He pushed on. The thickets started to clear, and then he crossed a road into the next block of forest.

At that point, the clouds had burned off, and the temperature was rising fast. The wind had dropped but was still in our faces. It was about eleven o'clock. The lions' speed had slowed dramatically; the trail showed an understep walk. From the tracks, it was clear the lions would be lying up soon. We came to an area where one lion lay down while the other walked further and then lay down, too. The lion in the back got up again and walked past the first one, and this was repeated four or five times. Joe misinterpreted the sign, thinking that the lions were scent-marking—that they had successfully taken over the territory from the dominant males. For this reason, he didn't expect them to be lying down.

The behavior of the lions clearly indicated that they were looking for good shade. They were obviously tired after running for their lives the entire night and well into the morning and being pestered by vehicles and cameras. No wonder they went through the densest block.

The landscape opened into grassland with only small scrubs. There was no shade in the vicinity large enough to cover two lions. It was hot. Half a mile further, there was an umbrella thorn growing in the middle of the grassland. This was the perfect spot for lions to rest—good visibility in all directions, good shade that would last all day, knee-high grass to disappear in. Five yards to the left of the tree, on the sunny side, was a termite mound about six feet tall.

As we approached the tree and mound, Joe veered to the right, directly toward the shade of the tree. He did not see the two patches of empty space where two large bodies squashed down the grass, visible from about forty yards. His eyes were glued to the base of the termite mound to ensure he did not walk into any danger hidden behind it. He missed the mane that was visible from about thirty yards and the slight movement of

Can you spot the lioness lying up to rest? ME

*a heaving rib cage at twenty yards. We tried to communicate with him
but were too close to make any noise: He remained focused on the mound.*

*With only about fifteen yards between Joe and the lion on the far side,
he remained transfixed by the mound. Then the lion picked him up and,
with a growl, took off in the opposite direction. The youngster closer to Joe
was up in a flash and ran straight at him while looking back in the direction of the growl. Joe jumped away, and the lion realized its mistake. It
changed direction and ran off.*

*It is a common behavior for growl-awakened lions to first run away
from the growl and then look to see where the threat is.*

—A. L.

LOOKING AHEAD

Even experienced trackers, especially when they are tired, fall into
the trap of looking only a short distance down the trail in front of
them. It is critical that you learn to scan the landscape constantly,
both up ahead and to either side.

Reading teaches us habits that are counterproductive to effective tracking. In the western world, we read from left to right, top to bottom, and this trains us when and where to "see" things. An effective way to break this habit is to force your eyes to scan from right to left. The first scan should be in the far distance, the second at mid-range, and the third at close range. This will mean that the area you are moving through is seen at least three times, every time from a different angle, before you get there.

It is easier and quicker to detect movement in your peripheral vision rather than in your focal vision directly in front of you. Learn to use your peripheral vision, as it will enable you to pick things up where you are not looking. You can, for instance, have your eyes pointing at but not fixed on a spot on the trail ten yards in front of you, but you can also see and confirm a footprint a few feet in front of you as well as the gap in the vegetation forty yards further on, which is the most likely route the animal has followed. Use your peripheral vision to notice the fallen branch that would snap and give your position away if you stepped on it.

While scanning ahead, look for obvious places on the trail that will hold a footprint well—a muddy or sandy patch. While doing this, keep in mind that negative space also tells a story. While looking ahead on a difficult trail with little or no sign, keep an eye open for the lack of sign in the easy places on the sides. This will confirm that you are still on the right trail, even if you do not see actual or obvious sign. This often happens when you trail an animal that had walked on a road that had vehicle traffic on it after the creature walked there. You will not see tracks obliterated by the vehicles. There is thus no physical evidence of a trail to follow. You have to scan the sides of the road while walking on the vehicle tracks until you find where the animal left the road. As long as there are no tracks going off the road, you are still on the animal's trail.

Learn to look for textures, shapes, and colors that are out of place. It is often just an odd angle of a branch or an upside-down leaf that will indicate the trail. Look for movement, a flicker of a tail, or the slight twitch of vegetation that will give the location of an animal

A male lion resting in the shade, spotted in the distance. We were making ample noise in an attempt to scare it away, but rather than running, it just watched us approach. ME

away. These subtle movements are more often picked up by peripheral vision than by focal vision.

The seemingly magical abilities of top trackers are directly linked to their ability to collect data this way. Practice using peripheral vision as often as you can. It is part of our survival and defensive make-up. Watch other vehicles in your peripheral vision as you drive. You might catch a vehicle slipping into your blind spot or an oblivious driver turning into your lane.

STOPPING TO LISTEN

While moving on a trail, it is difficult to pick up sounds around you unless they are very clear. If you are alone, you can freeze as soon as you detect the sound, allowing you to identify it and determine its location. When there is more than one person on the trail, however, the chances of everyone freezing immediately are small. This makes it much harder to determine the source of a sound. Learn to freeze *and* give a predetermined signal to others on the trail to do the same. Then wait. Do not move. If you need to, cup your hands behind your ears to enhance your directional hearing. Spend a bit of time, five minutes or so, to make sure of what you heard before moving on.

Before you enter a thicket, it is wise to stop for a minute or two to listen for potential danger or animals that might spook and give your presence away. If you have to go through a large dense area with limited visibility, stop every now and then so you can detect the slightest of sounds made by animals ahead. Do this too at the edge of a gully or the crest of a ridge, and as you approach water, a wallow, marsh, rocky outcrop, or reed bed.

AN AWARENESS OF WIND DIRECTION

*W*e both stopped in our tracks when we saw the gray rump of a rhinoceros only eight yards in front of us. My first thought was that it was dead. It was a cold late-winter morning with a strong wind gusting from behind. The rhino was lying on the trail on which we were walking. The guests behind me were not so quick to stop, but I managed to get them to a halt without making too much noise.

Amos indicated to me with a hand across his throat that he also thought the animal was dead. I was about to signal to the group to move back to safety so Amos and I could investigate when the wind pushed again. As the tall thatch grass and round-leaf teaks parted, the animal lifted its head, facing downwind, away from us. The small head with the tiny round ears of a black rhino bull sank back to the ground. Amos and I both immediately recognized the animal, and I felt a surge of adrenaline, as well as a renewed sense of urgency to get the group out of there. One stubborn fellow, a surgeon from Johannesburg, started to come forward to see what was happening. I signaled to Amos to take him and the others away while I stayed between the group and the rhino. Fortunately, everybody followed him.

Watching the sleeping creature, I couldn't understand why it didn't react to us being so close. Somebody behind me tripped over a branch. It snapped loudly, but the animal only lifted its head for a few seconds and then laid it down again. I took a good look at the stems of the tall grass bending in the wind. I noticed that the ones bending directly away from me were still about five feet on my side of the rhino. I could see a slight arc in the grass directly next to the animal's head. The wind was not blowing directly at him but slightly to its left. The wind was strong enough to carry our scent past the rhino's head. The animal became aware of the noise we made, but perhaps it blended so well with the sounds of the gusting wind and the rustling leaves that the rhino could not differentiate our sounds from any other.

Eventually, we circled downwind to a low outcrop about a hundred yards away. Fifteen minutes later, the wind momentarily died down, and the rhino immediately jumped up with a snort and spun around. He stared at the spot where we'd been standing. It was clear from his behavior that he had picked up our scent. Later, as the wind increased, he was convinced we had departed and settled down again.

—A. L.

If your intention is to locate an animal without it becoming aware of you, it is important that you are acutely aware of wind direction. Most animals have an acute sense of smell and will pick up human scent from a long way off. Noise will also reach an animal easier if the creature is directly downwind, meaning that the wind is blowing from the tracker to the animal.

There are different ways to detect wind direction, and it doesn't really matter what method you use as long as you do not give away your presence doing so. Some trackers prefer to throw sand, dust, or dry plant matter into the air to enable them to see wind direction. This is fine, but the sudden movement might catch the attention of animals, or even the animal being trailed if it is close by. If you use this method, be careful not to get dirt in your eyes or, if you are carrying a rifle, not to dirty its action, as this might cause a malfunction.

Robert Bryden using sand to test the wind direction in Kruger National Park. AL

To use this method, pick up dry leaf or grass matter and gently release it at hip height by rubbing it between your fingers. For better accuracy, extend your arm across the wind. Do not extend your arm to the downwind side of you as the turbulence created by your body will give you an inaccurate reading.

Another method to see the wind direction is to use an ash bag, a small linen bag filled with wood ash that serves to dry sweaty hands. (In South Africa, this is normally a Horse Shoe Tobacco bag filled with ash from the leadwood tree, which is very fine and almost white.) The bag is given a gentle shake into the wind to release a bit of its contents. The fine white powder is carried by the slightest breeze. A nasal-spray bottle filled with unscented talcum powder can be used, too. Just enough powder will be released when you give the bottle a gentle squeeze.

In dry environments, a tracker can simply flick a bit of sand or dust into the air with the tip of a shoe as long as it is done quietly. The effectiveness of this method is directly influenced by the height and density of the ground cover on the trail. Tall or dense vegetation around the spot where the dust is flicked might create turbulence, which will influence the drift. It is wise to wait until the dust floats clear of the vegetation and is picked up by the actual wind current.

Some trackers will simply look at vegetation bent by the wind. This is a good method to use when in relatively dense cover and the wind is swirling. Above the canopy, there is normally a steady wind, but, due to turbulence, it is not easy to detect the actual direction. Look at the treetops. In more open terrain, it is less accurate to look only at vegetation movement.

It can be better to learn to feel the wind rather than see it. Doing so takes a lot more practice but can be very accurate once you have mastered it. This method relies on either the fine hair on a tracker's skin or the cooling effect on the skin as air moves over it. The experienced tracker often uses both these sensations without thinking about them. The hair on the back of the neck, face, and edges of the ears is very good for detecting air movement. When you feel the wind in your face, turn your head into it until you feel it equally on both ears. You are now facing directly upwind. If you feel it on the back of your neck, turn your head until you feel it equally on the backs of both ears. You are now facing directly downwind. This method works very well in light to strong winds—if a hat or other clothing doesn't prevent airflow. In warmer climates, or in very low winds, it is often better to use the cooling effect as an indicator. If exposed skin is not damp, wet your index finger and hold it up. The side that cools first is facing upwind.

You often see guides wiping their hands on the seat of their pants as they progress down the trail of a dangerous animal. Rifle stocks have checkering to absorb sweat to ensure a good grip in stressful situations. It is human nature to have sweaty palms when under stress. This can be one of the most useful tools to determine even the slightest air movement. Pivot your hand at hip height until the sweat on the inside of your hand cools. The palm of your hand is then facing upwind. If you are carrying water, simply wet the palm of your hand.

Although the wind can change, swirl, or stop at any time, it is important to note that it does have some general tendencies.

- If there is no or very little wind, there will normally be an updraft up the slope of a mountain from early morning until the afternoon. Then, especially in winter, there will be a downdraft as cool air flows back into the valley.
- During low wind conditions, scent is often carried wide but not very far. Under high wind conditions, scent is carried far but not very wide.
- The prevailing wind in an area is normally very stable.
- In a relatively flat woodland landscape, moderate to strong winds will often swirl slightly as the turbulence created by the trees sucks air in behind them. This will give the impression that the wind is blowing in the opposite direction, but this is only a micro-scale phenomenon. Usually, after swirling around a tree, scent is sucked up above the tree line and carried by the prevailing wind.
- Moderate to strong winds in mountainous terrain will often create a strong backdraft on the lee side of a ridge. This will carry scent over the ridge and then back up the other side of the slope, giving the impression that the source is on the far side. This characteristic can be very dangerous as it might cause a stampede in your direction away from the perceived source.

Whatever method of determining wind direction you use, use it often so there is no doubt in your mind about where your scent is being carried. Be proactive, test the wind often, and use it to your advantage when you are on the final approach toward an animal, or when you have to avoid a potentially dangerous thicket, gully, or other obstacle. The same applies to sidestepping other animals en route that might jeopardize your stealth.

KNOWLEDGE OF WILDLIFE BEHAVIOR

Most animals are creatures of habit. To be a successful tracker, it is important for you to be a keen scholar of nature. An effective way of obtaining the basics is by reading everything written on a particular species (for starters, see Elbroch and Rinehart 2010 and Estes 1992). Watching wildlife documentaries will also help to give you the general tendencies of the daily routine of the animal you intend to trail. But do not rely on these alone. Animals do not read the books or watch the films. Most books on animal behavior are based on studies of small populations, under very specific conditions, with limited observations and interpretations. The more we trail animals, the more we learn about a species, and the more likely we are to wiitness behaviors not included in published literature. Tracking can provide a unique perspective on wildlife.

Animals have different routines in different populations and different seasons. They also often have different routines in different herds or groups within the same population. These routines can easily be disrupted by other animal activities or human pressure. The only way to learn the routines and their variations is to spend time

A red fox's den is the central point of radiating trails. ME

A red fox. ME

in the field studying a particular animal. Some of the best trackers we know may not be able to pass a theoretical exam on animal behavior, but when asked to interpret behavior on the trail, they can provide the most accurate description of that particular species you've ever heard.

Regularly tracking individual animals teaches you much about specific individuals. A predator might follow a regular route through an area, and when it does, it is most likely heading for a specific place or area to bed down, feed, or hunt. This will also give you an intimate knowledge of the specific environment that individual animal moves through.

Use this knowledge to your advantage. It can help you understand other dangerous animals in the area. Let's say you are trailing a single male lion that had been patrolling its territory. It is almost noon, and the trail takes you into a low-lying area next to a dry riverbed. It is peak summer, and the pans and wallows next to the river have been filled by recent rains. The dense vegetation cuts the visibility to only a few yards in places. The breeze is in your face. It is hot, and you have to strain your eyes to see the sign in the mottled light created by the bright sunlight and deep shade. The trail takes you parallel to the river, along the game trails linking the pans and wallows. This is an absolute danger zone, as buffalo, rhino, and elephant will often cool down during the heat of the day in these wallows. If you do not know this, you will most likely not be careful enough and could end up walking straight into a sleeping buffalo bull.

You might see tracks of hyenas going to or coming from a specific area over an extended period of time. This might indicate a den. Hyenas will regularly den inside an old termite mound, using the burrows created by an aardvark. In varied terrain in the northeastern United States, bobcats almost always sleep on south-facing slopes in rock jumbles. In winter, lions and leopards often sun themselves on the north sides of termite mounds. White rhinos will often be found on eastern slopes on winter mornings warming themselves in the sun. Chirping birds might indicate large animals, and circling vultures, condors, ravens, and other scavengers might indicate a kill site. In the Lowveld, leopards will often use gullies and other drainage lines to conceal themselves when they are hunting. In mountains, they tend to walk just below the crest on the lee side, peering over the crest from time to time. Cougars use the same strategies; they zigzag when hunting and move in straight lines when traveling with a destination in mind.

While on a trail, the tracker will most likely cross the trails of other animals of the same species as the tracked animal or a different species. They might be those of a dangerous or nondangerous animal. They might be fresher, of the same age, or older than the trail being followed.

Good trackers will constantly be aware of what is happening around them and not be focused only on the trail. When you are tracking with others, have them test you on other animal signs you have passed, and test them when they are in the lead.

ANIMAL BEHAVIOR THAT SERVES AS A WARNING

Wild animals can pose a threat to humans for various reasons—the only rule about this is that there are no rules. There are, however, certain tendencies. For instance, a cougar is more likely to charge when she has small cubs with her (though it is still a small chance), but she is also more likely to break off her charge than an injured male lion. An elephant bull in musth will act more aggressively toward humans than when it is not in musth.

Regardless of a tracker's ability to follow footprints systematically, the importance of recognizing potential danger is also important. The ability to interpret the sign visible in the trail that indicates potential danger relies heavily on trackers' knowledge of animal behavior and their ability to integrate this knowledge with what they observe. Often, trackers are eager to move fast on an easy trail, and it is often then that they miss signs of danger ahead.

A lioness napping upside down. ME

A warning sign might be very subtle, like the slightly shorter stride of a leopard as it slows down toward the end of a long walk. But often obvious and clear signs are overlooked: the leap-frog of members of a lion pride as they go down one by one, the drops of urine on a trail from an elephant bull in musth.

It is important for trackers to be constantly analyzing all the evidence along the trail, and for trackers to be open-minded enough to revise their ideas. Make sure a small mistake early on isn't followed by a bigger one, one that might be fatal.

Warning Signs, Alarm Calls, and Smells

On a trail, there are often telltale signs, smells, and calls that indicate danger ahead. The signs can, to a certain extent, be learned from a reference book, but their application requires practical experience. Look for sign relevant to the trail, but also that of other animals in the area. You might be trailing a lion, but a very wet mud trail leaving a wallow in the late morning will almost always indicate that a buffalo bull or rhino is lying up close by. Look for abnormalities in tracks that might indicate an injury—maybe a limp, or blood. Look for urine drops.

The obvious alarm calls of chipmunks, jays, crows, impala, kudu, and the like are relatively easy to learn, but understanding and interpreting them is more of a challenge. Then there are sounds that are harder to detect: a branch brushing against the thick skin of a rhino, the thud of elephant dung hitting the ground, the groan of a lion rolling over. These are not sounds you can learn from a book. You have to see and hear the animal making the noise. You have to spend time in the woods.

The same applies to learning what smells might indicate danger. Animal feces and urine have distinct smells, but knowing what smells are relevant to the trail requires practice. Learn to link smells to other sign. If you are trailing rhino and you smell rhino dung and notice dung beetles rolling their dung balls away from it, it is most likely not all that fresh. If the dung beetles are still flying in, however, it is fresher. If you are trailing a cougar or leopard that has just made

Vervet monkeys, one of many sentinels that betray the presence of both trackers and their quarry. AL

a kill but has carried the carcass off, you might end up catching a whiff of fresh blood or rumen that might give its position away.

LEAVING THE SPOOR AND PICKING IT UP AHEAD

It is sometimes necessary for a tracker to leave the trail to avoid danger. This will obviously be the case when there is a strong possibility that the animal being trailed is close by but hidden by vegetation or broken terrain. It is then wise to leave the trail to get a better view from a different angle. But at which point should the tracker leave the trail? This will depend on the trail itself, as every situation is unique, and the tracker must learn the answer to this question almost entirely from experience. The tracker might have picked up some visual sign on the trail that indicates that the animal is about to bed down, or some telltale sound that indicates something close by. Or the trail might go into a thicket, and visibility be reduced to a few feet. In this case, it is *always* wise to circle around the thicket on the downwind side as long as there is better visibility from that side. If there is not better visibility, or the terrain does not allow it, proceed carefully along the trail. Try not to move upwind from the trail, as this will most likely give your presence away. An inexperienced tracker might circle upwind from the potential danger if visibility is better from there. Another common error is to leave the trail just to end up in a denser place with less visibility. If you move to the downwind side and realize it is not going to help you, move back to the trail and proceed very cautiously.

The same tactics should be used when the tracker detects dangerous animals along the trail. In a case like this, it is important to circle wide enough to remain out of sight of the animal. If you simply encounter a dense patch of vegetation that might hold a dangerous animal but all indications are that the animal has continued on, move downwind to get a better view, but then get back on the trail without wasting time. Experience will soon teach you when to be more cautious and when doing so will simply waste time. You will soon learn that animals such as bears, lions, rhinos, and leopards will lie up on the lee side of solid objects such as termite mounds on cold, windy days. They favor deep shade on hot, sunny days.

If the wind is blowing straight down the trail of a dangerous animal and you suspect that you might be getting close, turn off the trail and make a loop on the downwind side. Circle back to the point that would intersect the trail while scanning for the animal and the trail. Look for sign up ahead so you do not have to actually go to the tracks. If you cut the trail again, leave it in the same manner and make another loop. Do this with great caution so you do not give yourself away.

Other dangers that should be avoided if possible are extremely steep slopes or other physical features in the landscape that might be dangerous to traverse or dense stands of poison ivy or other hazardous vegetation, such as cacti, acacia, and so on. If possible, circle downwind, but do not be too concerned if the terrain does not allow this while the trail is cold. If the trail is hot, always take the wind into consideration.

Sean Robertson at left and evaluator
Adriaan Louw watch the white rhino Sean
successfully tracked during an evaluation
at Garonga, Makalali Private Game
Reserve Conservancy, South Africa.

WAYNE TE BRAKE

DETERMINING WHERE DANGEROUS ANIMALS ARE
Life is full of risks and dangers, whether you are driving, hiking, working in a city, or tracking a cougar. Tracking wildlife always holds some risk or danger. And it is not necessarily less risky to trail mule deer in a national forest in California during the hunting season than to trail lions in a game reserve in South Africa.

Trackers must develop the ability to locate a dangerous animal without putting themselves, the people with them, and the animal in unnecessary danger. You have to take risks, but there is a fine line between acceptable and unnecessary risks. Determining where that line is comes with experience, and one of the best ways of gaining this experience is to walk second in line while an experienced tracker leads. Observe what they do and how they do it. Sit with them afterward and ask why they made the decisions they did. Then take the trail yourself with an experienced tracker watching you, and correcting you. Accept their valuable advice on where and how you should move.

There are two general pitfalls you must avoid so as to not put yourself in unnecessary danger:

- Becoming so relaxed in the field that you become unaware of potential danger. Even experienced trackers start to believe that nothing wants to harm them or that animals aren't really dangerous. Then one day they overstep the fine line and end up inside an animal's attack zone.
- Relying on your rifle to keep yourself out of trouble. There is no excuse or reason to purposely jeopardize the life of an animal that you are not actively hunting, yourself, or anyone who might be accompanying you in the field. *Never walk into a situation with other people and a rifle if you would not be comfortable walking in alone without a rifle.*

Seeing an Animal Before It Sees You
You need to see the animal you are tracking before it sees you, and you must see wildlife that may betray you en route. It is not unusual for a tracker to walk right past an animal or even a herd without seeing it. It is only when the animals detect the presence of the tracker

Ekson Ndlovu squats low to spot a black bear in Sequoia, California.
NATE KEMPTON

and start alarming or stampeding that the tracker realizes it, but then it is too late. The alarm and flight notify everything else in the area that there is a human, or at least potential trouble, nearby. Although this situation is not always unavoidable, it often occurs as a result of a lack of alertness on the tracker's part.

The first priority is to be aware of all the animals in front, to the sides, and even behind you. Knowing where animals are, you can take necessary steps to ensure that you will have as little impact on them as possible.

It is important for the tracker to maintain the ability to look for and identify the presence of other animals in the area. A tracker too focused on the trail in front of him will often not see animals further down the trail and walk into them. The spooked animals will flee, and their alarm calls will blow the tracker's cover.

When you do spot the animal you are trailing, freeze immediately and take a few seconds to make sure it hasn't seen you. Also look for other animals that might be associated with it. If it hasn't seen you, slowly move behind cover or sink to your haunches to reduce your profile. Then, if you have to approach closer to get a better look, plan your route from there.

7

Stealth

Ekson Ndlovu signaled to us to stay put while he figured out what had happened to two male lions after the game-drive vehicles full of high-profile foreign guests had left. The lions had been lying up near the shoulder of one of the smaller roads but had then moved into the thickets after the vehicles departed so they could rest. They knew that in the afternoon the vehicles with their camera-wielding tourists would be back.

A full-time tracker in the Lowveld of South Africa, Ekson is a short, friendly Shangaan in his late forties—one of the old-school trackers who live for the bush. He is an amazing tracker yet very humble. His phenomenal sense of humor has often lifted everyone's spirits during a tracker evaluation. He is a great favorite among his peers, the guides working with him, and their guests, and an absolute ace on a leopard's trail.

That morning, while on the trail of the two male lions in their prime, Ekson had taken us through much of the Thornybush Game Reserve. Although it was in the middle of the dry season, the grass cover was still very dense in some areas. The lions had walked through open woodland, grassland, riverine thickets, and dense woodland, and sometimes simply down one of the many dirt roads that crisscross the reserve. They had walked far the previous evening and wanted to sleep undisturbed. They left a nice, challenging trail. Ekson was being evaluated.

He called us together and explained at a whisper that the lions had moved back across the road and into the thickets on the far side, and that we had to be very cautious as the site was almost directly downwind. The light breeze was pushing in a southwesterly direction, and he pointed out the large pug marks heading into a magic guarri thicket.

He led us at ninety degrees off the trail to the right, and then back to it in a big semicircle of about fifty yards. When he was about ten yards away from the line of the trail the lions would have used if they had stayed on course, he signaled to us to stop. Carefully, he snuck in, and immediately back out to us again, signaling for us to follow as he started the next semicircle. Checking the wind constantly, he completed the loop, and the next, and the next. Pointing out obstacles that we must avoid, he made sure we all moved quietly.

Peering around a guarri on his fifth loop, he looked back at us with a big smile and indicated for me to come forward. As I looked over his shoulder, I saw a big paw poking through the knee-high grass as the lion stretched. It was only about eight yards away, oblivious to our presence. It was only when Ekson pointed at something closer that I noticed the second lion only five yards away, fast asleep. I signaled to Louis and the others, and one by one, Ekson showed them. He then led us away, behind cover and out to the side, using the wind to his advantage with the lions still off in dreamland.

—A. L.

GOING BAREFOOT

The ideal way to stalk an animal is to go barefoot. But to do this you need to toughen up your feet and walk barefoot all the time. Even when your feet are tough, wearing shoes continuously for just a short period of time will make your feet soft again. It is also better to wear shorts if possible, since long trousers tend to make noise when rubbing against grass and bushes.

Today, of course, stalking barefoot is mainly an academic exercise. In most modern situations, you can track animals wearing boots with soft soles. Now that most Bushmen hunt with dogs and horses, few still stalk animals barefoot. Only when they are hunting with the traditional bow and poison arrow do they usually go barefoot. To hunt an animal with bow and arrow, Bushmen hunters need to stalk to within twenty-five yards of their quarry. In areas where animals are hunted for subsistence, they become very skittish and flee the moment they detect the presence of humans. When feeding, animals

!Nate preparing to shoot after a long stalk on his belly. ERIC VANDEVILLE/ROLEX AWARDS

constantly look back to see if there are hunters following their trail. !Nate explained that when you hunt kudu, the kudu is also hunting you. When looking for a safe place to rest, they double back downwind from their own trail so that they can smell any hunters following them. Hunters need to leave the spoor, looping downwind in order not to be detected. In the relatively open Kalahari, it requires a lot of skill to hunt animals with the bow and arrow, and often hunters fail. Only about five percent of attempted stalks result in a successful kill. To be successful requires a lot of patience and persistence. Although it is very difficult to hunt with bow and arrow, it is the most versatile method, since most species, from steenbok to giraffe, can be hunted with it.

When going out on a hunt, even the Bushmen wear shoes to walk long distances in the hot sand. Traditionally, before they adopted western-style shoes, they made sandals out of thick leather hide. But they spend so much time walking barefoot in hot sand that their feet are very tough. Once they have spotted the animal they have been tracking, the shoes come off and they strip down to their shorts. Before adopting western-style clothing, they wore leather thongs. Even as recently as the 1990s, one old hunter, Tso!oma of ≠Xade, still wore a leather thong underneath his clothing, stripping down when stalking an animal. Cloth often becomes snagged on thorns, he explained, so a leather thong is much better for stalking.

Before stalking the animal, the hunters come together and discuss their strategy in soft whispers. On the initial approach, they might need to cover quite a bit of ground before getting down to stalking. They will approach from the downwind side, keeping bushes between themselves and the quarry. When a few hunters work together, they communicate with hand signals. When they cannot see each other, they might use bird calls and whistles.

To stay hidden, hunters might be forced to cross areas of thorns. To do this, they have a special technique: They put their foot down directly on the thorns, which barely penetrate the toughened sole (tolerating a degree of pain and discomfort without flinching is part of being a traditional hunter). The thorns are only a problem if they were to pick up the foot and then put it down again, forcing the thorns deeper into the skin. Instead, they brush their sole lightly on the ground, dislodging the thorns, before putting it down again. In this way, they can move across thorns without being distracted, concentrating on the animal they are stalking.

As the hunters move closer, they crouch down, focusing on the animal while feeling the ground with their feet. Stalking barefoot enables them to feel for dry leaves and twigs without taking their eyes off the quarry. Moving barefoot also seems to make them more alert, as if feeling the ground with their feet makes their other senses more acute. Wearing boots seems to have a blunting effect on alertness. When moving forward, they slowly bring their foot down, first touching the ground with the outside ball and then gently rolling onto the rest of their foot. When bringing their foot down, they balance on the other foot so they can first feel the ground before moving their weight forward.

If the bushes are very low, the hunters go down onto their hands and knees to crawl closer, always keeping vegetation between themselves and the quarry. In long grass, they may even go down on their stomachs, pulling themselves forward with their elbows. Stalking an animal can sometimes take a long time. Whenever the animal looks up, the hunters freeze, waiting for the animal to relax. Only when the animal continues feeding will they slowly move forward, careful not to make any sudden movements.

In open grassland, hunters must approach the animal in full sight. This is done by making themselves resemble animals, leaning over with their backs almost parallel to the ground and their arms close to their sides. Hunters might also stimulate an animal's curiosity behavior, which is characterized by an animal standing motionless, looking toward an unusual object. In some situations, the animal might actually approach the object while maintaining a fixed stare at it. Some hunters wear a white ostrich feather in a head band. When they stalk an animal, its curiosity is stimulated by the feather blowing in the wind. While the hunter remains motionless, the animal may move toward him, moving into range of his arrow.

The most difficult moment comes when the hunter must take aim. While stalking, the hunter can stay hidden behind bushes or long grass, looking through the vegetation. But to get a clear shot, the top part of the bow and the hunter's head must move from behind the bush into an exposed position—this is often the critical time when the quarry sees the hunter and flees. The hunter needs to take aim and release the arrow during the few critical moments before the quarry is aware of him. Often two hunters stalk together to increase their chances of getting a hit. The first hunter will take aim while the second hunter crouches behind him. The moment the first hunter releases his arrow, the second hunter sends off a rapid shot, increasing the chances that one of the arrows will hit the target.

WALK-AND-STALK HUNTING

Tracking is essentially hunting, and tracking and hunting have both played prominent roles in human cultures (Liebenberg 2006). Since our goal as trackers is to find an animal, we are for all intents and purposes hunting it. This fact is helpful to realize, and to practice. The best way to outsmart animals is to practice a walk-and-stalk style of hunting. When you encounter an animal, sneak up to it and stalk it as a predator would. Do this often enough and you will learn how to get close to animals without giving yourself away. Realize that hunting is not about killing the animal but rather about outsmarting the animal's well-developed senses. Walk-and-stalk hunting is the best way to observe wildlife and really learn what they are about. Learn to be comfortable in the woods. Get dirty, and allow animals to approach you, keeping safety in mind. Ultimately, you want to be able to stalk up to animals, view them, and pull out without them even knowing you were there. But to get there, you will need to spend time in the woods—lots of it.

Minimizing Noise

Western civilization is polluted with man-made mechanical and electronic noise. There are few places in the world where such noise doesn't have an impact on wildlife. Few of us are privileged to be able to track in these areas. Most tracking takes place in areas with some form of noise pollution, from vehicles, airplanes, water pumps, trains, and so on. But these are external factors to the trail itself. The bigger issue is that many of us have become desensitized to noise. In some workplaces, "white noise" is deliberately generated so employees can better focus on work and not be distracted by what is being said in the next cubicle. While tracking, however, we must be ultrasensitive to both the noises we make and the noises being made around us. Animals do make noise when they move, and the bigger the animal, or the faster it moves, the greater the noise. But these are natural sounds—hooves hitting the ground, a branch pulled from a tree, or dung splatting on the soil. Rhythmic, mechanical sounds stand out in natural environments. Boots hitting the ground, water sloshing in a half-empty container, backpack buckles hitting against a button are all readily identifiable as unnatural.

Footwear. Here are some guidelines for selecting footwear that will minimize noise when tracking:

!Nate illustrating the use of hand signals. Each animal is represented by a signal; the speed of the animal and the age of its tracks are also conveyed between trackers. ME

- Hiking boots provide more support and protection than shoes but are normally heavier, stiffer, and noisier.
- Any spare or empty space inside shoes will act like an amplifier. Make sure they fit properly.
- Soft leather uppers are less noisy than synthetics but are heavier and less weather resistant and not suited for wet and cold climates. They are, however, more resistant to grass seeds and thorns than synthetics are.

- The best type of sole for tracking is soft and very flexible, but, unfortunately, this type of footwear provides poor protection and support. Crepe soles are very quiet but heavy and don't always give good traction. Also, crepe soles dissolve in diesel, petrol, and engine oil; if you wear crepe soles, be careful at the gas station.
- Find shoes or boots that fit you like a glove. They must be comfortable to walk in all day. The lighter and softer, the better. In colder areas, you will most likely need different shoes for different seasons.

Clothing. It's fine to wear nylon gaiters to prevent snow from getting into your boots, but don't use them in dry climates. Wool or leather gaiters are a good alternative. Synthetics are extremely noisy—brushing against each other or against vegetation. Modern raingear is also incredibly noisy. Consider wearing layers of wool in wet weather instead.

If you wear long pants, use cotton in warmer climates and wool in colder climates. Avoid synthetics and canvas. Heavy-duty canvas workwear might be durable, but unless it's been through the wash a thousand times it is too noisy to wear when tracking. If you hear a swish-swash sound when you walk, you are most likely brushing your legs against each other. Practice walking in a way that this doesn't happen. Your walk must be quiet. It is always less noisy to wear shorts, as long as the climate and environment allows for it. It is also better to wear many thin layers instead of just one or two thick items when it is cold. This allows you to peel off clothing as needed.

Clothing that makes noise when it brushes against a branch should also be avoided, weather permitting. Cotton or wool are best, and stick to earth tones: brown, beige, olive, green, khaki, or even blue. Avoid yellow, red, pink, and all other bright colors. *Definitely avoid white.* There is no sense in being quiet if an animal can spot you from a mile away. Remember, too, that if you wear layers, they all should be in neutral colors.

Gear. Backpacks should have as few unused loops and straps on them as possible. Anything that can catch on branches should be avoided. Cameras and binoculars should be properly secured so they don't swing from side to side. Keys and other metal items should be securely stored inside the backpack. And the canteen—if you can't afford a modern Camelbak, fill a number of small containers with water—small enough that you can empty a single container in one go. Do not walk around with a canteen that sloshes. To animal, it sounds like a half-full water cart.

Walking Quietly

Learn to walk in such a way that you cannot hear yourself. Practice over and over. The best method is to put down the outside part of the heel first, then roll down the outside edge of your foot, and then roll onto the palm of your foot. If the sole of your shoe is soft enough, you will feel a twig before it snaps, and you can curve your foot around or over it.

If you have to negotiate rough terrain, do so at the place where you will make the least noise. Learn to roll through dense brush instead of dragging it with you. Do this by first pushing against branches to your left with your left flank, then turn into the left to get your back against the branches on the right. Then turn to the right to get your back against the branches to the front left again. Work your way along, repeating this action. It is less noisy, and you will not become ensnared as easily. If you need to go underneath low-hanging branches, be prepared to take off your backpack and carry it in your hands to lower your profile.

Learn to use hand signals. You do not need a complex system of signs. If you need to communicate more information, make sure the person you talk to is close enough so that you need only to whisper. The human voice travels far in the woods, and there are always ears that will pick it up and betray your presence.

LOW IMPACT

Ideally, the tracker should move through the landscape without disturbing anything. But this is virtually impossible. We have a profile that draws attention, we make noise when moving, and we smell. Wearing the correct clothing can reduce noise and visibility, but

Peeking between some bushes to look at lions. ME

knowing when and how to move is equally important to reducing your impact.

You must be alert so you can detect the presence of animals in the area and also predict where they might be. It is far easier to deal with an animal once you know where it is. If an animal is unaware of you, or at least hasn't seen you, it's best to freeze the moment you detect it. If it doesn't have its head up, slowly sink to reduce your profile. Once you have done this, take some time to find out if the animal is alone. If not, the rest of the group might be even closer to you and will reveal itself when its members move around. Once you have established the whereabouts of the group, use the cover of vegetation or the terrain to circle downwind from it, even if you have to backtrack a fair distance. It's important to have a good idea where a trail will come out on the other side of the animals, as you now have to pick it up again on the downwind side. This might sound easy, but it takes a lot of practice, and patience.

If an animal sees you but doesn't run away, stopping or kneeling is often the worst thing to do. This is what hunters often do and so the animal will immediately sense danger. It will either flee or alarm others or even approach while staring at the spot where you went down. This will attract the attention of everything in the area. Unless it is a dangerous animal that spots you, it is best to keep moving in an upright posture. If there is a good distance between you and the animal, veer off to the downwind side and walk around it in a semicircle. If you are close to the animal, or you cannot move to the downwind side, turn around and walk away. Do not sneak, and do not stop until you are out of sight. If you do the wrong thing, you will most likely trigger the animal to flee.

If you didn't see the animal in time and it has run off, alarming as it went, remember that the entire area is now aware of you, the intruder. Some trackers might simply pull up their shoulders and continue on the trail, but it is wiser to stop and give things time to settle down. Wait five minutes or so. If you cannot see the animal making its escape, listen to where it's going. In dense bush, you can often follow it a long way by its sound. Listen and look for other movements that might give away the presence of other animals.

Keep productivity in mind when you weigh your impact on animals. It is senseless to spend an hour working your way around a herd of impala when you know the trail you are following is a day old. But don't go charging in and turn the bush upside down. Simply work your way through the animals in a way that causes the least disturbance. Do not act as if you are stalking them. As the trail grows fresher, make sure you are more cautious, and at the end, make sure you do not give your position away.

Use Cover to Approach

Once you have located the animal you are trailing, it is important to not let it know you are close by. Here are a few guidelines:
- The first priority is to stay downwind, or at least in a crosswind position. Never go upwind from the animal.
- Use vegetation to conceal your approach, as long as you can do so quietly.

- If available, use "dead ground"—an area not visible to the animal because of the lay of the land. This might be on the other side of a hill or inside a gully. The advantage of using dead ground is that you can move relatively fast; a disadvantage is that you cannot see the animal, and it might move off.
- If cover is sparse, or if you have to move in front of cover, it's always better to remain in the shadows than in direct sunlight.
- During early mornings and late afternoons, it is better to keep the sun behind you and in the face of the animal.
- If you have to move in the open in good light, do so *very* slowly. A sudden movement is easy to pick up in good light.
- If you have to move in the open in low light, do so quickly. A slow movement is easy to pick up in bad light.
- Always keep the size and abilities of the other people with you in mind, and make sure they understand what is expected from them.

Remember, these guidelines apply to both approaching your quarry and leaving after you've seen it. Remain undetected by using cover on your exit route.

How Close Is Close Enough?

How close is close enough is a difficult question to answer, as every encounter is different. Your intentions will be a major factor. If your goal is simply to confirm the identity of the animal you've been trailing, you likely don't have to get that close, and you don't need to stay long. If your intention is to study the animal, you might need to stay longer, and you might have to get very close. Remember, safety is always a top priority. But you should approach animals closely to continually improve your skills. Push your limits. Remember stealth—do not compromise it. Use cover. Use the wind.

Keeping the Quarry Unaware

It doesn't matter why you track animals, but you have to be able to observe an animal and then leave without it becoming aware that you were there. To do this, you need to know the habits of the ani-

Two leopards in Sabi Sands, South Africa. AL

mal. You might be in a well-camouflaged spot under a tall tree thirty yards downwind from a rhino in a mud wallow, but if you do not know that at some point he will get up and walk to that tree because it's his rubbing post, you will end up in trouble.

A field guide might tell you that a moose will circle downwind when it detects something close by but can't identify it. Practical experience will teach you that you better get out of there quickly by quietly circling back to a new position further downwind or it will pick you up and disappear.

Selecting Your Exit Route
As you move on a trail, take note of your surroundings and create a mental map of the area. This will be helpful when you need to move out of the area undetected. It is also vital in case you need to get out of the way of a dangerous animal. Take note of all gullies, ridges, dense patches of vegetation, or other places that create dead ground and could conceal you if you need to get out of sight.

Also take note of high ground, such as boulders, termite mounds, steep riverbanks, or any other place that might provide safety in case you are detected by a dangerous animal. If you are walking down a dry riverbed with steep banks, make sure you are aware of the nearest escape route behind you. An animal will very seldom come after you if you retreat to high ground, especially if you've opened an escape route for it to flee.

Once you have encountered the animal you were trailing and it is time to leave, do so undetected. Of course, this is not always easy. The wind might change, or the animal might move and see you if you move away from your concealment. This can normally be avoided if you have enough experience and knowledge of that particular animal and the landscape, as you will be able to predict its movements and therefore act proactively.

When you leave the area, stay downwind, or at least crosswind, from the animal. Try to stay out of sight as far as possible, keeping track of the animal as much as possible. If it moves, adjust your route. If it looks in your direction, freeze immediately. Most mammals have difficulty identifying a shape that isn't moving. If the animal has spotted you and does not pose a threat, it is usually best to quietly walk away.

If it's a dangerous animal and you are concealed but the animal is moving in your direction, it is often best to stay where you are, especially if you are in a safe spot. If, for example, you are hidden among large boulders or the branches of a fallen tree and a white rhino is walking toward you but is not yet aware of you and its route will take it upwind, it is better to stay put. If the animal is coming toward you and its route will take it close and downwind, and your position is not that secure, it is best to let the animal know you are there before it gets too close. Break small twigs with your hand. This will let the animal know there is something nearby, and it will most likely go the other way. Exercise great caution.

8
Learning to Track

We were walking on a lion trail at Royal Malewane: Wilson, me, and another young tracker. The pride had walked down a road, and their tracks could be seen thirty yards on. For me, this was a practice session I arranged with Wilson, and I was stopping at every little trail crossing the road to make sure one of the lions didn't break from the pride and leave the road. Each time I did this, Wilson asked, "What are you looking at?"

"I'm just checking that one of the lions didn't turn off."

"Where are the other tracks?" he invariably asked, and every time I pointed them out on the road, he quizzed me: "So why are you looking there?"

A few months later, the scene repeated itself. A different pride of lions on a different road, but I was still doing the same thing. The only difference was that before I started veering off to look for a potential track on the side of the road, my hand was already pointing at the tracks on the road, preempting Wilson's, "Where are the other tracks?"

He wasn't planning to spoon-feed me; he knew I had to figure it out for myself. But at that point, I still hadn't figured out what I needed to figure out. Wilson allowed me the freedom to make mistakes and then simply pointed out the results. He forced me to push through my limitations. I had to realize that I did not trust my own abilities.

Our next session a few months later was very different. I picked up very fresh lion tracks on entering the reserve, but instead of heading out that way, Wilson took me to a buffalo track. It was a single bull that had been in the area for a few days. Judging from the tracks, it had been *harassed by lions the day before. Wilson knew full well I was aware of the risks involved in tracking such a bull.*

The lush summer vegetation was dense. It took me a while to figure out what was happening on the trail, as the buffalo tracks were a maze of old and new sign. While I worked, the bull picked up our scent and jumped up from where it was lying, some seventy yards away. It threw its head back and ran off downwind. I was ready to call it a day when Wilson insisted that we go to the spot where it had been lying. We waited five minutes, then Wilson told me to follow.

Reluctantly, I started down the trail again. Lone buffalo bulls will normally move away from humans but can be very dangerous if pushed— they will eventually stand and fight. The trail took us out of the sickle-bush and into a dense stand of mature tamboti trees and raisinbush shrub. Still heading downwind, we saw that the tracks had slowed to a walk. I pointed out where the bull had turned to look back on his trail and then run off again.

"Carry on," Wilson said.

I thought to myself, "Are you trying to walk us into trouble? Is this your way of making sure I quit tracking altogether?"

Again the trail entered very dense vegetation, and, holding my rifle with both hands in front of my chest, I slowly moved forward. I felt the cool breeze on the back of my neck. After three or four hundred yards, the vegetation opened up. The trail was clearly visible for quite a distance. The saucerlike hooves had plowed up the muddy soil as the bull ran. Forty yards away was a dense stand of magic guarri. It looked like the trail was heading straight past it, but my head was telling me something else. I stopped and looked long and carefully. Then I saw the bull. It was stand-ing inside the guarri, possibly waiting to ambush us. I pointed it out to Wilson, and, with his thumb up and an "okay," he indicated for me to pull out and head back. I was still upset when I left Royal Malewane the next day, not understanding why Wilson had asked me to follow such a dangerous animal.

A few months later when I was being evaluated again, I followed the bulk of a lion's pride, taking note of the individuals veering off, feeling calm and confident in my knowledge that they would eventually rejoin the group. The next morning, I walked a perfect trail.

What had changed?

Cape buffalo. AL

It was only a year or so later, during an evaluation, that I saw one of my peers making the same mistakes I had made. Insecure of his abilities, he was grasping at every little detail, and even some that didn't exist. He was checking and double-checking every possibility, only to miss the obvious. He was hoping to find the lions by chance. Soon he became agitated with himself and the rest of us. Eventually, he gave up. In a rage, he expressed his frustration with the evaluators and the evaluation process. It was obvious he lacked the calmness and humbleness that would take him to the next level.

And then I realized that had been Wilson's lesson for me. But he didn't sit me down and talk to me about it. He simply created the opportunity for me to learn on my own.

—A. L.

For traditional hunters, learning to track is a natural process that begins in early childhood. Those who are not full-time hunters might find it difficult to reach the level of skill and expertise attained by traditional hunters, whose survival depends on their tracking abilities. Any intelligent person, however, should be able to master the basics of tracking. Of course, reading a book will not in itself make you a master tracker—tracking demands practical skill acquired through many hours of practice and experience over a long period. And once this skill is acquired, it must be maintained through continued practice. It will soon become ineffective if it is not exercised.

The average person should by practice and experience be able to become a fair tracker, but the really outstanding trackers are probably born with the latent ability. Qualities required include good senses (or good glasses for poor eyesight), acute observation, physical fitness, patience, perseverance, concentration, alertness, a good memory, an analytical mind, an understanding of nature, intuition, and a creative imagination.

Apart from the tracker's own ability, the ease or difficulty of tracking depends on other factors as well. The type of ground, vegetation, and weather conditions will determine the degree of skill required to recognize and interpret spoor. It is, for example, more difficult to track on hard, stony ground than in soft sand. In overcast weather, spoor lacks depth, while rain can completely obliterate it. One must also consider the extent to which similar tracks might confuse or blur spoor in areas with high animal densities.

THREE-PHASE METHOD

The best way to learn how to track is to track with an experienced tracker. Interacting with an expert will help you develop a critical way of thinking that is important in solving problems in tracking. Expert trackers, however, are few and far between, so most people need to start off by teaching themselves, which is time consuming. But it is also more exciting to make new discoveries on your own. When teaching yourself, a good place to start is by studying your own tracks. This can be done with a method comprising three phases which, repeated often enough, eventually fuse into one.

Phase One

Lay out a trail for yourself, marking the point where you start. Go back to the starting point, then move forward and carefully study every sign of your own trail. Take time to memorize each little detail, even the smallest scuff mark or bent blade of grass. Study pebbles or stones that have been dislodged or dirt transferred onto the rocks you stepped on. Look for each and every sign you left behind. After completing the course, which may take quite a long time at first, return to the starting point.

Phase Two

Your course now consists of two trails, and since you've been over it twice, you should know where it is going. For the second phase, walk over the course at a fast pace. Look well ahead of you, trying to see as many signs as possible.

In phase one, you concentrated on recognition and interpretation, ignoring speed, momentum, looking well ahead, and anticipation. In phase two, you already know the spoor and must now concentrate on aspects that were previously neglected. At first, you will probably miss most of the signs, but after repeating phase two several times, you will start to recognize more of them. Although you already know where the trail is going, you need to look ahead at the terrain and visualize how you moved through it, all while looking for signs well ahead.

Repeating this two-phase exercise, you will improve the speed of phase one while finding more signs during phase two. This exercise should be repeated over different types of terrain, starting off easy and gradually working toward more difficult types.

Phase Three

When you have developed the ability to track down your own trail, you should get someone else to lay out a trail for you. This spoor will obviously be more difficult. The object of the exercise is to develop an ability to anticipate and predict an unknown trail. This is easier to do with another person than with an animal because you can, without much difficulty, identify with that person and think where you would have gone if you were in his or her position.

In phase one, you concentrated on each and every sign. In phase two, you concentrated on speed, momentum, looking well ahead, and anticipation. In phase three, you should try to follow the trail by anticipating and predicting the person's movements while looking at only a few signs. Look at the terrain ahead, trying to imagine the most likely route the person would have taken. Look for signs well ahead, ignoring those in between. Don't waste time looking for signs on hard, rocky ground but look for them further ahead where the ground may be softer. You'll save a lot of time taking shortcuts. If you know the area well and are able to predict where the person might be going, you could simply go to that place and track the trail from there. For example, the person might be hiking down a rocky hill, and in the valley, the tracks might be easier to see in soft ground. Or there may be a riverbed ahead where you can pick up the trail. If you lose the spoor, several likely routes should first be searched for signs. Should this be unsuccessful, work in a complete circle to look for fresh leads. You might also walk out in a wide perimeter around the area, using natural boundaries where tracks would be obvious, such as paths or riverbanks.

While it is relatively easy to anticipate and predict the movements of another person, it will be much more difficult to identify with an animal if you do not know it very well. African trackers in the Lowveld suggest starting with large, hoofed animals, such as buffalo, moose, or horse, then gradually decreasing the size of the animal as you improve. Then switch from hoofed to soft-footed animals.

The best way to learn how to interpret animal tracks is to watch an animal and then go study its tracks. To learn to track an animal, it is easiest to start by following the trail, studying all the signs in detail in order to get to know the animal's habits. Start by studying tracks, gaits, and activities in easy terrain, such as barren dunes along beaches, in arid regions, or in snow. This will help you visualize tracks and signs in terrain where footprints are not obvious. From terrain with soft substrate and sparse vegetation, move on to soft substrate and denser vegetation. Once this has been mastered, try hard, stony substrate with sparser vegetation. Then try hard, stony substrate with dense vegetation. Eventually, as you get to know the animal, you will be able to anticipate and predict its movements so it won't be necessary to look for all its signs. An experienced tracker who knows an animal and the local area doesn't need to follow everywhere it went. Anticipating its movements by looking at the terrain ahead, the tracker might be able to predict its course, leaving the spoor at places and picking it up further ahead to save time.

It is also very important to be able to determine the age of the spoor. The tracker must know whether a spoor is fresh enough to follow up or too old, in which case you will never catch up with the animal. You should also be able to tell if the spoor is so fresh that the animal might be very close, since the animal might be alarmed if you do not approach it stealthily. Only a very experienced tracker can establish the age of a spoor with reasonable accuracy. The rate at which the sun, wind, or rain erodes or blurs spoor can vary considerably. A detailed knowledge of local weather conditions is therefore essential. A tracker must also have a thorough knowledge of animal behavior.

The best way to acquire the ability to determine the age of spoor is to study the aging process systematically. To do this, lay out a succession of footprints next to each other every hour during the course of a day. You will then have examples of spoor that are one hour old, two hours old, three hours old, and so on. Compare the different-aged spoor, which will illustrate the aging process in detail. Repeat this exercise in different soil types, terrain, weather conditions, and seasons to determine the rate of aging in different conditions. When done repeatedly, this exercise provides the experience necessary to develop an intuitive aging ability.

An alternative exercise is to mark known tracks in the field as you encounter them. Nate Kempton suggests that beginning trackers carry popsicle sticks in the field to do this, and when they see a deer or other animal in the bush, they should mark its fresh spoor, writing the time and date on the stick. They can then recheck the tracks periodically to see how they have degraded or otherwise changed.

PROPER TRACKING TECHNIQUE

Trailing is not about following footprints; it's about finding animals. Footprints, scat, and scrapes are merely evidence confirming that the tracker is still on the trail. Although the systematic following of footprints forms part of trailing, it is not trailing itself, merely a tool used by a tracker to follow the trail. To understand this, it is essential that trackers master the basics of trailing or they will forever be limited by the systematic following of footprints.

In the beginning, it might be useful to practice finding every track in a trail so as to learn to see subtle signs. The identification of every footprint, however, is often too slow to create the momentum needed to catch up to an animal. It also limits your ability to move into a speculative or intuitive thought process.

Walk on the Trail

Following accepted tracking etiquette, trackers usually try to step next to instead of on the trail so that others can enjoy what they have found. When learning how to track, however, it is important to walk directly *on* the trail, as this will enable you to see what the animal saw while it was walking. This makes it easier to put yourself in the animal's place. In most cases, humans are taller, or at least on a different eye level, than the animal being trailed. Therefore, the tracker is not on the same vertical plane as the animal. By walking next to the trail, you also take yourself out of the horizontal plane, further reducing your ability to see through the animal's eyes.

If the sign is difficult to detect, make a little mark on the ground with a stick as you walk over the track. This will allow you to find it later if you want to come back to it. The only time you should walk next to the trail is when the angle of the light is making it impossible to see the sign. Even then, though, it's better to step off the trail from time to time to confirm sign than to walk next to it.

Some experienced trackers do not necessarily walk on the trail—they simply follow the path of least resistance. If an animal goes through a bush, they walk around it. If an animal moves in a zigzag path, feeding from bush to bush, they follow a more-or-less straight path in the general direction of travel, picking up the trail whenever

The slender stick at the lower edge of the photo is pointing to a female leopard's track, a very difficult trail to follow. ME

it crosses their own path. If the vegetation or landscape dictates that the route of least resistance is the same as what the animal followed, as is often the case in densely wooded regions, the experienced tracker will often walk on the trail.

Keep Your Head Up

One of the biggest drawbacks of systematically following footprints is that you continue to look down for fear of missing a single footprint. It is fine to look down during a particularly difficult section of trail after you have already established that the animal didn't follow the most obvious route. Other than that, though, keep your head up.

Practice walking in a way that you never lose sight of the horizon in your peripheral view while looking for sign fifteen to thirty yards in front of you. Drop your eyes momentarily to confirm a sign that you picked up earlier, but then look ahead as soon as possible. This will allow you to see in advance if there is a change in direction so you can maintain your momentum. It will also allow you to see the most obvious route as you are moving toward it.

Follow the Most Obvious Route

Animals and people generally use the route of least resistance to move between two points. This will often entail walking through openings between stands of brush instead of through the brush itself. With their heads up, trackers see these natural openings or paths in advance; they can then direct their search for sign toward those areas.

Don't Be Distracted

If taken seriously, trailing is physically and mentally demanding. It requires endurance to remain on a trail all day. But the most challenging sections are often interspersed with easy sections. You must be very careful not to become sidetracked or lose focus when things are easy. More mistakes are made during easy sections of the trail than at the difficult stages simply because the tracker loses concentration. It is important to understand that you shouldn't focus on the footprints in front of you but on the trail in the landscape. Take note of the landscape as you move through it. Scan the area in front of you as you move, but don't allow distractions to take your time and energy away from the trail.

Don't Be Afraid to Make a Mistake

If you lose the trail, stop and coolly assess the situation. Sometimes people move so far from the trail they cannot locate their last con-firmed sign and so must give up the trail altogether. It's okay to make a mistake and lose the trail. It happens to the best of trackers. We are all human, and it is important to understand that any trail can become so difficult that it is almost impossible to find it again after it's lost.

Accept input and use help. If two or more trackers are on a trail, focus on teamwork. If you are in the lead, take responsibility, and don't be afraid to allocate the searching of specific areas to others. If you are in support, don't turn things into a competition. Help your colleagues move faster and find the animal.

Don't Lose Momentum

A common mistake is for trackers to pick up sign fifteen feet or so out and then keep their eyes fixed on that sign as they move for-ward. Once there, they stop—and then start looking for new sign fif-teen feet further along. This creates a stop-start, stop-start rhythm, which usually leads to frustration. Always try to maintain your momentum as much as possible. Work at a speed suitable to your abilities, the terrain, and the difficulty of the trail itself. Competent tracking is all about maintaining flow.

Taking Breaks

Of course, you will need to rest from time to time. Select an area in which to do so very carefully. You must be safe and invisible to wildlife. More importantly, realize that after losing your momentum it will take some time to get it back. When you restart, begin slowly. Too often we make silly mistakes just after taking a break because we lose the direction of the animal and the flow we gained earlier in the trail.

Use Your Senses

If you do not work hard at maintaining a total awareness of your environment, you will most likely chase the animal off without even knowing it, or worse, end up walking right into it at close quarters. It is important to learn to use all your senses, not only in the positive, but also in the negative. If a black bear walked down a dirt road but traffic has destroyed its sign, and you don't see bear tracks leaving the road, it is the *lack* of sign that indicates that you are still on the trail. Scan the area in front of you. Look for sign, but at the same time, look for movement and obvious gaps in the vegetation in the distance that might indicate a likely route. Listen while looking at the trail, be aware of wind direction, and pick up smells. Create a total image of your surroundings as you move on the trail.

Become Part of the Landscape

Animals are extremely sensitive to human intruders. We have been hunting them for millennia, so don't expect them to simply stick around when they realize they are being tracked. Learn to be inconspicuous in the field. Keep your voice down. Dress appropriately. Make no sudden moves. Tread lightly. Give the wilderness time to adjust to your presence. If you create a disturbance, allow things to settle down before carrying on.

Know the Animal

Study anything and everything about the animals that you plan to track. Observe them moving and find out where they bed down, what they eat, when they eat, and all their other habits and behaviors. Trailing them then simply becomes easier. You will also continue to learn more about the animal by trailing it—intimate knowledge of

Senior tracker Patson Sitholé, moving smoothly with eyes up, predicting the path of a female leopard. ME

an animal comes from both scientific study and practical field observations, creating a far better understanding of a species.

A good place to learn about animal movement is to watch wildlife documentaries. Find something with a lot of footage of the specific animal you want to trail. Turn down the volume, as the commentary can be distracting. If you want, put on music. Watch how, where, and why the animal moves. Study its foot placements, feeding height, scent markings, and everything else you can. This will make it far easier to locate and interpret the animal's signs on the trail.

Don't Give Up

If your intention is to track and find an animal, some trails are not worth spending time and energy on simply because they are too old, difficult, or confusing. This is part of tracking. But if you want to be a competent tracker, you must have perseverance. Keep working trails until you can regularly stay on the same trail and find the animal. You will most likely go through stages, each with a ceiling or "hump." Keep working—it's the only way to get over a hump. A good way of doing this is to change trailing environments. Do something else. Travel. Change your trailing buddy and get new input. Then go back and work your area again.

TRACKING TOOLS

Native trackers in Africa do not use any equipment to aid them while tracking, other than perhaps a short bit of hard grass stem trimmed to size and used to measure the width of the metacarpal pad of a leopard track. Tools that at first seem very useful in learning tracking can, in time, become hindrances. Rather than relying on measurements to differentiate between similar species, use their distinctive morphologies, the shape of their footprints. The tiny toe 1 nub on a red squirrel's front tracks is distinctive and a surer way to differentiate its tracks from a gray squirrel's than by measurements alone.

*I have a running joke with Shangaan trackers in the Lowveld about a
walking stick I bought from an old herdsman. This stick travels with
me when I do tracker evaluations, as it is perfect for circling tracks and to
sit on. People have begun to joke that this stick gives me my "power."
During one evaluation, while our Land Rover negotiated a few sharp
kinks between some granite boulders, my stick flew from the vehicle and
clanged on the rocks. The vehicle came to a sudden halt. The spontaneous
chit-chatter on the vehicle came to an equally sudden halt. As I looked
around, eight Shangaan trackers started at me with big eyes. I jumped off
and climbed over the rocks to retrieve my stick. Fortunately, it was in one
piece.*

"No problem," I said. "It is not broken."

"Mtagati (magic)!" someone said, and we all had a good laugh.

—A. L.

WALK BEFORE YOU RUN

We are often hampered in our development by process, and the biggest single contributor is our misunderstanding regarding the application of the systematic following of footprints and speculative trailing. Often during basic trailing classes, I have heard trackers say "but I can't see the line!" At the other extreme, folks with decent knowledge of wildlife or with well-developed intuition want to leap ahead on the trail, and then find themselves without the physical skills to confirm that they are still on the trail. Speculative skills are only useful when joined with the physical skills of identifying and following footprints. Walk before you run.

9

Safety

The bite of winter had been pushed out by a late-morning sun by the time Andre Morgan picked up the lion trail on the sandy track. Much earlier in the morning, the trail had taken us all over the reserve as the animals moved almost the entire night, probably in an attempt to stay warm. The multitude of game drives and other management vehicles that had been out since dawn didn't make things any easier; they had obliterated large sections of the trail where the lions had made use of the roads. The tracks that were visible were frosted over and thus from earlier in the night. The cold steel of my rifle was almost frozen to my hands.

Andre was a field guide at one of the lodges at Entabeni, a privately owned game reserve in the picturesque Waterberg. This tall, slender man in his early twenties grew up hunting on his parents' farm. Joining us on the trail was Jacqui Glover, also a field guide in her early twenties, who was to qualify the next day as a level III tracker, becoming the first female to ever do so.

The pride of lions we were trailing was the only pride in the reserve. With the boundaries of their territory delineated by an electric fence and no spotted hyenas to compete with, they had very little to do other than feed themselves. They were tracked on foot almost every day so high-paying clients could view them from the safety of game-drive vehicles. They were also regularly captured and tranquilized for management and scientific reasons. The constant pressure gave them something of an attitude.

It was July, the coldest month in the South African Bushveld. We were dwarfed by the sandstone cliffs towering to the northwest of us. This part of the Waterberg consists almost entirely of sandstone, its weathering creating deep, loose, sandy soil at its base. The ground was covered with dead leaves, and under the canopy of the broad-leaved woodland, very little grass and forbs grew. The landscape was draped in gray, brown, and yellow; a black frost a few weeks earlier had killed off all the green.

The trail of the pride was heading straight down the two-track road, into the wind. Unlike the other roads they had used during the night, this one was not capped, as it was seldom driven. The area toward which the lions were heading was secluded, a good place to escape from vehicles and people. The soft sand muffled the sound of our progress. Andre was moving comfortably on the trail. I followed with Jacqui behind me. Visibility varied between twenty and sixty yards in mottled sunlight.

The bush went quiet—a telltale sign that we were not far from the lions. I saw a sunny patch about ten yards in diameter ahead and to our right, about sixty yards away, but the vegetation didn't allow good visibility. As we cleared a small thicket to our right, the patch became more visible. In it, hidden in the shin-high grass, were the lions, fast asleep. We could see only their yellow flanks along the top of the grass. Andre didn't see them, but he stopped when he realized I had stopped. His eyes scanned the area ahead. Eventually, he whispered, "I can't see anything, but I know they're here because I know you can see them."

At that moment, some wildebeest stampeded a few hundred yards away, downwind but out of sight of the lions. A head popped up above the grass. We stayed frozen, hoping the lioness would not see us. She stared in the direction of the commotion for half a minute or so, then rolled over to go back to sleep. Unfortunately, when she did, she was then facing us, and for a brief moment it was almost comical to see her facial expression change. A low growl erupted, and five more heads popped up, including that of the big male.

The lions were facing in different directions, some half lifting into a sitting or low-standing position. Then one of the adult lionesses also spotted us as a youngster moved off to the back. The scene changed in

A large lioness stands tall to assess an intruder. AL

seconds—*every lion focused on us. I ordered Andre to get behind me and stand still. The male, notoriously aggressive toward people on foot, started his approach with a low, threatening walk, growling with lips up and canines exposed. The females joined him, two of them flanking his right and one to his left. It looked as if their support had spurred him on; he immediately approached more boldly. All we could do was hope he turned away before we did.*

A typical lion encounter on foot is somewhat anticlimactic. The animals are either completely unaware of your presence (which is, of course, ideal) or they leave in a hurry. If they do decide to charge, it is normally only briefly: an explosion of fur and teeth before they turn and leave.

Seeing the females flanking the male, I quickly realized this was different. I took a step or two forward, but the lions kept pushing closer. By now, the females were spread out, and the formation was about twenty yards wide. I realized we were going to lose sight of the females behind the vegetation if we stayed where we were. To enable us to keep them in sight, we moved back past the thicket on our right. I also realized the line the male was following might take him behind the thicket, and that he would most likely charge the moment he lost eye contact with us.

I allowed him to come a few yards closer, hoping this would force him to come around the thicket and maintain eye contact. In preparation, I told Jacqui to get hold of Andre's belt so she could lead him out on my count, and I told Andre to do the same with me but to keep his eyes on the lions. With my rifle ready, we moved back one step, but the lions kept on coming. We moved one more step, but nothing changed.

The male was now about twenty-five yards away. The females were fanning out more to the sides. Then the male moved behind the thicket. We found ourselves at the point of no return, and I wanted more space quickly. I told the team to keep moving up the road. Then, exactly what I predicted happened: The moment we lost eye contact with the male, he charged, erupting on our side of the thicket not more than twenty-five feet away. We froze, and so did he when he broke through the bushes. We stared at each other for a few very long seconds, and then he pulled his head back into the thicket. We began backing out again, but he restarted his approach the moment the females caught up to him.

Little by little, we opened up distance from the animals. But their persistence made me call in the vehicle to pick us up. When it pulled in, the lions simply turned around and went back to bed down in the winter sun. They knew the vehicle posed no threat.

—A. L.

GENERAL SAFETY

When tracking animals, one will inevitably encounter dangerous situations. They range from severe storms and landslides to intense heat and threatening animals. It is therefore necessary to prepare for such an encounter so that you can avoid them as much as possible.

Given the nature of their work, professional conservationists, rangers, and researchers must expose themselves to danger. Sometimes, it might be necessary for them to take calculated risks, otherwise they will never get their work done. A calculated risk is one where you have the odds stacked heavily in your favor. Trackers who take unnecessary risks are not exhibiting bravery, but stupidity, or a cavalier disregard for animals (which are inevitably killed if they act aggressively or attack a person).

In 2007, a white rhino bull was shot in self-defense by a guide while he and a colleague were tracking the animal. They located the animal at about fifty yards, where it was lying under a tree. As they pulled out, the wind changed, and the animal immediately charged from about a hundred yards away. There were no tall trees nearby for them to climb. In their attempts to get away, they changed position four times, but the animal homed in on them nonetheless. The guide gave the animal every opportunity to break off the charge but, in the end, shot it from just five feet away. The guide dove clear, and the animal's shoulders landed where he stood when he fired. In this case, there was no sign of aggression prior to the start of the attack, nor was there a history of this particular animal being aggressive toward humans.

In 2009, a leopard was shot by a guide while he was tracking the animal. The animal was hiding in some vegetation, and the guide had walked passed it five times at a distance of less than ten yards. The leopard charged, and the guide shot it at eight feet. In this case, the leopard had a history of remaining stationary when being tracked. An incident was once reported of a tracker lifting a fallen branch off the trail of the leopard in dense vegetation only to find the leopard lying underneath it. Fellow trackers and guides blamed the guide for overreacting when he shot the cat. Their reasoning was that he should have known that particular leopard had developed a habit of charging from very close, but then stopping at about fifteen feet from the intruder. The leopard would then relax and allow an intruder to walk away and bring guests in with a vehicle to view it.

We will never know if the leopard would have stopped, as the fifteen feet were already halved. The more important issue is that none of the trackers, guides, or lodge operators took control of the situation when the cat started to charge trackers on a regular basis. Strict guidelines and protocols should have been imposed much earlier, banning the tracking of this animal in areas where visibility was restricted.

Recreational walks in the wilderness are becoming increasingly popular, allowing people to gain first-hand experience of nature and develop positive attitudes toward conservation. Participants should, however, at least know about the possible dangers involved so they will not give way to irrational fears. The inexperienced naturalist should at all times be accompanied by an experienced ranger or tracker.

Your first priority should always be to avoid confrontations. The advice given in this book for handling dangerous encounters is intended only as a last resort in the event of an accident. Never test a dangerous animal. There are always exceptions to the rules. While animals may generally conform to certain characteristic behaviors, individuals have their own personalities and some might deviate from the norm. Although the authors have tried to ensure that the information given is reliable, neither they nor the publisher assume responsibility for any action taken as a result of information contained here.

Shooting dangerous animals should be left to experienced rangers who know what they are doing. Unless you are an excellent marksman and know exactly when and where to shoot an animal, it might be better not to shoot at all—there is nothing more dangerous than a wounded animal. Even

A male cougar snarls at being approached too closely. ME

if unarmed or armed with only a knife, the appropriate reaction can save your life.

The inexperienced naturalist who plans to spend a lot of time in the wild may develop through several learning stages. Initially, they will probably experience irrational fears due to a lack of knowledge of wildlife. Such a state can cause panic and have fatal consequences. You should avoid this at all cost by gaining as much knowledge as possible. Over a period of time, when nothing serious happens, some people grow careless. Such an attitude is equally dangerous because then they can be caught off-guard and lose control of the situation. As trackers begin to encounter dangerous animals and no serious incidents occur, their familiarity sometimes breeds recklessness. Should you reach the stage when you disregard natural fear, you are in even greater danger than before.

You might be lucky enough to survive a few close shaves, but sooner or later your recklessness could prove fatal. And if you are

Approaching lions with cubs must be done with utmost care. ME

unlucky, it could happen sooner rather than later. It would be best if after a few close shaves you become increasingly cautious, appreciating real dangers for what they are. Experience should diminish irrational fear *and* help you develop respect for dangerous animals, based on rational fear of real danger. If you are well informed, the appropriate attitude can be adopted from the very start, and the dangerous early learning stages can be avoided.

Sometimes we end up going too far. I was evaluating tracker Million Mathonsi in the Thornybush Game Reserve, tracking a pride of lions. We eventually arrived at a dense thicket where females had been going in and out over the course of several days, which indicated that their cubs were inside. From fresh tracks, we could see that the lionesses had gone off to hunt, leaving their cubs hidden. Million was keen to show me the cubs, but I hesitated, thinking that I should pull him back and conclude the evaluation. Then my own curiosity got the better of me, and I allowed him to continue. We carefully approached the thicket from the downwind side, slowly moving into the thicket until we found the cubs. Million smiled broadly at the sight. We silently backed out and moved to safety.

It was quite an experience, and we excitedly laughed about it. But afterwards, master tracker Wilson Masia, who had been watching us from a safe distance, took me aside and reprimanded me for putting our lives in danger. If the adult lions had returned while we were inside that thicket, they would have fought us. This places the lions at a completely unnecessary risk, since we would have had to shoot one or more of them. And even though I was carrying a rifle, they might have killed one of us. Wilson then went on to tell me how he, when he was young, once tracked a leopard and found her den. Excited by his find, he put his head inside to take a closer look. When he got home, he told his father what he had found, but he too was reprimanded by his father. Tracking is something you learn through experience, and no matter how much you try to caution young trackers, it seems that at least once they will go too far. Sometimes we allow our curiosity to get the better of us, but it is important to consider carefully and temper our curiosity.

—L. L.

Natural fear is important but needs to be kept under control. It keeps you alert and, when you are confronted by a dangerous animal, intensifies the senses, making you think faster. Fear suppresses emotions and pain, and the adrenaline it provides gives you additional strength. However, you do still need to prepare yourself psychologically for a possible confrontation. No matter how small the chances are, you should always be prepared for the worst. When it does happen, you won't have time to plan your reaction. When you are suddenly confronted by a dangerous animal at short range and an intense sensation of fear shoots through your body, it is difficult to react in a rational way. As well, every muscle in your body will tense, including your vocal chords, so your voice will become a high-pitched squeak. In order to sound assertive when shouting at a charging animal, you have to force your voice down. A high-pitched, panic-stricken voice might well encourage a wild animal to attack. Fear will also make the animal appear much bigger than it is, and time will seem to stand still. Yet you must react instantly and intuitively, and your intuition must override your instinctive urge to flee.

To prepare yourself psychologically, visualize animals attacking you and, in your imagination, act out the appropriate response to that particular animal. This mental exercise should be repeated until it becomes second nature. It must become part of your intuitive way of thinking so that when the worst happens, you will be mentally and psychologically prepared to react, without having to think.

You also need to train physically. Train your body so you will be able to endure days of walking in broken country. It is not good enough to be fit enough to walk half an hour on a trail. It helps to keep your gear light, basic, and appropriate. Don't overburden yourself with unnecessary gear. More people get in trouble because they carry too much, not too little.

It is important to understand that every animal has a comfort zone, which experts call the "psychological defensive zone." This is best described by the discomfort you experience when you are forced to share a crowded space, such as an elevator, with a group of strangers. Animals experience the same discomfort when their personal space is penetrated by a predator or human intruder. They perceive it as a threat to either themselves or their young.

Although it will vary, animals in general have three distinct zones around themselves: the alert/curiosity/flight zone, the warning zone, and the attack zone. An animal relies on scent, hearing, and sight to discover an intrusion, and the size and shape of these zones will differ depending on the species, character, and mood of the animal, as well as the prevailing circumstances of the area and the encounter.

If the outer zone is entered, the animal might become inquisitive or curious at first but will then choose to move off. If you trespass on the fringes of the outer zone, you will often illicit an inquisitive response—animals might approach in an attempt to identify you. If you maintain the distance and do not show any interest in the animals, they might even carry on with whatever they were doing. Most animals will give way to humans and move to avoid confrontation.

If the second zone is penetrated, the animal will begin to feel threatened and respond by eliciting warning signs intended to persuade the intruder not to come any closer. Hissing, snarling, puffing up, growling, baring teeth, tossing the head, bristling the hair on its back and neck, raising or swishing the tail, flattening the ears, breaking branches, kicking or pawing the ground, spitting, or rattling quills are some of the methods used by animals to warn off intruders. If these initial warnings are ignored, they will be increased in intensity.

If you penetrate the second zone and then move off, the animal will in most cases calm down and also move off, usually in a hurry. If, however, they feel uncomfortable or suspicious, they will run off. If you enter the attack zone—by mistake or intentionally—expect trouble. The animal now feels so threatened that it sees attack as the best form of defense.

These zones apply to all animals: big, small, wild, tame, and domesticated. All animals can be potentially dangerous. In fact, you must be extra cautious with habituated wild animals as they have lost their fear of humans and often associate us with food. Remember, too, that all animals with young are *extremely* protective. Greater caution must be exercised when encountering them with or near their young.

A female cougar stands stiff-legged and tall, laying back her ears to indicate discomfort and agitation at being approached too closely while she cares for her kittens. ME

*W*hen I started my career as a wilderness trails ranger in the Kruger National Park, I had some big-game experience. As a nature conservation student, I was involved with predator research that included lion-capture operations. I had worked in the Kruger as a research assistant for a year and another provincial park for a year and a half. But taking on the responsibility of protecting the lives of paying guests on wilderness trails brought an entire new dimension to it all. It was a daunting and sometimes terrifying task.

One of the ways I prepared myself was to mentally rehearse getting charged by animals. Every day, after an incident or an encounter with a dangerous animal, I would replay it in my mind, looking at it from different angles, visualizing what would have happened if the animal had not turned but pushed the attack. I often role-played this with my colleague Amos to get his input. I especially did a lot of this in those first few weeks of 1992, when I started on trails, and Amos and I had to forge a relationship that would keep us alive.

Mental preparation proved valuable on a trail once in March 1992. The trail group consisted of two couples, each with two teenagers. On the first morning's walk, we had trouble with a buffalo bull and a herd of elephants. Early the next morning, lions caught a kudu inside the camp's fence, and some of them remained in the camp at wake-up time. As we started the second morning's walk, we were charged by a buffalo bull. He broke the charge off at five yards, when he sank his head and front legs to his chest, into loose sand and water in the riverbed. After breakfast, we were charged by a white rhino cow and calf, and on our way back to the vehicle, a leopard jumped up underneath my feet as I was about to cross a stream. Finally, in the last ten minutes of the walk, we were charged by another buffalo bull but managed to open an escape route for him and made it out intact. The adrenaline was definitely flowing.

The incident with the rhino cow and calf especially illustrated the importance of mental rehearsal to control fear and do the right thing. Adrenaline is part of our survival makeup, and we need to learn how to use it to our benefit.

Shortly after breakfast, we were walking down a gentle slope. The landscape was relatively open, but further down the slope was a dense stand of round-leaved teak. As we were about to enter it, some branches *broke in front of us, and we heard what sounded like a freight train coming toward us.*

Amos had a few days off, so Sandros Chivodze stood in for him as second rifle. The two of us stopped immediately, but the group pushed a bit further before they stopped. This meant that Sandros ended up next to me on the right, with our guests to my left.

At about thirty-five yards, the rhinos broke cover, the calf running in front of the mother. Sandros and I both chambered a round, and his magnum barked as he fired a shot. This infuriated me. "You fool," I thought, "you should know that you don't fire a deterring shot at white rhino—they only zoom in on it. And you know you should wait for my command before you fire in any case!"

Standard operating procedure dictated that the first- or lead rifle always fire first, or gives the command to the second rifle to fire a warning shot. It is only if the first rifle is out of action that the second rifle is to take charge.

The next thought that went through my mind was to check where the bullet struck, to make sure we hadn't wounded the rhino. The bullet struck the ground about twenty yards from us, very close and directly in line with the calf. "Thank goodness it didn't hit the animal," I thought.

I saw where Sandros's cartridge case landed as he cycled the bolt of his rifle. I heard the zing as the bullet ricocheted off the ground, and then I saw the bullet strike the ground again with a cloud of dust on the other side of the rhino. It missed again! I then saw Sandros moving around to my back to take up a position in front of the guests.

The animals were now coming in fast, zooming in on the rifle shot. I saw one of the guests turn to run, but her husband pulled her back into the group. The calf was heading straight at me, and the cow, a few yards behind him, was aiming straight at the guests. I realized it would be senseless to shoot the calf because then I would definitely have to shoot the cow as well. The calf was large enough to run me over but would most likely not kill me. I envisioned a line ten feet from me and decided that if the calf reached it, I would shoot the cow.

I drew a bead on the cow's brain and waited. The calf approached the line, but at that moment, the cow started to swing her head from side to side, her horns making a swip-swip. I readjusted my aim. And then about five feet away, the calf turned, just missing me.

A white rhino with a calf. CAY-UWE/ISTOCKPHOTO.COM

I felt a wave of relief as I realized I had gained a bit more time. The cow then lifted her head a bit, pulled her ears back, and turned toward me. I kept my aim to the last, then lifted the rifle out the way as she would have knocked me over had she ran into the muzzle with her shoulder. She came past me at less than an arm's length.

We watched as the animals kept running past us, up and over the ridge. I checked that everybody was still in one piece, then we set off at a brisk pace for about three or four hundred yards to a small rocky outcrop. There we stopped for water, and to let our nerves settle.

All of this happened in a few seconds, but it felt like a lifetime. I could replay the events vividly in my mind, envisioning it all over the sights of my rifle. Adrenaline, if correctly channeled, sharpens the senses so well that you can remember everything with astounding clarity. The bullet from Sandros's rifle travelled at a speed of about 1,950 feet per second and had gone 66 feet before striking the ground. The entire argument I had with Sandros in my mind took place in less than one-thirtieth of a second.

Sandros never told me if he fired the shot intentionally.

—A. L.

10

Tracking Different Animals

hat follows are accounts of specific animals, most of which can pose a significant danger to trackers. While the fundamentals of tracking apply to all wildlife, here we discuss nuances particular to specific species. When appropriate, we also describe potential dangers and the animals' methods of perceiving threats and communicating warnings, and, finally, make suggestions for evasive action in case of attack.

SNAKES

One day while walking in the dunes at Arniston, I found puff adder spoor making a straight line in the sand. It moved in a caterpillarlike progression, indicating a leisurely prowl. Its belly muscles moved the large ventral plates forward in alternate waves, gripping the ground to draw the body forward. I knelt down to inspect the ridges in the spoor to see which way the ventral plates had pushed back the sand.

Once the direction was determined, it was not too difficult to follow the spoor. Where the snake went into thick bush, I moved around to the other side to avoid going through myself. I reached a bush with no spoor coming out. I searched the undergrowth, carefully edging my way into the bush.

A thorough search revealed nothing. Yet the snake had to be in that bush. It simply could not have disappeared without a trace. The more I searched, the more my curiosity grew. And then it suddenly appeared in front of me out of nowhere. I had searched the spot several times and must have looked straight at it, but simply didn't see it. Only when I recognized the chevron pattern on its back did the snake jump into focus. Although I knew what I was looking for, I was unfamiliar with that particular color morph, so the preconceived image I had in mind simply did not fit.

The way snakes are camouflaged when they lie still is uncanny. A few times I tracked snakes until the spoor disappeared only to discover the snake itself lying in full view right in front of me. Usually, I freeze when I see a snake and pin it down if necessary. But on one occasion I saw my big toe almost touch a horned adder and felt an electric jolt that sent me flying through the air and landing flat on my back.

—L. L.

I have trained myself to stand still when I detect a snake, so this is what happens even when I see one in my peripheral vision. But I have also trained myself to move in the opposite direction when a snake strikes at me. I do not play with snakes, and I do not pick them up, but I do tolerate them around me. One day while tracking a rhino, I was moving relatively quickly through a dry, open wetland with hip-high grass. I instinctively launched myself up, and to the right, clearing the grass. While already in midair, I realized I had glimpsed the big pink mouth of a puff adder coming up at me from the left. After I landed a few feet to the right of it, I took a look in the grass, and it was the biggest puffy I'd ever seen. It had managed to strike almost a yard off the ground.

—A. L.

Tracking Notes

Senses and Speed: Most important is snakes' well-developed sense of smell, which they do with their tongues in combination with their Jacobson organs. Diurnal snakes have relatively good eyesight but cannot detect an object unless it moves. Some snakes have heat receptors that guide them toward warm-blooded prey. Snakes "hear" by feeling vibrations through the ground. Some snakes, such as adders, are sluggish, while others are fast. All of them can move relatively quickly when disturbed, however. Because they are exothermic, they might not be able to move at all when it is very cold.

Warning Signs and Dangers: Snakes tend to move away from humans as soon as they detect their approach. Most species are non-venomous or only mildly venomous. It is rare for snakes to actively charge a human, and then it will last only until a safe escape route opens. Some snakes, such as puff adders and vine snakes, rely on camouflage and do not move away. When cornered or alarmed, cobras and mambas tend to rear up (cobras form their trademark hoods). Adders hiss, and rattlesnakes rattle. Most snakes will make warning strikes before they actually bite.

Method of Attack: Most snakebites occur when a snake is cornered, trapped, or stepped on, or hurt during an attempt to capture or kill it. At close range, they strike at movement. Venomous snakes bite to inject venom only when they are seriously threatened. Some snakes, including rattlesnakes, are able to control the amount of venom they deliver. A rattlesnake can bite without delivering any poison, or only a small dose. Young snakes (smaller than adults)

A coiled western rattlesnake ready to strike. ME

have less control of their venom and are therefore the most dangerous. Cobras might spit, and their venom will cause a painful burn in the eyes. Some large constrictors will anchor themselves onto their victims with a bite and then coil around them to suffocate them.

Avoiding Conflict and Evasion Techniques: It is usually relatively easy to stay out of trouble with snakes. Freeze when you detect a snake close to you until it moves away. Learn to identify the snakes in an area and, if they are venomous, what type of venom they have. Do not try to catch or handle a snake unless you are trained and have a good reason to do so. Do not tease a snake. Do not pick up a dead snake—some species feign death as a survival mechanism. Step onto logs and rocks instead of over them, as snakes often hide underneath. If you sleep on a trail, open your bedding only as you go to bed. An unoccupied sleeping bag is a great hiding place for snakes.

COUGARS

We could hear her signal in the drainage below us, a moist strip of cottonwoods in the midst of vast desert. The signal emanating from her collar was strong and clear, but the rapid two-note "beep-beep, beep-beep" meant that the battery was running out of juice. We changed the frequency and heard the signal of her kitten, which was nearing two years old and expected to disperse to her own home range at any time. Without the aid of trained hounds, we would have to catch the older female the old-fashioned way—by trap or snare—in order to replace the battery in her collar. And this meant predicting her movements well enough to catch her. We could have attempted to bait her, but since we'd run out of road-killed deer, we hoped instead to find a fresh kill and use it to lure her.

The next morning, we found her in the exact same place, and on the subsequent morning as well. This was sure sign that she had killed something, and that it was nearby. Mike Puzzo, the other biologist on the project, was hosting a workshop for people interested in mountain lions and so we brought them along to look for her kill. We drove around to the other side of the drainage, parked, and approached her position on foot.

I crossed one of her trails very near where we knew she rested with her kitten. Their signals were still strong and crisp. Her tracks moved away from the riparian area and across an open stretch of scrub desert toward a gully in the Cigarette Hills. I signaled to Mike, who led the others up the slope, and I began to follow her trail. She crossed the open stretch in a trot, which meant it was likely dusk when she moved. She entered the gully quickly and then began to climb, winding a bit to take advantage of larger boulders with surer footing. As we approached the crest of the hill, she cut south, paralleling the top, but remaining just below the crest and invisible to any animal on the other side. She crossed through an old barbed-wire fence where it had fallen. Then she padded across the rock jumbles and down into the drainage.

Mike and the others reached the crest and proceeded to head straight down the other side. I pointed out her direction, and they spread out to search for signs. I watched as Mike pointed to some large juniper bushes halfway down slope, ideal places to hide a cached carcass, keeping it safe from aerial scavengers and shielding it from the sun. An eager participant raced down the slope to investigate the bushes, and I silently wished him luck.

Watching the group work over the area, I slowly picked my way down the boulder-strewn hillside, following the route I thought the cougar might have taken. The man below yelled that he'd found nothing under the junipers. Strange, I thought, for that was certainly my best guess as to where the carcass was stashed. Then we found it—the cached remains of half a mule deer out in the open, halfway between the crest of the hill and the junipers. The cougars had attempted to cache the remainder of the deer with dried yucca leaves and scant debris.

We chatted about cougar-feeding ecology and the kill for some time, and then I started to backtrack the attack up the hillside. The trails were still clearly visible, and I was able to lead the group through the chase down the hill to the kill site. The mule deer was stotting, jumping on all four feet at the same time, as though on a pogo stick. The deer moved down the hill at great speed, leaving dark gashes in the desert crust in between boulders, chollas, and yuccas. The cat streaked in from above, angling alongside the deer. She used a small boulder to launch onto the deer's back—and then there were no cougar tracks for ten yards or so, just the deer's. I could envision her reaching forward in a flash of motion, hooking the deer's head with her claws and yanking it back so she could bite the throat. The deer crashed down so hard that it broke an antler midtine on a large boulder. The cougar appeared to be unhurt; it dragged the deer around to the other side of the boulder and began to feed. She was soon joined by her kitten. The tracks told the story, and the remains of the deer were the tangible conclusion.

—M. E.

Cougars are most active during the twilight periods, when day and night meld. They also move frequently during periods of darkness. When cougars inhabit areas where humans are present, they become more nocturnal. Even then, though, they may move short distances at any time of day. Most of the day, however they rest, conserving energy in preparation for hunting prey larger than themselves. During the heat of summer, cougars require shade and rarely leave their beds. In the desert Southwest, they lie in the deep shade of large boulders or in thick brush. In cooler temperatures, they consciously select beds in which the sun will reach them. They bed under cover, but where the sun breaks through the brush, such as on the southern sides of ridges.

Cougars patrol their territories and hunt using a walking gait, giving them a stealthy and fluid grace. When traveling, they often take the paths of least resistance, including trails, dirt roads, and sandy washes. When they hunt, cougars weave through cover and zigzag across the landscape, using both wind and terrain to their advantage. In steep country, a cougar will hunt from the ridges, moving along them, traveling just out of sight of the next drainage. Periodically, it will loop up to the crest to scent and listen for prey below. Then it will loop down and around to move into the wind toward its quarry. Alternatively, cougars weave across the landscape, pausing every few hours for intervals up to an hour in areas where prey species frequent, waiting for a target to appear.

Wandering is fundamental to cougar natural history. In southern California, it is not unusual for cougars to hunt areas intensely from

Multiple cougar trails pointing to a kill site, which was twenty yards further along the trail. ME

several weeks to a month, then disappear and not return to them for two or three months' time. Females with kittens may only move a couple of miles per night, while a typical adult moves four to five miles. On occasion, a traveling animal will cover up to twenty miles at a time. Cougars trot to cover ground quickly and bound and gallop when fleeing. Communication between cougars is primarily olfactory in order to prevent fighting between such potent carnivores. Chemical communication through scrapes, scats, urine, scratching, and rubbing is essential in maintaining territories as well as relaying information about sexual status and availability. A cougar scrapes with its hind feet only, first with one foot and then the other, to create a neat pile of debris and soil at one end of parallel swaths of exposed earth. Both males and females create scrapes, although males do so far more often than females. Some scientists believe that females only scrape when they are in heat and use scrapes to inform males that they are in estrus, but they clearly play a territorial role as well.

Scrapes are often made in softer substrates, such as pine or leaf litter, or where other debris has accumulated. They are found most often where topography funnels movement: under ledges, along

Scrape made by an adult male cougar. ME

ridges, in dry drainages, and at forested mountain passes. They are also found around kill sites. In some areas, numerous scrapes accumulate over time. In Arizona, under a large Ponderosa pine, I saw cougar scrapes completely covering an area at least twenty by thirty feet. Where adult male ranges overlap slightly, cougars leave scrapes along territorial boundaries. In areas where they overlap greatly, such as the Southwest, scrape sites are sprinkled more broadly across their ranges. They function like community bulletin boards, perhaps emphasizing dominance and advertising which male is presently using that area.

Cougars are specialist hunters of mule and white-tailed deer. They lie in wait, or stalk, slinking low to the ground with ears alert until their prey is within a striking range of approximately fifty feet. When they are this close to their quarry, their chances of catching it are great. When close, cougars pounce, leaping onto their prey or pursuing it until they are able to do so. They grip their quarry rodeo-style, clinging tightly with sharp, protractable claws, including the enlarged claws of "toe 1" on the inside of their front feet and the equivalent of our thumbs. With their victims bucking and struggling beneath them, they deliver a killing bite to the back of the neck or skull. On larger prey and animals with antlers or horns, cougars hook

A cougar feeding on a mule deer in a snowstorm. ME

A freshly killed mule deer, opened in characteristic fashion by a cougar. Note the clumps of fur plucked first, followed by the removal of the ribs to get to the internal organs. ME

their heads with a paw and yank them to expose their necks. Then the cougar bites and severs the windpipe, killing their prey by suffocation.

Once an animal has been killed, a mountain lion generally drags it downhill to a secluded spot, leaving a conspicuous drag line on the landscape, unless the prey is too large to move. Once under cover, cougars pluck their prey, pulling great tufts of fur from one side behind the rib cage. Then they open the carcass and remove the rumen like a surgeon, setting it aside before any serious eating. Sometimes, a cougar will start with the meat from the inside of the hind leg adjacent to the hole in the abdomen. More often, it will first shear the ribs close to the spinal column, moving up toward the head. Once the ribs are consumed, the cat gorges on the protein-rich internal organs. After the initial meal, cougars often cover their prey with debris, called caching, though they sometimes just leave it as it is.

An adult male cougar. ME

Cougars defend their caches from other animals, but there is only anecdotal evidence to suggest that they defend caches from humans. Certainly you should be cautious if investigating their kills. Cougars may bed immediately adjacent to their kills or up to a mile and a half away. When they feed on a carcass on successive nights, they often bed in the same area each day, and their trails will be seen both coming and going—one of the surest signs that you are near a kill. Remember to look for scavenging birds above and the trails of smaller terrestrial scavengers that might lead you to the carcass, especially if the cat has moved on.

Tracking Notes

Senses and Speed: Cougars have excellent hearing and eyesight. They can run up to forty mph for short distances, but it is their lightning-quick acceleration that helps them catch prey. Vertically, they can leap more than ten feet, and horizontally, up to twenty-five feet.

Warning Signs and Dangers: Curious cougars swish their tails from side to side and may sit to watch you. Do not encourage a curious cougar, because it might cause an actual predatory attack. Cougars that crouch and pump their tails up and down are signaling an imminent attack.

Agitated cougars point their ears backwards and flatten them against their skulls. They also growl in a low rumble. If a cougar is unable to run from an intruder, or if the intruder continues an approach, it will intersperse growls with long, high-pitched hissing. These sounds are produced with the mouth wide open to reveal the canines. Aggressive lions might also stand stiff legged with their heads raised, hackles erect, and tails twitching. Agitated lions might also bluff-charge (also called a warning charge), though this is rare and most often exhibited by females with kittens.

Method of Attack: Cougars are stalk-and-ambush predators. When close enough, they leap onto their prey or pursue it until they are able to do so. They cling to their quarry with sharp, protractable claws, including the enlarged claws of "toe 1" on the insides of their

A cougar, head held low and ears erect, exhibits curiosity as it approaches. ME

front feet. With their victims bucking and struggling, they deliver a killing bite to the back of their neck or skull or sometimes suffocate them with a bite to the throat.

Avoiding Conflict and Evasion Techniques: Encounters with wild cougars are rare, and attacks on humans even more so. They do occur, however. Cougars are ambush predators. If you see one, it generally means it will not attack since it has lost the element of surprise. Should you encounter a curious or aggressive cougar in the wild, yell and make lots of noise, throw rocks or anything available, and make yourself appear as large and intimidating as possible. Pick up a large stick to use as a weapon if one is nearby. Cougars typically flee when they realize you are human.

Do not allow a curious or approaching cougar to circle behind you, and do not break eye contact with it, as it might take that opportunity to charge. Should the cougar attack, fight hard; cougars often abandon prey that does not easily succumb. And keep fighting: Cougars focus-lock on their prey for several minutes regardless of the abuse they suffer. You must make the cougar realize that the cost of attacking you outweighs the benefit.

AMERICAN BISON

Tracking Notes

Senses and Speed: A bison's sense of smell is acute and seems to aid in the detection of predators. It can hear and see quite well and is able to discern moving objects at 1.2 miles and a man on a horse at 0.6 mile. Bison can run up to thirty-seven mph.

Warning Signs and Dangers: The tail is an important means of communication among bison. When bison are grazing, it sways peacefully back and forth; during sexual and aggressive encounters, it is raised horizontally or even vertically. The height of the tail is a graded signal and varies along a continuum: The higher it is raised, the greater the intensity of the animal's stress or aggressive intent.

Method of Attack: Bison gore with their stout, hooked, tapered horns, which can break ribs and puncture organs. Bison can be shy and retiring or aggressive and dangerous. Unfortunately, they do not always communicate their intentions clearly; fatal attacks have been made without preceding threat displays in both wild and captive animals. Bison have been seen throwing intruders up to thirty feet with a quick hook and twist of their shaggy heads. Several patterns are clear: The older the bison, the less tolerant and more unpredictable it becomes. Females are less predictable during the calving season and males during the rut.

Avoiding Conflict and Evasion Techniques: When a bison charges, climb a tree or retreat into water, such as a river or pond. Or place boulders, trees,

American bison, exhibiting the tail-up threat.
MEGAN WYMAN

or other obstacles between you and the animal. Otherwise, you must dive out of the way at the last moment. Should a herd of bison charge, you must worry about being trampled as well as being gored.

BEARS

*M**any mornings I have the opportunity to walk out my front door, cross the driveway, and, after a short stroll, find a fresh black bear trail to follow. This has given me chances over the years to get to know several individual bears, not just from following trails but also from direct observation. One in particular is a young female I began bumping into several years ago. An irregular blond patch on her rump and her slight build helped me identify her. Her small tracks soon became a regular feature of the woods we share. I was sure the first time I saw her that she had not been on her own for long. She seemed nervous, and the slightest sound set her on edge. During our first encounter, I had been trying to stalk close enough to see her after I heard her bed down. More than a half hour had passed without the slightest sound from where I last heard her thirty yards away, and so, with the breeze in my face, I eased forward. Deep sword-fern made for an agonizingly slow stalk. After another half hour, I made it a few yards closer. Then a fern raked across my pants leg. This noise was all it took to send the young bear whooshing twenty feet up a Douglas-fir.*

She was barely fifteen yards away, looking at me, then at the ground around her, then away. I could see the agitation in her face; it seemed she was annoyed at her choice to climb rather than flee. I took a step back, and she climbed a bit higher, shaking her head and grinding her teeth. I talked to her softly and began easing away. At my retreat, she calmed a bit, her face peering at me from around the giant tree trunk.

And so it went with her for several seasons after that. I would follow her trails and occasionally see a patch of black moving in the green. On occasion, I'd notice a face staring at me from through the low crotch of two trees. (Her hiding like this always left me wondering just how many black bears have let me walk past them. They are excellent at hiding and

A young black bear peering down from the crown of an aspen. ME

can disappear into the woods like a ghost slipping from sight right before your eyes.)

After coming home from work one summer evening I had a feeling I should take a walk up the hill and see what I could see. I set off on the trail that threads the woods between our home and one of the clear-cuts on the hill above. All sorts of plants that bears enjoy were springing up on the hillside: an array of clover, grasses, blackberries, and fireweed. Not far from the edge, I noticed the rounded compressions of two large pads overstepping through the fallen maple and alder leaves. Flattened miner's lettuce and flagged stinging nettles pointed the way. The breaks and bruises were still bright green and damp with juice, suggesting that they were fresh. The trail was coming from a neighbor's property and headed up toward the clear-cut. I followed it up to the logging road above, where I saw that the bear left the woods and walked out onto the road. Before walking out myself, I studied the clearing. When I was sure that all the dark fir stumps were indeed stumps, I stepped out. The beautiful compressions so easy to follow in the leaf litter gave way to dull gray crushed rock. Confident that she would be headed up rather than down, I began looking in the dust that settled in tire ruts. A pad here, a pad there, betrayed by the shine of dust grains compressed to the same plane—my suspicions were confirmed, and I eased up the road. I had an idea of where she might be going and so didn't need to search out tracks in the gravel. Just seeing one every so often would be enough. When she left the road, the vegetation along the edges would indicate where.

I didn't go far. Less than a hundred yards up the road, the little bear came into view. A large slash pile had screened us from seeing each other. Her appearance happened rather suddenly. I had been on her trail for maybe twenty minutes, and now there she was, head down, inhaling greens, oblivious to me watching from fifty yards away. This was the kind of trailing I like! Or so I thought. I quickly realized how exposed I was. Fortunately, she turned her rear to me and continued to feed, allowing me to slink to the road's edge and try to blend in with the logging slash and blooming foxglove. From here, I considered what to do. I could sit and watch her feeding until she wandered off, or I could watch her from a little closer. I had the breeze in my face. She was slowly moving away, allowing me to crawl out of sight to the road cut below her. This would put me within about twenty yards of her, which seemed close enough.

I made my way through the ditch to the cut. Downwind and well hidden, I watched for half an hour. She was methodically raking blossoms from the flower spikes of wall lettuce. The delicate yellow flowers disappeared behind her incisors. Occasionally, she would eat the whole plant, but she definitely favored the blossoms. Seemingly content, she wandered around from plant to plant, coming within about ten feet of me at one point. Watching a bear eat is always something, but listening to them really adds to the experience.

In my hiding spot, I was well concealed, but I had not considered that she might come back down onto the road, and that is what she did. Not five yards away from me, she half bounded, half slid down the embankment. I was completely exposed. I flattened my back against the cut. She didn't give me a glance, landing on the road facing away, a direction in mind. Slowly, she began walking up the side of the road, stopping to inhale every wall lettuce plant along the way. I followed. The circumstances for stalking seemed too good to pass up. I had a little trouble keeping pace with her and staying silent at the same time. The gap between us began to grow. As she walked, I tried to keep up; when she stopped, I would drop lower and stop, too.

I was confident that I could follow her until the gap grew too wide and I would have to call it quits. It would be dark soon, and I did not want to spook her. She was about thirty five yards ahead, and it looked as though she would head for an upcoming trail off the bend of the road. Then, out of the corner of my eye, I noticed a face staring at me. I slowly turned my head to see a coyote, front paws resting on a stump, its neck craned out, looking at me. I had been so focused on the bear I had not noticed the coyote in plain sight. I think the coyote had been focused on the bear, too. We were eye to eye, with only a few feet between us. This was all the reason the coyote needed to leave: It nearly did a back flip trying to swap ends and crashed away through the slash. I winced, tuning my head to see the young bear accelerating into a gallop. I don't think she turned her head, just broke and ran, crashing into the woods at the bend. I looked up to see the coyote on a switchback above, loping out of sight. I looked back to where the bear disappeared. Little plumes of dust hung in the air, indicating her departure.

I figured I might as well enjoy the rest of the evening and reflect on what had happened. I walked up to the bend where the little bear took to the woods. Examining the tracks in the clover, I decided it wouldn't hurt to follow her trail into the woods a bit to see where she might be headed. Not far down into the draw, her pace slowed as she negotiated the blow-down and began walking from log to log. Soon she hit a game trail and continued up the draw. With the light growing dimmer, I turned and headed back up toward the road. I planned to walk up to a landing and enjoy the sunset before heading home.

I didn't make it to the landing. A snap from the clear-cut above caught my attention. Far too loud for a deer, I knew it must be another bear. I studied the hillside. Sure enough, a hulking, jet-black body materialized and began angling down the hill toward the bend in the road I had just left. I thought if I headed back down I might be able to see this guy up close. I quickly moved down the road, hugging the edge to stay concealed from above. The switchback in the road cut into the forest, and it was here, where the little bear went into the woods, that several trails converged. And this is where the big guy was headed. I found a boulder to hide behind and watched. I heard twigs snapping as the big bear approached. By now, the woods were so dark I could barely discern his outline. He came within about fifteen yards of me and paused to sniff the wind. His nose went up and swayed from side to side. He was overlooking the spot where the smaller bear and I had passed only a short time before. The evening downdraft spilled down the draw, bringing him the smells of our passing. He scraped at the duff under a fir tree, clearing out broken branches, and plopped down on his haunches, nose still swaying. Then, off to the side of me, I noticed another face rise and then quickly drop back down into a fallen tree. It was the little bear; she had backtracked and was now spying on me.

"Now this is interesting," I thought, "I'm between two bears. Only one knows I am here, and it's getting dark quick. Now what?" I didn't have to wait long to find out. The big one clambered to his feet and began working his way down into the dark timber below. This was my invitation to exit, and I took it gratefully. I still needed to walk past the small

bear, however. I stayed to the far side of the road and slowly slipped past. I heard a slight shift in the branches at the tree. I waved goodbye and walked home in the dark.

—Brian McConnell
senior tracker

When you look for bears, one thing to keep in mind is that their world revolves around three things: food, reproduction (mating and sows caring for young), and sleeping. Food is the top prior-ity. Diverse habitats support bears, and they eat a wide variety of forage: The list of plants that bears will eat is truly dizzying. Both black and brown bears are also predators of fawns and calves each sum-mer and are adept at finding large carcasses to scavenge. Aside from coastal popula-tions with access to salmon runs, both bear species pre-dominantly eat plant matter, however.

Learning their preferred foods in your area and when and where these foods are available is an excellent way to begin looking for a bear trail. Identifying fall berry patches and mast crops can be especially productive. You will know when you have found the right place because their trails become well worn, and ample scat will litter the

A black bear feeding on aspen leaves. ME

A "bear nest," which is actually signs of a feeding bear breaking branches to harvest nuts in early fall. ME

area. Bears can have extremely large home ranges, so finding food draws can be valuable for not only finding bears but also becoming familiar with their sign.

Bears are most active around sunrise and sunset, often napping in day beds in between. Regular bed sites usually offer ample shade and cover and have numerous scats off to the side. Timbered draws and drainages near water are favorite spots. Beds are often found on lookouts above open parks of woods that take advantage of the view and daily updrafts.

Bears often use paths of least resistance when traveling across the landscape. They usually make and maintain their own trails, but do use those of other animals, including humans. Bears will use roads to travel, sometimes for long distances. Abandoned logging roads and seldom-used jeep trails through the woods are often well used by bears. Look for sign such as bitten and clawed trees, scat piles, and zigzagging depressions created by scent-marking bears.

Such patterns emerge because bears walk in the same footsteps over and over along a stretch of trail, forming dirt or mud ovals worn into the ground. These will vary in size and depth by the species of bear, substrate, and number of years the route has been used. The depressions are found around the edge of wetlands, leading to water holes, bite trees, bed sites, or important feeding areas. Wherever they are found they indicate frequent use by bears.

Remember, though, that from time to time, bears, unlike many other animals, will slip through bushes rather than go around them. Black bears will squeeze through much smaller areas than you might expect they would, and doing so seems to be a trait of some individual bears. One particular sow in California clambered through bushes at least in equal proportion to going around them and thus the search for the "most likely route" worked only about half the time.

The tracks of bears can be difficult to discern in anything but clear substrate. They typically leave large oval compressions, wider at the front end, tapering toward the back. When following a bear, you should first determine if the animal is foraging or traveling between a bedding and foraging area. When bears forage, their trails meander, and they feed nearly continuously as they move. Of course, this movement depends upon the food source, but plant foods, including fallen mast crops and fruits, allow bears to wander. Should bears be feeding on manzanitas or acorns, their trails weave from bush to bush, circling over themselves as the animals

Signs of biting bears. ME

move through the area. This makes for difficult tracking. When bears have a destination in mind, they travel in much straighter lines, often on paths of their own or made by other species. Traveling bears are much easier to predict and follow.

Always keep food foremost in your mind when tracking bears—where they are on the landscape, what they are eating at that time of year, and so on. Also keep in mind that black bears are skittish creatures, pausing frequently when unsure of themselves. If they smell or hear danger, they abruptly change directions. Smaller bears usually avoid larger bears, which forces them to forage in areas with less food. In arid regions, also keep in mind the sun. Black bears cannot tolerate hot temperatures and choose secluded cover with ample shade to spend most of every day. In cooler climates, bears plop down in more varied areas along foraging routes, but in hot climates, they often reuse the same beds again and again. Bears also frequent wallows and stream pools to cool down.

Sometimes the sound of crashing brush is the only indication that you have just encountered a bear. They usually yield to humans

A black bear cools off in a shallow creek in California. ME

but can be unpredictable. Encountering one up close or by surprise can be unnerving and dangerous for both parties. They do, however, often signal their intentions with visual cues. A large part of their social communication is through posturing, looks or nonlooks, and expressions. Even when a bear is charging, it might be signaling intent, looking for clues to continue through or put on the brakes. Bears will woof a low and loud call when surprised or unsure about a noise or movement. A loud *woosh* might indicate that you are being or about to be charged.

To the casual observer, bears might seem somewhat unaware. But this behavior could indicate that they are actually aware of your presence and giving you space to pass. Their hearing is excellent and their eyesight is very good. And their sense of smell is amazing. If the wind carries from you to them, you will not go undetected. What happens after that is up to the bear.

Avoid areas in which surprise encounters can occur—brushy streamsides or tall berry patches. Bear trails become tunnels in such places and force you to crawl your way through—not a good place to bump into a bear. If it becomes clear that you might be following a sow with cubs, it would be wise to avoid a confrontation. Females with cubs are extremely unpredictable, especially brown bears.

Be mentally prepared for what will happen or what you will do if you find yourself confronted by a startled or charging bear. Stay calm and do not run. Avoid direct eye contact; it's a sign of aggression. Turn your head to the side to diffuse the situation, but keep the bear in your peripheral vision. Try speaking in a calm voice; loud is okay, but avoid screaming. Try to keep a confident tone in your voice and movements. Retreat slowly. Often a charge will be just a bluff, and the bear will either stop short or veer off to the side.

—B. M., M. E.

Tracking Notes: Black Bear

Senses and Speed: Black bears have excellent senses of smell and hearing, which they use to detect other animals and food at great distances. They can run at speeds up to thirty-five mph for short distances.

American black bear. ME

Warning Signs and Dangers: Bears use explosive woofs and huffs to scare off potential competitors or when they are afraid. They also rattle their teeth, "jaw-pop" in an intimidating manner, or utter a long huff as a challenge. The position of the ears is an excellent clue about their intentions: Curious or alert bears hold their ears erect and forward. Playful bears spread their ears so they stick out to either side. Aggressive bears, including those on the defensive, pull their ears back flat against their skulls.

Threat displays are generally sequential and predictable. A bear will stop and stare at a competitor or potential predator with head held low and ears back. It may pant audibly or otherwise vocalize discomfort. With ears flattened, upper lip curled, and snout narrowed, bears stick out their "elbows" to appear larger and then charge forward in a great explosion of air. They either veer off into cover at the last moment or stop short of their target with a great slap of their forelimbs on the ground or a nearby tree trunk and an intimidating, explosive exhalation of breath. Such a display is often the surest sign that they don't mean to attack. Bears also walk with stiff front legs in an exaggerated gait to exhibit discomfort and fear. In an extreme state of stress, they also bite and claw trees as a displacement behavior.

Method of Attack: Most reported encounters do not involve physical contact but rather bluff-charges and other noncontact aggressive displays. Physical attacks occur most often when people are crowding or feeding bears. While brown bears more frequently attack people than black bears do, black bears more often kill people to eat them. Very rarely, a black bear hunts people as it would large game, and its hunting behavior is markedly different from the visual and auditory signals that precede loud bluff-charges. Hunting bears stalk their victims, often approaching from behind, in an attempt to sneak into striking distance without being detected.

Avoiding Conflict and Evasion Techniques: Should you feel threatened by a black bear, be loud and assertive. Yell and throw things. Pick up a large branch to use as a weapon but do not corner the animal. Give it a clear avenue of escape. Bear aggression is typically a display of fear, and the animal will escape if it has the chance. If a black bear attacks with the intent to kill, however, do not lie down and play dead. Fight for your life.

Tracking Notes: Brown Bear

Senses and Speed: Brown bears have excellent senses of smell and hearing as well as sharp eyesight. They can run up to thirty-five mph for short distances.

Warning Signs and Dangers: Huffs, snorts, and jaw-pops are used by nervous brown bears attempting to unnerve an intruder (and they usually work). Brown bears might also bluff-charge in combination with these vocalizations, storming in, drawing up short, then turning and walking away.

The height and orientation of the head and body and the position of the ears are important signals. Brown bears raise their heads and use a stiff-legged walk in both submissive and aggressive exchanges. Dominant or aggressive bears maintain frontal orientation, stretch out and lower their heads in the direction of the target, and flatten their ears backwards. They also open their mouths to display their impressive canines as they approach. On uneven terrain, they assume a higher position.

Threats follow three distinct stages: confrontation, bluff-charge, and fight. Brown bears also "jaw," a low-level exhibition of aggression during which they lay their ears back, partly open their mouths, and growl. After jawing, they bluff-charge. Then they fight. Bears stand on their hind legs to box and grapple their opponents with their front paws. Fights are vicious and fast. They swipe with their claws at the victim's head and shoulders and aim bites at the head and neck.

Method of Attack: The vast majority of brown bear attacks are nonpredatory, meaning they are not trying to eat you. Instead, they are territorial or defensive in nature and are often accompanied by the displays described. If a bear makes contact, it is at the end of a swift and short charge.

Avoiding Conflict and Evasion Techniques: Brown bear behavior can be unpredictable. They are most passive when food is abundant

Brown bear. PHOTOGAGA/DREAMSTIME.COM

and when they are in large congregations. Precautions around brown bears must always be taken, however. Do not interfere with a brown bear's cubs, or in any way separate them from their mother. Do not feed brown bears. Do not challenge a brown bear defending a food cache. Do not surprise a brown bear at close quarters. If you see one before it sees you, either retreat from the area quietly if you are at a safe distance or make noise to let it know you are there. Lastly, do not follow a brown bear closely or harass it. If you are charged, wait until the bear moves away, and then retreat slowly from the area. Do not continue to follow.

If you are charged by a brown bear, do not move. Never run. Should the bear make contact, curl up into a fetal position and cover your neck with your hands. Some people go directly to a fetal position when the bear charges, which is fine. Others argue that you should attempt to intimidate the bear, making yourself as large and loud as possible. This is not the recommended course of action, but it has proven effective in driving some bears away. The strength of a brown bear is incredible, and even though attacks on humans are rare, a swipe of a paw is enough to maim or kill.

DEER

The patchy morning clouds glowed. Tinged with pink and gold, they told of the coming of a new day. The late August morning held the feel of summer slipping into fall. Still, I was sweating from the uphill creep to the top of the mountain I call home. I checked my pace to shed my shirt and admire the ravens gliding down from their roost. I croaked a low call to them, but they ignored me. I continued up the clear-cut, checking deer trails as I crossed them. A few looked interesting, but the color was not there, and a slight crust spoke of exposure to dew and subsequent sun. Too old to follow. I went on my way.

I wanted to make it up to the ridge top to where I knew larger bucks collected. Scattered clearings offered an abundance of succulent forbs on which to fatten up and grow bone, and the heads of the timbered draws held many bed sites. Picking my way along the uphill edge of the clear-cut,

I soon found what I was looking for. Tracks—well over three-and-a-quarter inches long. They told of a big blacktail. The contrast of the duff and the bright new bruises on the crushed and kinked stems of the trailing blackberry indicated that the heavy-bodied buck passed not long ago.

I collected my thoughts, had a sip of water, and began picking my way along the trail. Leaves rocking in the light breeze showed the night's downdrafts spilling down the hill. This current should hold until mid-morning, giving me time to catch up to a napping buck. He picked his way through a thicket of ocean spray and young fir and found his way up to a well-used game trail that cut the side of the hill. I followed this trail for a short time, then the buck's trail left the game trail and began switching back and forth up through low exposed rock outcroppings that created a series of shelves. These were covered with succulents that showed signs of heavy browsing and held a spiderweb of trails. I was rewarded with a rare sight in the woods of northwest Washington: clear tracks. I had the opportunity to confirm the trail's age. Inspecting the various substrates offers clues to the age of a set of tracks. I've learned to continually check this; tracks age even as you watch them. The contrast and sharpness of these tracks against the red dirt around them was undeniable—I was right behind this deer.

The relentless scolding of a Douglas' squirrel from a nearby fir cut the air. I rose from my crouch, letting go of the need to study the buck's tracks and training my ears to the timber beyond the squirrel. Squirrel alarms, while pesky and sometimes downright disastrous to a stalk, can also be a useful tool. They have alerted me to the presence of other animals many times. But this one served as a reminder to slow down. By now, I was confident the deer was probably bedded, and I would need to proceed at a snail's pace if I were to have any hope of seeing him.

Easing slowly from tree to tree, I slipped through the lodgepole. The trail in the duff cast shadows on the toe of each track, almost the reverse of lighting the way. Where the ground was firmer, scuffed and overturned needles were crimped and kinked from a hoof wall rolled from the toe. His trail was still side-hilling a bit but also angling up into the breeze that was sifting down through the timber. Soon, however, the draft would switch as the morning sun created thermals and updrafts carrying scents up the hill. This buck's bed would be in a place where the deer could monitor this. The trail proved my suspicions. It hit a dark cedar draw and began going straight up. The breeze would soon turn. I hoped I wouldn't be going up much longer but decided to keep following for the time being. I slowed my pace even more, half expecting to hear a deer crashing away through the brush. Knee-deep salal made for a slow approach before I slipped into the shaded draw. Not far up, a game trail bisected the deer's route, and he took this to continue on in his original direction, meandering slightly but angling upwards. Within a hundred yards, however, the trail switched back almost a full one-eighty and began angling up toward the head of the draw—right through some thick cedar tangles. "I'm being set up," I thought. Elk commonly do this, deer also, especially wise old bucks—doubling back to their beds, dragging you through thick brush within earshot of where they are laid up. It's very effective, and very frustrating.

Sure enough, the dense cedar opened to more mature trees. Several cone middens put me on the lookout for another squirrel. Random tracks caught my attention, suggesting that this approach had been used before. While I paused to listen and sort out the confusion of older sign, a movement caught my eye—the twitch of an ear, a very small ear. A Douglas' squirrel skittered to the base of a large tree. Finding a perch and eyeing

A bachelor herd of mule deer. ME

me tentatively, it began consuming a pinecone. I moved carefully, a step or two to reach a tree upon which I could lean to watch and listen. Looking past the squirrel for the route to take if the coast became clear, I saw him. He was less than thirty yards away, bedded and peaceful. His soft and fuzzy-looking rack still covered in velvet was massive. Rolls of fat rippled in the curve at the base of a large and thick neck. Healthy and beautiful—a sight to see, dappled in spots of sunlight flashing through the conifers. I watched. An eternity passed. Occasionally, he would stare me down. Only my face and shoulder were visible around the tree, but it was clear he was aware of something, just not too concerned. After a time, he stood. Instinctively, I felt for a bowstring that wasn't there; only the anticipation of the coming season met my fingers.

After stretching for a bit, he slipped off directly away from me, uneasy with my presence but not spooked. I turned and began the long walk home. In the distance behind me, a squirrel sounded an alarm.

—*B. M.*

I have heard it said that following deer is easy because their hooves cut into the ground. While I agree that following deer trails can be easy and that anyone who practices seeing and following sign can do so, a deer's trail can go from easy to difficult within a few steps. Understanding deer behavior can make following their trails a little more predictable. An arid-country mule deer might roam several miles in a single night while a suburban-fringe–dwelling black-tail might find everything it needs in a few acres. A farm-country whitetail might be somewhere in between. A buck in November might stray far and wide, with no logic to its movements. The same deer in the summer might routinely follow the same trail at the same time every day. Trails between food sources and bed sites might be relatively straight and the deer making them moving purposefully. But trails in a feeding area might create a confusing maze that overwhelms you with sign to interpret. A lot can be learned from unraveling the trails in such areas, but sometimes it's wiser to skirt feeding area edges, cutting trails coming and going until you find the one you want.

The characteristic trail of a walking mule deer buck. ME

A well-used mule deer trail in tall grass. ME

When following trails to or near known or suspected bedding areas, pay special attention to noise levels, wind direction, and your general presence in the woods. Stalking deer on their beds is not easy. Deer do not like to be caught napping, and they usually choose bed sites that prevent this from happening. Beds are often in brushy places difficult to approach, and they usually offer the deer some type of thermal protection, either warmth or shade. Typically, deer can observe travel routes to their bed site, and they position themselves to take advantage of wind direction. When deer bed in groups, for example, they each face a different direction to cover all possible approaches. Deer seldom tolerate being disturbed in their beds and will for some time avoid a bed in which they were disturbed. If you spend any time following deer trails, you will eventually spook deer. Be considerate of their space and don't pressure animals you have bumped from a bed site. But it's worth noting that an alarmed deer might trot off only a hundred yards or so, depending on visibility, to put a safe distance between itself and a threat. Then it will turn and face what spooked them. It might try to get you to move with head bobs or by lowering its head and pretending to feed, only to snap its head up to catch you moving. It might even approach you to try to get you to move. Sometimes, during a staredown with a deer, I will mimic them. This seems to calm them a bit. If the deer is still concerned, it might stamp a forefoot to release a warning scent from interdigital glands; it might also huff loudly. If, however, it catches your scent, it usually means the game is over. Time to find another trail and start again.

—B. M.

MOOSE

Tracking Notes

Senses and Speed: Moose hear very well. They can detect movement at considerable distances but do not see stationary objects easily. Their sense of smell is good. They can run at speeds up to thirty-five mph.

Warning Signs and Dangers: As in other members of the deer family, the moose's basic threat is a hard stare. They freeze, stare at the threat, and then either incorporate a head-high, head-low, or antler threat. The head-low threat from cows is considered a high intensity "scare threat," the last signal before an attack. Antler threats are specific to bulls after they have shed their velvet. Bulls tilt their heads so their noses point down and the greatest surface area of their antlers is exposed. In the low-antler threat, with ears laid back and hackles up, the bull's nose can nearly touch the ground.

Bull moose.
PAULTESSIER/ISTOCKPHOTO.COM

During the "challenger gait," bulls walk with long stiff-legged strides, present their bulky profile, and sway their antlers from side to side. Moose are generally nonthreatening toward humans. Rutting bulls and cows with calves can be dangerous, however, and moose-watchers would do well to recognize threats and displacement activities that indicate anxiety.

Method of Attack: Head-high threats might be followed by charges and attacks with a stiff foreleg. Or a moose may rise up on its hind legs and attack with the front legs (called boxing). The head-low threat might be followed with a charge and head butting. Males also use kicking attacks, especially when their antlers are absent or still growing. And they also use a backward kick of the hind legs, like a horse, to defend themselves.

Avoiding Conflict and Evasion Techniques: Put trees and other large obstructions between yourself and a charging moose. Climb trees if you can. In one encounter, a woman was trapped in her cabin for several days by a cow moose with calf. Every time she tried to sneak out of her house and reach her car, the cow would emerge from the woods and charge her. After several days, the moose finally left.

—Kurt Rinehart and M. E.

ELK

*T*hings did not look good for following a trail. I kicked at the blank dirt washed out to a dull tan by my flashlight. Barely a scuff. Frozen solid. I might as well be looking for tracks on concrete. I doubted I would see a fresh trail crossing the dirt road I was walking in on. The steady breeze that came down the valley all night meant there was no frost out in the open. Elk trails cut into the frost—stringing from the meadows and leading quickly to a bedded cow—were a luxury that I would not find this morning either. Perhaps in the timber things would look different; they sometimes do. I turned off my light and took a long look at the twinkling stars. The darkest hour, just before dawn, on cold November mornings has always held a special magic for me—a hunter's sky.

I began a brisk, dark walk down the dirt road. I wanted to make it to a trail that cut through the timber before sunrise, a good quiet place to slip along and maybe catch an elk moving to bed. I had a growing feeling—a feeling I've come to trust when hunting—that this morning I would get close to an elk. Some people say we create our own realities. Believing this has never hurt my chances. Leaning against a tree, I waited for it to become light enough to see into the woods. The breeze had died with the dawn and my breath hung gently around my face. As the morning brightened, I noticed that some low areas flanking the road and the edge of the woods held a fair bit of frost heave—no surface frost, just gravel, sticks, and twigs vaulted on miniature columns of ice. In the gravel and sparse grass, I saw old tracks distorted and rounded by the freezing and thawing that indicated the coming and going of elk. I noticed several of *the ice sculptures had been crushed and tipped over. When I walked over to examine the tracks, two trails materialized. Frost-lifted stones had been pressed back down. Rounded toes had rolled pebbles from their mini towers, toppling ice formations. Two elk trails—made by a cow and yearling. And they were headed in the direction I had planned to hunt.*

The next couple of hours, I slowly worked my way down their trail. Moving in slow motion. Taking a step, waiting two moments. Becoming a tree for a while. I had to remind myself of this pace. When squirrels and juncos ignore you and bobcats walk by at ten yards—that's where I wanted to be.

The elk had traveled down the abandoned road quite a ways. The road was covered with moss and fir needles, not a place to easily see tracks, but the shadows of fresh toe scuffs were just visible. I guessed at their destination and about where they would be. Soon the trail on the road gave way to older tracks that did not look quite right. I backtracked a few steps and found hoofprints cutting frozen beargrass and twigs dislodged from the frozen duff. They cut off through the woods, leaving the old road and heading toward a favorite elk creek-crossing.

Things were hushed underneath the old hemlocks. Nuthatches and gray jays shook off the cold. Trails cut into the duff became more apparent as I neared the creek. The cow and yearling tracks still showing here and there met one of these trails in front of me and began nosing their way down the switchback to the river. I grew anxious. Below was a small clearing and seep at the well-used crossing. There could be elk there feeding or bedded under the immense firs flanking the wet meadow. I watched from the ridge and waited awhile. I could see the tracks of two elk, the ones I followed, cross the mud of the seep below. I thought about spending the rest of the day sitting here. It was such a nice place for an elk to happen by. After assuring myself nothing was watching, however, I decided to continue following the trails. I dropped down the embankment and walked to the creek edge. To my relief, I didn't see fresh tracks going across. I was not looking forward to crossing the thigh-deep, icy water. Spending the day hunting on this side was fine with me.

I walked back and picked up the two trails and followed them up the opposite ridge. The hill was flanked by deep trails from generations of elk snaking their way down to the river. I found fresh scat, not steaming, but

A bull elk bugling. LEE KIRCHHEVEL/DREAMSTIME.COM

not cold either. The pellets spilled their way up the trail. I followed to the top of the ridge. Here, the terrain flattened, and the old-growth hemlocks gave way to younger firs. Scattered among the trees were small clearings with beargrass that showed signs of heavy grazing. The two elk wove their way through the maze of brushy clearings. I delicately picked my way through the frozen branches, avoiding the open as much as possible, choosing the lesser of the two evils: making a little noise instead of being seen moving. These small openings were sheltered enough from the night's breeze for frost to develop. In places, the elk's trail seemed to glow like a green stripe painted on the frosted ground.

A snap caught my attention. I strained to listen. Then the noisemaker appeared—a red squirrel darted past a few yards ahead. I waited for it to disappear then inched forward again, going only a few steps, half-eyeing the squirrel. Another twig snapped. Then all was silent. I was crouched over, looking past the squirrel, when I saw the long, chocolate-colored legs of an elk stroll by ten yards away. I was too close.

All I could do now was stay frozen and hope the still air did not drift its way. Another snap twenty or thirty yards away told of a second animal. A soft mew call from the cow floated my way. A tawny flank drifted through an opening, but I didn't dare lift my bow. Too much brush separated us. All I could do was await the inevitable, which came quickly as the elk closest circled by and caught my scent. The stillness was replaced by the deep thud of elk hooves and branches snapping as they trotted away.

Time to start over. The squirrel squawked an alarm as I collected my thoughts, and then I crept forward to see what the two elk had been up to. They had fed in a small circle and were working their way back toward me when my scent spooked them. With half the day left to hunt I decided to follow their trail and see where they went. I waited a bit then set off.

Deep hoofprints cut through to crusted duff leading back toward the bluff that fell away to the creek below. Sure enough, the elk found a trail that led straight down to another popular creek crossing. I stood at the water's edge, staring at the wet stones glistening on the far shore. They had gone straight across. I found a stick for balance, shucked my boots and pants, bit my lip, and followed. Once across, I sat in the sun and let the feeling come back to my legs while I ate some lunch. Then I pressed on. The elk had calmed and transitioned into a walk. Then they entered a hardwood flat and began feeding along the way. Beyond the shade of the conifers, the sun had warmed the flat enough so that the alder leaves had lost their frozen crunch, allowing me to slip quietly along. Soon, the cow and yearling's trail met the trails of several other elk. A slight breeze was forming, and the elks' trails were heading into it. The going was quiet, but I felt very exposed, stalking in the open from alder to alder. The trails crossed a small stream, and they fed along its edge. A clump of grand fir offered me cover to flank the direction they were headed. I crossed the stream, content to leave the tracks and look for the elk. This proved to be a wise decision—I did not go another hundred yards before I saw the sil-houette of the cow outlined against the dimness of overhanging branches. She was facing away, but I was sure other eyes were watching. I slunk behind a young fir and looked for the others. I heard an occasional chirp then saw eight cows bedded under two giant cedar trees, with a couple more standing and feeding along the edge. And there was one large, impressive bull. He was facing my direction, half-heartedly horning a small alder, antlers methodically rising and falling against the brushy tree. The rut was, for the most part, over. He seemed to be acting out of habit more than in earnest. Then he let out a hoarse bugle, jarring me from my trance.

I could have stayed put and waited, but there seemed to be enough cover to slip to within easy bow range of some of the closer cows. (The bull was tempting, but it was a cow permit that I had in my pocket.) The wind blew lightly in my face but I didn't trust it to stay that way all day. I crept forward on hands and knees to another young fir tree, about thirty yards from a feeding cow.

Things seemed to be perfect. I was downwind and in bow range. A bull was bugling. The sun was shining. What could go wrong? I slowly rose and peered around a fir branch and saw the closest cow staring at me. I dared not move. Expecting her to bark an alarm and elk to scatter, I stood and waited. My muscles were aching. Finally, she lowered her gaze and went back to browsing. She was broadside, with her head buried, grazing. Arrow nocked, I drew and peered through a leaning fork in the trunk of an alder tree. This fork created a Y that I needed to shoot through. I used my sight pins to see if the trajectory would pass through the fork a few yards in front of me—something I have done before, something I have practiced. I had all the time I needed. The cow continued to feed. She took a step forward, and I released the arrow. To my horror, it ricocheted loudly off the fork and careened harmlessly into the ground. Stunned, I watched elk scatter. As the crashing faded, I looked up to the tree fork and saw the fresh red bark on a burl knot protruding down a few inches. This is what my arrow smacked. How could I have not noticed it?

All I could do was silently apologize to the elk for spooking them, pick up my arrow, and laugh at myself. I had learned a lesson I have sadly had to learn over and over while hunting: Don't rush things.

I walked back to look for elk on the other side of the river.

—B. M.

Elk leave ample signs of their presence on the landscape: mazes of trails, feeding areas littered with tracks and scats, multiple beds, rub trees, wallows, and mineral licks. It is this abundance of signs that often presents problems in tracking them. Often traveling in numbers and using regular travel routes, elk can create a maze of signs to sort through while trying to stick to a fresh trail. Identifying individuals can help. Trusting one's ability to age tracks becomes a necessity when following elk in such areas. Look at feeding sign and scat. If the trail is fresh, the pleasant barnyard smell of elk urine will greet your nostrils. At times, it's common to smell elk before seeing them.

Knowing their feeding and bedding habits and travel routes to and from these areas offers a way to decipher the maze of tracks you might see in one area. The amount of sign can vary with the habitat and season. Roosevelt elk in coastal forests may not range in their daily travel as much as their Rocky Mountain cousins. That said, animals only go as far as they have to to meet their needs. High, moist, summer mountain meadows or snow-free, south-facing slopes and good foraging and cover will see regular use by elk herds. They tend to move up and down in elevation between summer and winter ranges; some herds travel fair distances between these two areas. Exceptions to this are the old bulls that head up into snow-covered mountains to seek solitude and recover from the fall rut. Pressure from humans and other predators, such as wolves, will also influence elk movement.

Elk stick to and make new trails for travel routes between bedding and grazing sites. This is also seen where terrain dictates movement, such as low saddles to cross ridge lines or at river crossings. But trails that lead straight from meadows or clearings that hold grazing sign and are aiming for heavy timber are a sure sign of elk heading to a day bed. Elk will feed in cycles, in the morning before bedding for the day and then again in the evening before bedding some during the night. Night beds can be out in the open, often right where the animals were feeding. Cows are often less picky about selecting bed sites than bulls. Day beds are generally in patches of timber that afford a view of approaches or the back trail. Thickly timbered draws are a favorite place for elk to spend the day. Daily updrafts will carry the scent of anyone approaching, and it can be almost impossible to get close to them without making noise. Sometimes, however, looping around an area in which elk might be bedded, getting above, and approaching from downwind may offer a view. Elk spooked off their bed will often travel quite a long distance before stopping again.

Much of the year, herd structures are separated into cows, subadults, and calves. Mature bulls are found in small bachelor herds. Tracks in spring and summer of all large animals may be all bulls; trails of medium-sized elk tracks with young are definitely cows and calves. This can be seen in bed sites also. Elk will often defecate and urinate when they stand to leave the bed, leaving valuable sign to interpret. A cow's urine stain will be toward the rump of the bed. A bull's scat will be noticeably larger, and urine will be projected toward the front of the bed and often sprayed about. Occasionally at bull beds, antler gouges can be seen in the ground behind the head and back of the bed.

Elk rub, where a male has rubbed his antlers and forehead during the rut.

Elk are very vocal, and their birdlike calls will often tip you off to their location. A bull's bugle will definitely charge the air. Chirps and mews can be heard from content traveling or feeding elk or in timber as elk try to locate each another. A sharp, loud bark is an alarm given by a cow. This is often given if you have been seen moving or heard but the herd hasn't yet figured out if there is definite danger. If you are safely downwind and remain still, they may calm a bit and go on about

Elk tracks. ME

their business. But from this point, they will remain on edge for some time. Another bit of noise or movement will send them packing.

The elk's sense of smell is supreme, and they rarely tolerate smelling humans. There is a large market for scent-blocking and scent-eliminating clothing and sprays. But the best advice is to pay attention to wind directions and be aware that fickle mountain air currents can change instantly.

When following elk on well-used trails where tracks are easy to see and a person can move quietly, I've noticed that trackers tend to move too fast. Then they spook the animals. Slow down and take in what is around you. A snail's pace may be too fast at times. If an animal is bedded, you might have lots of time to catch it. Enjoy the trail, and let it pull you along.

—B. M.

Tracking Notes

Senses and Speed: An elk's eyesight is relatively keen and can detect movements at a considerable distance. Its senses of smell and hearing are well developed. Elk can run up to thirty-five mph.

Warning Signs and Dangers: When elk are suspicious, they freeze in an alert posture. They use a stilted, high-stepping warning gait to alert other elk that a danger is in the area. They might also use high-pitched bleats or barks to sound an alarm.

Threat displays consist of head-high and head-low threats. Head-low threats are made with the head and neck held low and extended forward from the shoulder. The ears are laid back, and the muzzle is tilted slightly upward so the antlers are angled back. An elk's weapons include its head, antlers, and teeth. The bite threat is like a head-high threat with the nose raised up and lips pulled back to expose the upper canines. Bite threats are accompanied by tooth-grinding and hissing. Antler threats are made with the nose pointed to the ground so the antler tines bristle forward. Bulls may also use charges that end with a slap of the forefoot on the ground and a series of sharp grunts.

Method of Attack: Both males and females will charge intruders and spear them with antlers or head-butt them. The head-high threat might be followed by dangerous kicks of their powerful front legs.

Avoiding Conflict and Evasion Techniques: Elk are rarely dangerous, but rutting bulls are particularly unpredictable and occasionally attack people or even vehicles. Females protecting calves might also attack in their defense. Climb trees or place trees and other obstacles between yourself and the animal.

—K. R. and M. E.

Sparring elk. LIQUIDPHOTO/DREAMSTIME.COM

CROCODILES

Tracking Notes

Senses and Speed: A crocodile's senses are well developed, especially its eyesight. It is uncertain to what extent it can hear, but it does respond to sounds like the clicking alarm calls of birds. On land, crocodiles are quick and can easily outrun a human. In water, they can swim very fast and leap at least half their own length vertically and their total length horizontally out of the water.

Warning Signs and Dangers: Crocodiles see humans as prey. They will almost always enter water the moment they detect you.

Crocodile trail. ME

They might approach on the surface but will most likely dive when they get within striking range. A line of bubbles is sometimes all that is visible when they do.

Method of Attack: Most people are attacked by crocodiles when they are wading in the shallows, especially if they do so as part of a routine—someone fetching water at a specific time of day or a fishermen checking nets every morning. The crocodile will lie in ambush below the surface and then launch at the victim in the shallows or on the bank. Once a grip is achieved, it will try to pull the victim into deep water to drown it. Crocodiles often spin around while holding onto their victims, which normally breaks or removes limbs and disorients them.

Avoiding Conflict and Evasion Techniques: Don't mess with crocodiles. Be extremely cautious when crossing a body of water in crocodile territory. Cross at the most shallow spot and, if possible, at a rocky drift with good visibility. Crocodiles can hide themselves in very small bodies of water. Do not bathe or swim at night in a river or dam that might hold crocodiles.

If you are attacked, do all you can to prevent the animal from dragging you into deep water. If your hand is inside its mouth, try to open the valve at the back of its throat to let water into its lungs. If you have a knife, immediately dig out its eyes. If you see someone being attacked, call others and drag or carry the victim (and the crocodile if it won't let go) onto dry land. Wounds from a crocodile (as with other predators) will become infected very quickly, so immediate medical attention is important.

PRIMATES

Tracking Notes
Senses and Speed: Primates have a very good sense of smell, and their eyesight and hearing are also acute. Their speed varies with the species, but all primates are capable of running faster than humans.

Warning Signs and Dangers: Many primate populations have lost their fear of humans because we feed them or because they associate us with crops. This often leads to human-primate confrontations. Some primates are quite small, but, pound for pound, they are all far more powerful than humans. They are also equipped with large canine teeth. They use staring or direct eye contact to show dominance. The dominant animal will yawn regularly to show its teeth. Avoiding eye contact is a sign of submissiveness.

Prior to an attack, a primate might make short warning charges in your direction, often while flaring its eyes and showing its teeth. It might also vocalize. But be warned: Completely unprovoked attacks can occur without warning.

A male baboon. AL

If a primate is trapped in a car or building, it will act aggressively and vocalize loudly. It might exhibit a state of hysteria, defecating and urinating on everything while trashing the place.

Method of Attack: In most cases, primates attack to obtain food or assert dominance. The animal simply charges in and grabs what it wants. If it is met with resistance, especially from a woman or child, it will not hesitate to bite or claw its victim. If an attack is intended to enforce dominance, the animal will also not hesitate to bite and claw its victim, especially the lower limbs in the case of baboons and vervet monkeys.

Avoiding Conflicts and Evasion Techniques: Many confrontations with primates can be avoided if you do not eat or handle food within their view. Store all food securely and out of sight and close up dwellings and vehicles where animals might look for food. Avoid eye contact and do not laugh at primates. Baring your teeth could be seen as a challenge, especially if done by women or children. Never feed primates. If attacked by a primate trying to get food you are holding, it is best to drop it and hope the animal will take it without harming you. If an animal has gone into a room or a car and is trapped, open an escape route for it and allow it to leave on its own. Attempting to force it out will most likely increase the danger it poses.

AFRICAN ELEPHANTS

*W*e picked up the trail of the three elephant bulls in the car park of the camp, where one had broken branches of a jackalberry tree the previous evening. One of the others had joined the feast, and the tracks of their large round front feet were framed by the dark green leaves that were stripped off as they fed. The third bull had cut in from above the road, and his tracks followed the other two into the dense riverine bush.

We could hear the elephants feeding around the camp along the river until late the previous evening. Their low rumbling and the breaking branches were the only indications of their presence. They were so close to us, but we couldn't hear them walking. The only exception was when they started to cross the dry riverbed, and we could hear their heavy feet on the loose sand.

It was bitterly cold in the early morning, and the elephant tracks were perfectly preserved in the thick layer of fine dust on the road. It was the last day of a week-long trailing course, and all the students were eager to take up the trail. It took us from the car park directly into the dense bush. Here, the ground was littered with leaves and dead, trampled grass. It took the students some time to distinguish the fresh trail from the older elephant sign. Eventually, the odor of stale urine led us to the trail of a bull in musth. The elephants had drunk from the pool in the riverbed, and from there had moved up the bank on the far side. This section of the trail was challenging—the elephants stood in the water when they drank, and the thick layer of mud sticking to the underside of their feet kept them from leaving any sign. The coarse soil was also very hard, and in some places the only sign was a single pebble out of place.

Most of the knob-thorn trees were leafless, and there was very little ground cover. The winter sun eventually started to push the morning chill away. A few impala rams sunned themselves, their hair puffed up against the cold, giving them a dull color.

Louis Liebenberg examines signs of elephant feeding. ME

The elephants moved further up the slope to the east of the river, but the sparse grass cover and hard soil didn't make trailing any easier. There was only the odd sign every five or ten yards. Fortunately, they had started to feed again, and the freshly broken branches with stripped bark stood out like neon signs. We headed from feeding sign to feeding sign, seeing the odd footprint, scuff mark, or flattened grass stem.

The elephants kept moving parallel to the river for about two miles or so, feeding along the slope. Then the feeding signs started to dissipate. The trail was more difficult until it reached a well-worn game path. It then became clear that the animals were moving deliberately.

Another mile or so further, we started seeing fresh feeding sign along the way, but the bulls' tracks were still moving along the game path. They were heading toward a breeding herd of elephants. The bulls' tracks slowed down as the animals started meandering off the path again, presumably when they caught up to the herd. At the same point, the breeding herd had stopped feeding and taken off in a straight line, aiming for the dense reed beds of the river. We could only assume that they were moving away from the bulls, as the bulls' tracks also indicated that they were again moving fast on the trail of the herd.

We left the trail on the bank of the river. Later, we received word that the breeding herd was seen by a game-drive vehicle many miles away in a straight line from where we left the trail. The bulls were in hot pursuit.

—A. L.

Although elephants are massive, they can move without making a sound because of the thick layer of cartilage on their feet that acts as a shock absorber. When the foot is put down, the sole rolls or splays out; when the foot is picked up, the sole shrinks. The track of the front foot is round, and that of the hind foot is oval or egg shaped, with the heel at the wider end and the toes at the narrow.

When elephants walk through mud or down a sandy riverbed, they leave large, craterlike tracks, but on hard surfaces, they hardly leave a print. Their stride is much longer than a human's, so you need to look for tracks sufficient distances apart. When an elephant has walked through long grass off a game path, the pattern is easily identifiable and cannot be mistaken for anything else. When a herd of elephants walks through tall grass in single file, however, it leaves a highway that can easily be confused with that of rhinos or other large animals.

Elephants spend a lot of time feeding, and breaking branches often give their position away. Feeding signs vary widely, but the debarking of trees in the drier months is obvious at a great distance. Elephants are fond of water and will drink daily if it's available. They will often squirt water or mud over themselves to cool down and get rid of parasites. After a mud bath, they will often rub against a tall tree; keep your eyes open for fresh mud up to four yards off the

Bull elephant tracks. AL

An alarmed bull elephant. AL

ground. This is sometimes the quickest way to determine the direction the animal has gone after a wallow, as their tracks can be obscured because of the mud on their feet.

In hot weather, elephants rest in a stand of tall trees. They sleep lying down or standing, often leaning against a termite mound, river bank, or tree. During the rest, they are not always quiet. Listen for the *thub* of dung falling to the ground or a watery, bubbly sound as they pass gas. You might also hear rough skin rubbing against a tree.

When the animals are feeding, they move with a stop-start rhythm, and it can be possible to catch up to them. When the fruit of the marula tree is ripe, though, even breeding herds with small calves will run from tree to tree, all keen to get to the berries first.

Bulls often move slowly when they feed, but a bull in musth trailing a herd is almost impossible to catch up to. Their walking speed is at least double that of a human. Elephants are very mobile and will swim rivers or climb mountains to find food.

Tracking Notes

Senses and Speed: An elephant's senses of smell and hearing are very good, but its eyesight is relatively poor. It can run up to twenty-five mph.

Warning Signs and Dangers: An adult bull elephant that has become aware of a human or some other intruder but doesn't feel threatened will usually remain aloof. It will often continue whatever it was doing but leave subtle clues that indicate its awareness of the intruder: It might pick up food with its trunk and put it in its mouth but not chew it, or it may even drop it. It is busy sniffing the air while its trunk is raised. It might also act as though it's rubbing its eye while trying to pick up the intruder in its peripheral vision without turning in its direction.

Breeding elephant herds will normally huddle together when they detect a threat. Adult cows form a protective barrier around the calves. If they are unsure of the location of the threat or what type it is, they will lift their trunks to try and identify it. Warning charges from breeding herds are intimidating, as the animals often charge together.

One of the first signs that an elephant is uncomfortable with the presence of an intruder is a raised tail. If an elephant feels threatened, it will normally spin around in the direction of the threat, and, with spread ears, look down at it. If the threat does not go away, the elephant may turn and run away, trumpeting. If the animal feels cornered or is in an aggressive mood, it will likely give a warning charge. During this charge, the elephant normally runs at the intruder with extended ears, tail up, and lots of vocalizations. It often exposes part of its flanks to the intruder and will kick up a lot of dust and even throw branches and other objects. These charges often stop only a few yards from the intruder.

An elephant—especially a mature bull—that has turned away will often face away from the intruder and stand with one hind foot in the air, looking over its shoulder. If not chased, it will often spin around and charge.

Bulls in musth are often very aggressive. Musth is driven by a surge of testosterone. In natural populations, a bull will only come

The warning charge of a male elephant. AL

into musth starting at age twenty-five. For elephants between twenty-five and thirty-five, musth will last from a few days to three months per year. For older elephants, it can last up to seven months.

The signs of musth in an elephant are very obvious but can be misleading at the start or end of the period. The temporal gland secretes a sticky fluid creating a wet streak down the sides of the head. The bull constantly dribbles urine but the penis is sheathed. The urine stains the penis green and splashes onto the hind legs, leaving a powerful odor. The dribbling is normally visible in the tracks of the animal. A bull in musth "walks tall" by lifting its head, pushing out its chest, stiffening its forelegs. Its ears in a side-on view will cover the bull's shoulders. It will cover long distances in pursuit of breeding herds, is very aggressive toward humans and other animals, and will often tusk the ground and knock down trees for no apparent reason. Fights between musth bulls are very serious and can be fatal to the combatants.

Method of Attack: An elephant normally charges with its trunk curled up under the chest or tucked to one side. Its ears will be either held flat against its head or fanned out to the sides completely, resembling the blade of a bulldozer. Without making a sound, it will run straight at you. The elephant will either strike first with its trunk or simply crush its victim with its forehead. In extreme cases, it will kneel on, kick, tusk, and even throw its victim through the air. Other herd animals might join the attack.

Avoiding Conflict and Evasion Techniques: Take a warning seriously. Be especially cautious with bulls in musth and breeding herds. Make sure you stay downwind from the animals, and preferably out of sight. If an elephant gives a warning charge, it is extremely important to stand your ground: Running away can be fatal. Wave your arms, shout loudly, and throw sticks or stones at the animal. If you are in a group, stand together. If the animal stops, back off slowly, facing the animal all the time. If you are in a vehicle, do not pull out with the engine revving. Stay put until the animal stops, then pull out gently, and let other people in the area know they should avoid the animal.

The only effective way to stop a serious charge is with a bullet to the brain. You should only shoot within fifty feet. If made accurately, a shot will drop the animal in its tracks. If you realize that an elephant is actively searching for you, or just walking your way, use whatever cover is available to get downwind and out of sight. Do this as quietly as possible. Get to safe ground—on top of a rocky outcrop or big termite mound or on the other side of a deep gully. Generally, high ground is safe ground.

Victims who have survived first contact have saved themselves by crawling down aardvark burrows. Some held onto one of the elephant's forelegs. Others crawled out between the hind feet. Most people who played dead were left alone.

If an elephant enters your camp perimeter, give it space. It is far better to allow it to leave on its own than it is to force it out. Turn off the power and cut the electric fence instead of trying to force it out the gate. If you have to herd the animal, never do it without a rifle in your hands. In some cases, elephants react well to pepper spray, "bear bangers," raw eggs, or human urine, but always remember that elephants are unpredictable creatures.

Sometimes things can go wrong very quickly and you need to be prepared for anything. I was doing a tracker evaluation with a group of rangers in the Addo Elephant National Park, waiting at the edge of a clearing for a herd of elephants to finish drinking and bathing. Gradually, the elephants started to move on in small groups, until the last one went away into the distance. When the herd had gone, we went up to the water hole to look at the tracks in the wet mud. We were studying them for quite awhile when a young elephant bull suddenly appeared from the thick bush at the edge of the clearing. He must have been straggling far behind the rest of the herd and only now arrived at the hole. When he saw us, he came charging into the clearing in a playful mock charge. But one of the rangers panicked and started to run back to the vehicle. The sight of the running human excited the young bull, who now sped up his approach.

Since I could not carry a rifle in the national park, I had only one option. I had to move toward the charging elephant and place myself between him and the fleeing ranger, waving my arms and clapping my hands to attract its attention. I only had a few seconds to act and did not have time to think about it. At the last moment, the young bull swerved away from me and charged into the bush. It all happened so quickly that only afterwards did I fully realize what had occurred.

—L. L.

AFRICAN LIONS

It was about eleven o'clock, just before we went to bed, when the lions roared for the first time. Judging by the direction, the sound of the roars, and the last known position of the animals, I was convinced that it was the Machatons. This pride had been around for a while, with many generations of cubs growing up and game-drive vehicles and people tracking them on a daily basis. The pride was intensely studied in the 1970s and inspired Chris McBride's book The White Lions of Timbavati.

Pretty Boy the lion. AL

Since then, the pride has had its ups and downs, increasing in numbers when times were good and decreasing when times were tough.

In late April 2008, the pride consisted of two twelve-year-old females called Djuma and Singela, a young female, a young male, and a big male in his prime called Pretty Boy. The youngsters, as well as Pretty Boy, were the offspring of the two lionesses. Pretty Boy got his name because he never left his natal pride; he would simply lie low when the two territorial males came to visit. They were seldom with the pride, as their territory covered a large piece of land and included at least two other prides. At the age of twelve, these two males would still take on coalitions of nomadic males without hesitation. I once saw them successfully defend their territory against a coalition of five males in their prime.

As I crawled into bed, I was hoping the cats would talk a bit more during the night. Our clients were the owner and top managers of a large waste disposal company. We all wanted to track lions. For this, the Machaton pride was ideal; the members seemed to have a high tolerance for humans on foot.

At about one o'clock, they roared again, this time much closer. I estimated they were about three miles from camp, to the northwest. Half an hour later, they roared again, about two miles out. I dozed off. Around three, I heard two Egyptian geese flying over camp. Something had spooked them. They came from the direction of the neighboring lodge, less than a mile away. There was a pan with water there. I was hoping it was the lions that had spooked them as they went to drink.

At about four-thirty, I was woken by vervet monkeys alarming in the tall jackalberry tree in camp. A leopard or the lions were walking past or through the camp, an unfenced, luxury, tented facility on the bank of the Tlharhalumi River, a seasonal spruit that only flows after heavy rain.

The guests were woken at about five. We gathered for coffee around the fire and left at first light. Within ten minutes, one of the vehicles picked up the lions, which were still moving. They soon left the road and veered off back into the riverbed. All five were there. We watched as they disappeared into the dense bush on the far side, hoping they would keep moving.

After a thorough briefing, we headed after them on foot. We carefully worked our way through the dense vegetation on the riverbank and picked the trail up on the far side. The trail took us over a large open plain in the direction of a few seasonal pans that still had a bit of water. I worked on the assumption that it was the lions that had spooked the geese during the night and that they were not heading to the water itself but instead to the tree belt on our side of the pans. This would be an ideal place to lie up all day and, if the opportunity arose, kill something.

We saw the young female first. She was at the back. The rest of the pride had already moved into the tree line. We worked our way around on the downwind side and found the other four lions lying up next to one of the pans about fifty yards from us. They looked at us for a while. Then Pretty Boy rolled over onto his side. The others did the same and closed their eyes. Only the young lioness tried to keep an eye on us, but the warmth of the morning sun was making her drowsy. We left them in peace.

Back in camp, I walked down to the riverbed, and in the soft white sand, I saw the tracks of the young lioness. She had walked past our tents at less than sixteen feet.

—A. L.

Contrary to common belief, lions are not well-structured pride animals. That some prides have figured out how to lay an ambush while others are deliberately herding their quarry is true, but it is the exception rather than the rule. In some studies, a pride's hunting success rate can be as low as eight percent.

It is also a fallacy that the males leave all the hunting to the females and that they would starve if the females did not provide for them. Male lions are capable hunters. Once the males leave their natal pride, they have to fend for themselves for a few years before they are mature and experienced enough to overthrow the dominant male in their area or take over another territory. They normally specialize on big game, such as buffalo, giraffe, zebra, and wildebeest. A territorial male or coalition of males is also not necessarily restricted to one pride. If the dominance of the males or coalition is strong enough, they may occupy a territory large enough to overlap the territories of a few female prides.

Almost all the lion populations that have been studied have been heavily hunted. Even in the national parks, lions were once regarded as vermin—they were killed in the Kruger NP as late as the 1950s. All predators were shot on sight.

Today, it is not strange to see coalitions of six to nine males roaming as nomads, still not strong enough to take over a territory. One coalition of two old males allowed young males to join its ranks. It was reported by senior tracker Robert Bryden that this coalition grew to a total of twelve males roaming the area between Skukuza and the Sabi Sand Private Game Reserve. The old males died off, and some of the youngsters were most likely killed in fights or while hunting. It is possible that it is the six remaining males of the original coalition that became known as the Mapogo, which has killed nearly fifty lions and leopards in two years after taking over the territory in Sabi Sands. This included females with whom they mated, which they then killed and ate. They also killed elephants, white rhinos, and hippos.

Lions are opportunistic predators that will scavenge or kill anything they see as food or competition. But they have also devised a method of conserving energy: They do as little as possible for as long as possible. When it is cold, lions lie in the sun; if it is windy, they huddle up on the lee side of large termite mounds, boulders, or inside dense thickets. When it gets hot, they simply turn onto their backs, exposing the white of their bellies to the sun to reflect heat. If it gets unbearably hot, they get up and move to the nearest shade. There they move around the tree to stay in the shade as the day progresses.

Tracking lions is usually easiest toward the end of the dry season. In Southern Africa, most lion populations (with the exception of a few small privately owned prides) are found in the summer rainfall areas. With the rains normally only arriving well into the summer, the dry soil is quickly turned to dust during the winter. Open water is normally at its lowest by then, and daytime temperatures can be very high. The cats normally become active late in the afternoon, after sleeping in the shade the entire day. Activity normally starts with a lot of yawning, stretching, rolling around, and rubbing against each other. They might communicate with soft *umpf* sounds or roar while lying down. Then, normally initiated by one of the youngsters, they walk around a bit, maybe to water or in the direction in which they intend to hunt. In most cases, they will only start hunting once it is completely dark. If there is a moon, they often wait until it goes down before moving.

This does not mean they are never active during the day. They are, but usually on cold or rainy days. Patrolling males also sometimes disregard the heat and walk throughout the day.

Although they are soft footed, lions tend to walk quite heavily. Unless they are stalking prey, they flop their front feet with an outward flick of the wrist as they walk. Because of this, the tracker will seldom see clear tracks of the front feet, even when they do not walk with a direct register. Often only the three big lobes at the back of the metacarpal pad of the front foot leave a clear edge. The tracks of the hind feet are usually the only ones that are complete and clearly visible.

Lion and elephant tracks on an old 4x4 trail. AL

In private game reserves, where most lion tracking is done, there is often a well-established network of dirt roads used for the game drives. Lions often make use of these roads when they move around. Picking up their tracks on these roads is not difficult, and if you have the trail before other vehicles have moved on the road, it can be relatively easy to follow, even at speed. When the lions go off the road, however, it becomes more difficult.

It is common for lions to cut corners. When there is a bend in the road that circles around a gully or dry pan, lions often just walk straight through and join the road further up. If they are deliberately leaving the road to move in a different direction, it is often done at the junction of a game path. They then stay on the game path. When they are hunting, or their attention is drawn by something else (other members of the pride, territorial issues, predators, or anything worth investigating), they often take the shortest route. This might take them through tall grassland or dense shrubs or woodland, or even over steep mountains.

Although following a short section of a lion trail can be easy, tracking the animals with the intention of finding them without them becoming aware or you is a completely different ballgame. They are predators with well-developed senses and can smell, see, and hear a human approaching from a long way off. Because they often lie with their heads flat on the ground, they can also sense vibrations in the earth. You have to tread lightly when you trail them.

In soft sand or on hard substrate with a thin layer of dust, lions leave tracks that are relatively easy to see. The moment the substrate turns hard, however, they leave very little sign: sometimes only one or two toes or the three lobes at the back of the metacarpal pad are visible. If a thunderstorm is followed by a few days of sunshine, the granitic soils in the Lowveld form a very hard crust. If lions move across this substrate, it is almost impossible to see the tracks. The tracker then needs well-developed speculative skills—a systematic approach will likely fail.

When lions are searching for prey, they often walk into, diagonally to, or across the wind so it carries the scent of prey animals to them. They also use it to carry their own scent away from the prey during the stalk.

When young lions are still learning to hunt, they often visit warthog dens in an attempt to dig them out. Warthogs often den in unused aardvark burrows on termite mounds. They tend to stay inside until the outside temperature has risen. If you follow the trail of lions early on a winter's morning and see that they are heading for an aardvark burrow, never approach the entrance from the front. A warthog might just come out like a bullet, and it will injure you if you are in its way.

Lions often move just a short distance before they go down for the day, especially if their stomachs are relatively full. Other days, they might go twenty or so miles. When you are on a lion trail, be prepared for a long walk. You need to be extra cautious on a lion trail in the late afternoon. Lions that are scared of humans during the day will quite suddenly lose all fear the moment the sun sets.

Once the lions have made a kill, fierce competition among the pride members often leads to squabbles with lots of growling and snarling. This is often heard over long distances and is a good indicator of a successful hunt. After a while, the sounds of bones snapping under heavy jaws will give the feeding lions' location away. If there is enough meat, the animals will often hang around for a while, even for days. Some might be on the kill while others rest in nearby shade. Take care not to walk in among them.

When vultures are circling, they are often simply using rising thermals to gain altitude. This is *not* an indication of a kill. When vultures descend quickly, however, and then circle, it often indicates a kill—and that predators are still present. More and more vultures will dive in, the wind on their wings making sounds like a jet. If the vultures are landing in trees and not on the ground, it is almost certain that lions are still feeding. Take care not to be fooled by the position of such a tree—it is in the vicinity of the kill but not necessarily directly above it.

If the kill was large and the lions had moved off, hooded vultures in a tree away from the kill are normally a good indicator of where lions are lying up. These small vultures follow lions to feed on fresh scat. Because of the high protein content of a lion's diet, the first scat after they feed is tarlike and almost black. If lions kill something big, such as a buffalo, they will normally feed on it for a few days, and piles of dung will accumulate close to the kill, adding to the pungent aroma of the area. In some cases, lions bury the rumen after a kill. There have also been cases of lions burying the lungs and other organs of animals infected with tuberculosis, as if they knew they were potentially harmful.

Large quantities of skin and hair are consumed. Some of the hair, along with sharp bone fragments, is then regurgitated. In the lion's stomach, some of the hair will form a cocoon around indigestible fragments, such as teeth, hooves, and small pieces of dense bone. This cocoon can pass through the entire digestive track without getting stuck. These scats are normally found away from the kill site, as it takes much longer for them to pass through the gut. They usually turn white in the sun and are filled with hair and the other undigested fragments. While on the move, lions tend to defecate off the trail.

Male lion at a giraffe kill. AL

Never handle lion (or any other predator's) scat with your bare hands. Lions are host to a small species of tapeworm called *Echinococcus,* as well as numerous nasty bacteria. The adult tapeworm lives in the guts of predators, then migrates to the mouth, where it deposits its eggs. In social species such as lions, the eggs can be transferred from lion to carcass to lion. Humans can be infected, too, if they handle lion scat, bones at a fresh kill site, or lions themselves during capture. Because humans do not have a high-protein diet, the tapeworm migrates from our gut via the bloodstream to the brain, lungs, or liver. There it can form a cyst the size of a tennis ball.

Digesting protein requires a lot of water. It is not uncommon to find lion tracks heading for the nearest water after they have fed. Lion tracks to and from water will often give away the location of a large kill.

Mating lions are often away from the rest of the pride. If the dominant males form a coalition, some might be with a female in estrus while others are with the rest of the pride or patrolling the territory. More than one male from the coalition can mate with the female over a few days. They will copulate every fifteen to twenty minutes; copulation normally ends with a snarl or growl.

When a lioness is about to give birth, she will leave the pride and find a secluded den in a thicket, among boulders, or even inside a hollowed-out termite mound. Take care when trailing a single lioness, especially if you notice up-and-down traffic from one individual. You might be on your way to her den. Because lionesses often synchronize their estrus cycles and therefore give birth at the same time, they often have their dens close to each other.

Trackers usually give individual lions or at least the pride a name if they track and encounter them regularly. They also get to know certain characteristics of the individuals, even distinguishing individuals from their roar. Some lions might be aggressive; others might be skittish, running at the first sign of humans. Some might stay put until the tracker leaves the area, then move off before the tracker can get the game-drive vehicle in position to view them. In some cases, the trackers might not track specific individuals at all as they are simply too aggressive.

Mating lions. Their grunts can be heard at a considerable distance. ME

By tracking the same pride of lions regularly, trackers build up a large base of knowledge that enables them to make excellent speculative predictions. Lions are creatures of habit, often following the same general routes as they move through the landscape. The experienced tracker can exploit these habits to establish the whereabouts of the big cats.

Tracking Notes

Senses and Speed: A lion's sense of smell and hearing are good and its eyesight is very good, especially at night. It can run at speeds up to fifty mph.

Warning Signs and Dangers: Encounters with wild lions during the day normally end with a grunt and the cats running away. But their fear of humans disappears the moment the sun sets. Lions feeding, mating, or fighting; a lioness with cubs; old, injured or sick lions; and lions that have lost their fear of people because of baiting or other interference can be extremely dangerous.

A lion normally warns an intruder with a low growl. This will intensify as the threat increases. The lion will glare at the intruder with its nose lifted, its eyes staring. The ears will be pulled down to show the black markings on the back, and the tail will sweep from side to side. As the threat intensifies, the tail will start hitting the ground with up-and-down strokes. This can be followed by a warning charge that will stop as close as five yards from the intruder. The lion will normally run at the intruder in an arc to expose more of its flank, and with stiff legs, to appear larger. This will often be accompanied by a series of nerve-racking coughing grunts or slurring growls. If a lion's tail is twitching or jerking but its ears are still cocked, it is probably just nervous or excited, not angry.

When lions mate, their growls are initially soft and sound something like faraway thunder, increasing in intensity and eventually erupting in one or two very loud and ferocious snarls. A lioness with cubs may stay in the vicinity of water holes, where they hunt and stay until the cubs are big enough to move with the pride. Their presence is usually indicated by soft *umf* calls of the mother and cat-like *meow* calls of the cubs.

Lions' presence can be indicated by zebra and wildebeest that are hesitant to go near water; they might just stare at a thicket.

A pair of lions watch circling vultures. ME

Giraffes indicate the presence of lions by staring at a thicket, too. Lions do not roar while hunting, but at night, the alarm calls of birds such as lapwings and thick-knees can indicate their whereabouts.

Getting out of a vehicle close to lions is much more dangerous than actually coming face to face with a lion in the bush. Appearing suddenly out of a vehicle can frighten them, which might prompt an attack in self-defense.

Method of Attack: During a vindictive attack, the lion will charge directly at the intruder. At the start of the charge, the growling will intensify. The lion will come in low and will not attempt to jump on the intruder but rather pull him down with its claws in a sideways blow. Males tend to pin the victim down without biting if the victim doesn't struggle. Females normally do a lot of damage with their teeth.

If the lion is actively hunting a human, there will be no vocalization. It will hunt in the same way as if the human were normal prey. Once it catches prey, a lion will simply start feeding, and the victim will usually succumb to trauma and hemorrhage.

Avoiding Conflict and Evasion Techniques: If a lion warns you, stop in your tracks, face the animal, and start moving back slowly without taking your eyes off it. If aggression flares, stand still. Never turn your back on a lion, and never run. It will run you down—lions instinctively charge and kill a fleeing animal. If the lion charges, try to intimidate it by taking a step forward, raising your arms, and shouting at it. When the charge stops, start backing out again.

When camping out at night, you should have a big fire going, and someone should keep watch. While lions may enter a camp when everyone is asleep, the presence of someone who is awake usually keeps them away.

!Xo trackers of the Kalahari maintain that if a lion charges you, you must stand still and shout loudly and aggressively and throw sticks and stones at it. You must look it in the eyes and not move back or try to run away. If you react aggressively toward it, the lion will lose its nerve and back off. When it backs off, slowly move backwards. But if it charges again, stand still and shout at it. You must repeat this procedure, moving downwind, until you reach a safe distance.

If you are charged by a lion, it might happen very quickly, and you will not have time to think. Never be caught unprepared in such a situation. Condition yourself so that when it does happen, you will be able to react intuitively and instantly.

To call a lion's bluff, you need to work yourself up psychologically into an extremely aggressive frame of mind in spite of the fear you experience. !Xõ trackers deal with their fear by combining aggression with tension-releasing humor.

I was hunting with four !Xo hunters in the central Kalahari to study their tracking skills. Just after four o'clock in the afternoon, !Nam!kabe decided to go out with his bow and arrow to see if he could shoot a steenbok or duiker. I went with him, while !Nate, Kayate, and Boroh//xao stayed in the camp. About two hundred yards from our camp, !Nam!kabe shouted "lion!" and a lioness jumped up about forty-five yards in front of us, bounding off into the bush. Shouting to chase away any other lions that may be hidden in the bush, !Nam!kabe and I went to look at her tracks to see what she was doing there. As he studied the tracks, !Nam!kabe explained: "The lioness lay here, jumped up, and ran away. This is a large female—she lay here and saw us coming and was afraid of us. We found her here near our camp; she stays here. I do not know if she has eaten. Come, we must follow her tracks and see if she killed an animal, then we can chase her away and take her meat."

But as we followed her tracks, it was clear she had not killed anything. "What sort of lioness is this that cannot kill a gemsbok? She stays here among all these animals, but cannot kill anything. There are many gemsbok, there are many hartebeest, and the kudu are many. This lioness walks among all these animals to come and stalk our camp. She will not leave us alone. It is in the day. Why does she come and lie here with us like a dog? Let us leave the tracks and go and tell the others, because we will not sleep tonight. You and me, we do not sleep well tonight because we have to look after the fire while the others just sleep. We must go back and tell the others. This lioness is here with us—don't think that she ran away. She stalks us here in the thick bush."

When we returned to camp, the younger hunters decided to track the lioness. They took the tin we used to boil water, and put some stones in it so they could make a loud noise by shaking it. At about five o'clock, we set out with !Nam!kabe, his son !Nate, Kayate, and Boroh//xao, armed with spears and throwing sticks. From where we flushed the lioness, we could see from her tracks that she circled downwind to look at !Nam!kabe and me as we were studying her tracks. Kayate said we should chase her away: *"We must follow her tracks and shout at her to chase her away, because she is too close to our camp."* As we followed her tracks, they would start to shout at her and shake the tin, the shouting and noise becoming louder and louder, as they worked each other up, and then they would shout abusive insults at her and burst out laughing—alternating aggressive shouting with raucous laughter. After tracking her for a while, !Nate suggested that we not follow her tracks (to see where she had gone), but rather backtrack to see where she had come from. *"If she got our wind and came from a distance straight to our camp, then we will not be able to sleep tonight. And we cannot follow her when the sun is so low, because when we find her she will fight with us. We must go back to collect enough wood to keep the fire going all night long."*

That night, as we sat around the fire, !Nam!kabe told the story of when they encountered a lioness with cubs: *"A lioness with small cubs is not right in the head. My grandfather, father-in-law, and I were hunting spring hares with our spring-hare hooks. We were hitting tree trunks with our clubs, looking for honey [hitting the trees to see if bees fly out]. My grandfather was walking some distance ahead of us when he found the lioness with her cubs. When we caught up with him, he was fighting with the lioness, so we went to help him. As the lioness charged us, we shouted and threw sticks at her. Then she would go back to move her cubs away and then come back to charge us again. We threw sticks, shouting at her. She would go back and move her cubs a little further away and again come back to fight with us. Every time she came back we would throw sticks at her. And the last time she came so close she kicked the sand up in our faces! Then she went back to her cubs to lie in the shade of some large trees. We told her: 'If you are not right in the head, then we are also not*

The tracks of a lioness. AL

right in the head!' So we left her there and went home. When we hunt here in this place we must know that one day you will walk into a lioness with cubs, because the bush is very thick here."

Throughout the night, they told stories of tracking lions with safari hunters, and encounters with lions, times when they had to sleep in trees. Often they would laugh at each other when recounting their experiences. Then there were quiet times when we would just stare into the fire. And once in awhile, !Nam!kabe would feel a burning sensation under his armpits and say that the lioness must be near our camp, stalking us from the downwind side. Then all hell would break loose. They shouted and made loud noises, banging sticks against pots and tins, and shaking the tin with stones in it. Then they would throw sticks into the dark, down-wind from us where they thought the lioness might be. And when the shouting and noise reached a crescendo, they would hurl abusive insults at the lioness and burst out laughing. Then things would simmer down and we would be quiet for the next hour or two. This shouting, banging of pots, and throwing sticks into the dark was repeated a number of times through the night until the dawn finally broke.

The next morning, we went out to track the lioness to see what she was up to during the night. We found the place where she had lay down until sunset. From there she got up and circled downwind of our camp, coming toward us. But as she came near our camp, she stopped. !Nate pointed at her tracks: "She stood here and heard us making a noise. These are the hind feet and here are the front feet. As she stood and listened, she thought to herself: 'If I go there those people will kill me. If I do not go back, I will die here tonight.' Then she turned around and went back to where she came from."

We followed her tracks to see where she was going. It was important to see how far she had gone and whether she had left the area. We found the place where she had slept for the night. Then she got up and started to move on. Boroh//xao pointed out where she had defecated: "Look how dry her dropping are—they are like little stones. She has not eaten for days. This is why she has been stalking humans." She was walking with twists and turns through the thick bush, sometimes walking and sometimes moving at a trot. Boroh//xao explained: "She is moving through the thick

*bush where people cannot easily go in order to avoid us." We followed her
tracks for most of the day, and as we moved through thick bush, a loud
roar exploded a few yards from us. Everyone burst into loud shouting,
while aggressively moving in toward the noise. And then a few moments
later, they all burst out laughing. We had surprised a kudu bull, who gave
its loud hoarse bark. We were expecting to walk into the lioness any
moment and so the kudu sounded just like a lion.*

*At this point, they were satisfied that the lioness had moved out of
the area and was no longer a threat to us. It was getting late, so they
decided to see if they could hunt something on the way back.*

—L. L.

AFRICAN LEOPARDS

*H*ow long ago did the last vehicle come in?" Robert asked after greet-
ing us.

"About thirty minutes ago, why?" came the response from Andreas
Liebenberg, owner of Bateleur Eco Safaris.

"There is fresh sign of a leopard kill two hundred yards out of camp.
The drag mark is on top of the last vehicle tracks. Something small like a
duiker or steenbok. Shall we go and look?"

We were waiting for our guests to arrive later that afternoon. Within
a minute, Robert Bryden, Callie Roos, Andreas, and I were walking out
to have a look at the tracks. It was about two o'clock in the afternoon and
very hot. The drag marks were clear: The hind feet tracks visible in the
smoothed-out drag mark left by the prey were those of a female leopard.
We followed the trail off the road and through the short grass. At one
place, she had to go over a fallen branch, and Robert pointed out some
hair stuck in the bark. "Duiker," he said, rolling the hair between his
fingers.

Intuitively, we all knew that she would have dragged the carcass into
the riverine bush about a hundred yards away. We made our way carefully down the trail. About thirty feet or so before we got to the tree line,
the drag disappeared. She had picked up the duiker and carried it.

The trail left by a leopard dragging large prey. AL

Not wanting to be directly on the trail in case she was still with the prey, we moved a little downwind. The last sign was that she had gone a bit more to the left. We scanned the area, but didn't see any sign of her or the kill. I went a bit to the right, and Andreas kept a straighter course. Robert and Callie tried to stay with the trail, which had now become faint in the dappled light under the trees, where the ground was covered with fallen leaves.

Among the trees there was hardly a breeze. I picked up a whiff of fresh blood and stopped. Standing next to a dense raisin bush on the bank, I tried to determine where the scent came from. I was about to signal to the others that it was off to the left, where Robert and Callie were, when I heard a faint sound—a very soft, throaty cough coming from the cluster of reeds just in front of Andreas on the other side of the bush. Before I could signal to him, the leopard jumped out from underneath his feet and ran past me.

—A. L.

Many trackers are bold enough to take on a leopard trail in the South African Lowveld, but few find their quarry. The success of an individual tracker is based on his intimate knowledge of a specific animal. There are very few trackers who can regularly trail an unfamiliar leopard successfully.

The presence of a moving leopard is often given away by the rasping barks of vervet monkeys. They will sit in the treetops, facing in the direction of the leopard and barking continuously. If they are spread out, you will be able to pinpoint the location of the leopard; the monkeys will all be staring at it.

If a bateleur eagle and a tawny eagle are perched in trees close together, they are most likely indicating a leopard's kill. Leopards will often hide their kills from scavengers, but these eagles can usually find them.

Leopards tend to defecate on the road or trail they are walking on. The first scat after a kill, full of blood and meat, is almost black. Trackers Wilson Masia and Juan Pinto have located numerous kills in the bush by backtracking from fresh scat when the leopard had left to go and drink.

Leopards usually avoid humans and are normally not dangerous if you leave them alone. They are only likely to become aggressive when threatened or provoked. If wounded, cornered, or suddenly disturbed, they can be exceedingly dangerous. Stumbling across a female with cubs can be a life-threatening situation. !Xo trackers of the Kalahari maintain that it is dangerous to follow a leopard's spoor since it might ambush you if it realizes you are following it to where cubs are hidden.

They also believe that you can pass close by a hiding leopard as long as your eyes don't meet. But the moment it is aware that you have noticed it, it will flee or, if cornered, attack. !Xo trackers say that you must never look a leopard in the eyes since doing so will infuriate it. Pretend to ignore it, and it will most likely choose to avoid confrontation.

Only in the soft, wind-blown dune fields of the southern Kalahari is it easy to track leopard. On hard ground, or in thick vegetation, speculative tracking is necessary to follow a leopard. You need

Female leopard tracks. ME

Leopard and its kill. AL

to know its behavior and predict it movements. Tracking a leopard is more difficult than tracking a lion. Lions tend to move through the landscape in a fairly predictable way, and their heavy weight makes their footprints easier to see. A leopard moves stealthily, following the contours of a hill or moving along the sides of a dry riverbed. It treads lightly. In thick dry grass, you might see a perfectly clear foot-print on a small patch of exposed sand and then no sign at all for a hundred yards. You might follow the trail in easy terrain, only to have it disappear without a trace when the animal moves over harder ground. After tracking for hours, you might eventually find a thicket where a leopard is lying up—but you may still not be able to see it. The tracks might go into the thicket and not come out, but it is too dangerous to go in to see if it the animal is truly there. Only when you come back the next day and find fresh tracks coming out of the thicket will you know for sure that it was. Tracking leopard is hard work, and you often do not see it even when you find it.

The elusiveness of the leopard also makes it one of the most intriguing animals to track. I once tracked a leopard that had

Leopards often use roads and game trails to travel. AL

followed a hiking trail for quite a distance. I met up with a group of hikers who had walked right over perfectly clear leopard tracks. None of them noticed them simply because they were not "spoor conscious." To them, the leopard didn't exist. Yet to me, finding fresh leopard track in the wilderness added an extraordinary dimension to hiking in the wild.

Tracking Notes

Senses and Speed: A leopard's senses of smell and hearing are good, and its eyesight is very good, especially at night. It can run at speeds up to fifty mph.

Warning Signs and Dangers: Close encounters with wild leopards normally end with the cats running away. An injured or cornered leopard, or a female with cubs, can be extremely dangerous, however. If a leopard realizes that it has been seen, it may feel threatened and attack. A leopard normally warns an intruder with a growl. It will also glare at the intruder with its nose lifted and eyes staring. The ears will be pulled down to show the black markings on the back and the lips parted to show their teeth. The leopard will slap the ground with its front feet while growling and spitting. This can be followed by a warning charge that will stop as close as five yards from the intruder. The leopard will normally run at the intruder in an arc to expose more of its flank, and with stiff legs, thereby looking bigger. This will be accompanied by a lot of growling and kicking up of dust. Cases of a leopard running forward only on its hind legs have been recorded.

Method of Attack: During a vindictive attack, the leopard will come in low and fast, and often from a very short distance, and often without vocalization. Once committed to a full attack, only a fatal bullet will stop a charging leopard. It charges very fast and low to the ground. It embraces its victim, with claws extended, and makes full use of its powerful dew claws. The victim is mauled with teeth and all four clawed feet. The victim is often scalped as the leopard runs over the person after the attack. These attacks are seldom fatal if adequate medical assistance is available.

In certain parts of Africa, healthy leopards have preyed on humans, usually killing women and children. Such behavior is atypical of leopards in the southern African subregion. Old and sick leopards, unable to catch wild prey, may, on very rare occasions, hunt humans. If the leopard is actively hunting a human, it will not vocalize. It will hunt the same way it hunts other animals: stalking in very close, pouncing, and delivering a killing bite to the back of the head, neck, or throat. Human prey, in these cases, are usually killed instantly with a broken neck or crushed cerebellum.

Avoiding Conflict and Evasion Techniques: If you see a leopard and are not walking toward it, continue walking and do not look at it or stand still. Deliberately move your eyes away from it. If a leopard warns you, do not face the animal directly. Start moving away from it to the side. Making direct eye contact will most likely trigger

A leopard resting in a tree. AL

a charge. Never run. If a leopard charges, try to intimidate it by taking a step forward, raising your arms, and shouting. When the charge stops, start backing out again.

There have been cases in which people have successfully defended themselves against leopards with knives and even stones, hitting them on the head. In some cases, unarmed people have been able to choke the leopard to death or make it retreat by punching it on the nose. However, there are probably few people capable of such feats.

There have been numerous instances in which leopards attacked baboons, only to be mobbed by the troop and flee. The noise created by the troop was sufficient to chase the leopard away. Many times in private reserves a charging leopard has been shouted down, but apparently the leopards in these areas have become so used to people that they are relatively tame compared to leopards in wilder regions. In the Kalahari, for example, !Xo trackers maintain that shouting will not stop a charging leopard and that you will have to kill it to save your life. It would therefore appear that the reaction of leopards varies from region to region, depending on the amount of contact they have had with people.

!Xo trackers believe it is simply too dangerous to follow a leopard's spoor, since it might ambush you if it realizes you are following it to where cubs are hidden. And there is no doubt that following a wounded leopard is one of the most dangerous things a tracker could do.

SPOTTED HYENAS

Tracking Notes

Senses and Speed: A hyena's senses of smell, hearing, and eyesight are good. It can run at speeds of thirty-one mph.

Warning Signs and Dangers: Hyenas avoid humans during the day and pose little threat, unless they are already man-eaters. It is not wise for a single human to approach a clan of hyenas on a kill, but hyenas normally leave when a group of humans approaches. This changes at night, and hyenas often come into camps looking for food. Hyenas hanging around a campsite in the early evening will definitely come into camp once things quiet down.

Method of Attack: A hyena will simply walk into a camp at night and grab the first thing that looks like food and run. If people are sleeping outside on the ground and haven't washed their hands and face after eating, the hyena might bite a hand or face. If other hyenas are close by, they might join in, and this can be fatal. If hyenas are actively hunting humans, they will normally charge in and turn very close in an attempt to get you to flee. Then they will run after you and take you down.

Avoiding Conflict and Evasion Techniques: It is important to have a secure waste disposal system in camp. If you sleep out, you must take turns standing guard, preferably with two people moving around at all times. If a hyena wanders into camp, do not encourage it; actively chase it from the area by making loud noises and clanging pots. If you are mobbed by hyenas, stand together in a tight group and do not run or split up.

RHINOCEROSES

*W*ilson took us to a spot where he had seen a rhino cow and calf early
the previous morning. He pointed it out and told me to follow it.
Louis bent down to study the track of the cow and pointed out a promi-
nent line in the left hind foot running in an arch from the middle of the
notch in the back of the pad to the front of the outer toe. He wanted
to make sure we stayed on the right trail as there were numerous other
rhinos in the area.

Although it was summer, a cold front had swept through the Low-
veld, and it was chilly and overcast. By the time we started on the trail it
was late morning, and the sun had broken through the clouds. The tem-
perature was pleasant. The day-old trail took us down one of the small
dirt roads to a well-used midden, but the animals had passed it without
defecating. We followed, and soon after that, saw that they had changed
direction and veered off the road. At first, they had stayed on a game path,
but then the cow started feeding, and we encountered the first dung. The
big balls had been reduced by dung beetles to a flat bed of grass fibers. But
they were still wet inside. The calf had defecated a few yards from its
mother, and although its tracks indicated that it was small, its dung
showed that it was already feeding on grass.

There were also signs of other rhinos from the same time, their trails
overlapping and crisscrossing regularly. We decided to find the spot
where the two had left the area and confirm there that it is the right trail.
This took a while, but we found it eventually. The trail took us into dense
vegetation and then to the place the rhinos had bedded down for the better
part of the day. From there, it was on to more feeding, fortunately, with-
out distraction. But then everything became confusing as they exited the
area and entered a road that had been used by a number of vehicles. They
had entered the road diagonally to the north, so I searched for sign in that
direction. I didn't find any. Wilson turned to the south and suggested
that we look in that direction; he was certain the animals would have gone
to drink at a pan there.

Louis then saw tracks at a crossroad that he recognized as those of the
cow and calf heading off to the east on the side road. Fortunately, this was
the trail coming back from the water, so we had gained substantially on

them. The water was a few miles away, and many animals use the pan, so we would have spent a lot of time on the trail if we had had to find every footprint.

Louis led as the trail took us down the road for about half a mile. At another midden, the cow and calf defecated, and from there they went into a dense area with tall grass and shrubs. Louis moved on. The rhinos fed on the lush guinea grass growing under the knob thorns. We again came to a place where they had bedded down and estimated that it would have been where they had spent the night. The site was secluded and in dense vegetation on the lee side of a low ridge. It would have been a good place to escape the cold wind that had brought the front.

It was clear that the calf was the first to rise, as its tracks went around its mother twice, and only then did she move. Louis again confirmed that it was the cow's track that we had started on. From there, the trail took us deeper into the dense block, with almost nonstop feeding signs. A dung beetle flew past and dropped into the grass twenty yards ahead of us. We had fresh dung. Although it was already cold, the core was warmer than it would be if it were out all night.

Sparring young white rhinos. AL

The well-used rubbing post of a white rhino. A wildfire approaches in the background. ME

We pushed on, and about five minutes later heard the chirp of ox-peckers ahead. We moved forward, checking the wind, and about twenty yards ahead of us, we saw the rhinos. They were bedded down. We moved out, and only then realized that we had been on the trail for almost five hours.

—A. L.

Despite their size, white rhinos can move through the landscape without leaving much sign. They do leave good tracks on soft to moderate substrate, but often just a scuff mark left by a toe will indicate that a rhino has walked on hard ground.

When they move to water or between feeding sites, rhinos tend to follow game paths or roads, but when they start feeding, they can move in any direction. If it is an area with patches of good grazing available, they tend to move from area to area as they feed. In the wet season, the better grazing is often underneath trees, and that is where they go. In the autumn and winter, they will often eat the better-quality graze on and around termite mounds. If the trail is difficult to follow, it can be productive to follow the trail to a mound and then climb it to see where the next one is. The trail leading in that direction can often also be seen.

When rhinos walk, their hooves often leave a very clear scuff mark, but when they feed, they tend to lift their feet up and to the side as they swing from side to side, mowing down grass with their wide mouths. When this happens, they leave very little sign, especially if they feed on burnt or overgrazed areas.

A territorial bull will patrol its territory on a regular basis. When it does, it walks far and fast, spray-urinating at regular intervals. Following a bull on patrol is usually not difficult, but you might be in for a very long walk.

During the cold winter months, white rhinos tend to feed and bed down on higher areas during the night and feed on eastern

White rhinos circle up and face outwards when disturbed and unsure of the disturbance. AL

Enoch Mkansi marks the height of mud left by a rubbing rhino near a wallow in Londolozi, South Africa. ME

slopes in the morning. They will feed and rest in the lower areas during the day and head to western slopes in the afternoon. In the summer months, the movement is reversed: They rest on the ridges, where there is normally a breeze, in daytime and feed in the lower areas at night.

If a rhino has visited a wallow, look for the trail leading away from the water. Their tracks might be subtle if mud is sticking to the bottoms of their feet. Look for fresh mud sticking to vegetation or a rubbing post. This might be as high as six feet off the ground. You might also find mud that squeezed out of folds in the skin as they walked off. Don't be confused by mud left on vegetation by warthogs, which tends to be closer to the ground, no higher than eighteen inches.

Tracking Notes: White Rhinoceros

Senses and Speed: White rhinos have a good senses of smell and hearing, but their eyesight is very poor. They can run up to twenty-five mph.

Warning Signs and Dangers: The white rhino is temperamentally quieter and more placid than the black rhino. It is quite easy to sneak up on a white rhino if you have the wind in your favor. Because of their poor eyesight, it is easy to enter their personal space before they notice you. They can detect movement, however, especially if its combined with bright colors, at least a hundred yards away. If they pick up a foreign scent or sound, they will spin around to try and detect the source. If it is a group of rhinos, they will form a defensive star, standing huddled with their rumps together, facing in different directions. An animal that detects an intruder will often run off, circling downwind to investigate. This is not always the case, however, and a sudden and seemingly unprovoked charge can follow. In most cases, this is more a panic run than it is a vindictive charge and will most likely break off ten or twenty yards from the intruder.

Method of Attack: It is not easy to tell the difference between a panic run and a vindictive charge in their initial stages, especially in woodland, as a panic run can turn into a serious charge at the last moment. In open country, the serious charge will normally start from a greater distance. The animal will normally come straight in, head lowered, and horn and ears pointing forward. It might also roar and snort. If it has not yet locked onto its target, it will swing its head from side to side, with the horn slashing down vegetation in front of it. The rhino will normally scoop up the target, slam its horn into it,

White rhino. Note the broad square lip, long head, and pointed ears. AL

and throw it over its back. If it is a panic run, the animal will normally just knock the intruder down with its shoulder or flank and keep on running.

Avoiding Conflict and Evasion Techniques: Take a white rhino warning seriously. Be particularly cautious with territorial bulls and females with small calves. Make sure you stay downwind from the animals, preferably out of sight. If the animal runs at you, stand your ground—running can be fatal. During the initial stages of a charge, or even before the animal runs at you, do not shout or make loud noise, as this might provoke it. Instead, click your tongue. Once it is charging, wave your arms, shout loud, and throw sticks or stones directly at it. If you are in a group, stand together. Hiding behind a shrub or fallen tree is always a good idea, and remember, high ground is safe ground.

The only surefire way to stop a serious white rhino charge is with a bullet to its brain. This will drop the animal in its tracks. A white rhino might break off a charge at only six to ten feet: It is therefore important to hold your fire until the last second.

Unlike the black rhino, the white rhino tends to run away, often circling downwind to investigate an intruder from a distance. The odd white rhino might be dangerous, however, and may even track you down to charge you.

Tracking Notes: Black Rhinoceros
Senses and Speed: The black rhino has very good senses of smell and hearing. Its eyesight is poor. It can run at speeds up to twenty-five mph.

Warning Signs and Dangers: It is not easy to sneak up to a black rhino, as they often lie up in thickets. If they pick up a foreign scent or sound, they normally spin around to try and detect the source. An animal that has detected an intruder often makes short charges in its direction. This is not always the case, however, and a sudden and seemingly unprovoked charge can start from as far away as seventy yards. This is normally accompanied by a repeated loud snort.

Method of Attack: The black rhino is known for its nervous, unpredictable temperament and can be extremely dangerous. This is particularly the case with bulls that are associating with receptive cows and with cows with calves. When disturbed, the rhino will stand still with its ears cocked and head raised. It may utter a few snorts and trot away or approach with a lumbering gallop. Such a charge might be merely to investigate a possible source of danger. Human scent will normally make rhinos move off, but their reactions depend on whether they have been hunted or otherwise molested or left in peace. In areas where rhinos have been disturbed, they can become extremely vicious and dangerous. Black rhinos differ greatly in individual temperament.

A black rhino normally charges at high speed with its head up. Its victim is usually knocked over but not gored. Black rhinos must stop in front of their victims to lower their heads before they can use their horns as weapons. A black rhino will often stop in front of an intruder and then make repeated short charges in its direction, often retreating to its original position. This is normally the case if the intruder is standing still. If the intruder runs, the animal will give chase.

Black rhino with calf. AL

Avoiding Conflict and Evasion Techniques: If the animal runs at you, it is extremely important to stand your ground, as running can be fatal. Shout loud and throw sticks or stones in front of it—not at it. It will often chase after an object that bounces past it. If you are in a group, stand together. Hiding behind a shrub or fallen tree is always a good idea. If you can, climb a tree. Remember, high ground is safe ground.

Black rhinos normally react well to a shot fired into the ground, but be very careful that a ricochet doesn't hit it. As with white rhino, it might break off the charge at two yards. It is therefore important to hold fire until the last second. If it still comes at you, then throw some article of clothing or backpack at it to divert its attention before leaping sideways at the last moment so it charges past you. If you lie perfectly still, it might lose interest and leave you alone. Black rhino are very fast and agile; do not risk a charge if you can help it.

The last line of defense is to throw yourself onto your back, pull up your knees, and give the rhino a hard kick in its mouth as it comes at you. Black rhino specialist Peter Hitchins has saved himself by doing this on more than one occasion.

Black rhinos have different personalities, and trackers get to know individuals. Some will not turn around and some will charge anything that moves, even from a distance. It is sometimes possible to shout down a black rhino. Master tracker Karel (Pokkie) Benadie once had to face a charging black rhino cow known as Katrina in the Karoo National Park. He had two students with him, and, to protect them, he had no choice but to stand his ground: "We were out in the open, so there was nowhere to go. Next thing we saw Katrina charging toward us. I could not leave the students there, so I shouted at her and pelted her with stones, but she kept coming until she stopped right in front of us, kicking up dust. I kept shouting and throwing sticks and stones and anything I could get hold of. She grunted and snorted, and I shouted, but she kept on coming back at us. Finally, she turned and ran away and I led the students to safety."

Sometimes things go wrong when you least expect it, and you may only have a split-second to make a decision.

*P*okkie, J. J., and I were tracking Suurkop, a black rhino bull. A young
student, Karin, came with us to see how we track rhino. We tracked
for several hours over hard, rocky terrain. Often it was not possible to
find any tracks at all, and Pokkie and J. J. had to predict where he was
going. Each rhino had its own favorite areas where it would feed and rest
up in the afternoon. Eventually, we came to a large thicket of acacia karoo.
Tracks had gone into the thicket and did not come out the other side, so we
knew he was sleeping in there. The ground was hard, and the footprints
were not very clear. So J. J. decided to go in to confirm that it was in fact
Suurkop. I asked Karin to wait up on the ridge with Pokkie and me.

Pokkie and I had started a conversation while we waited for J. J., who
by then had disappeared into the thicket, when we saw Karin follow him.
We were not sure if J. J. realized that she followed him, so I hurried after
her to get her to come back. As I caught up with her, J. J. turned around
and said: "He's coming!" We heard the sound of breaking branches at the
other end of the thicket. I grabbed hold of Karin to stop her from running
and stood to assess the situation. The thorn bushes were thick on both
sides of the path, and we were standing in the rhino's route—we had a
split-second to get out of his way. Moving to the downwind side of the
path, I pulled Karin down and pushed her into a thorn bush, while
crouching down over her, whispering "keep still." Moments later,
Suurkop came rushing past us, barely five yards away, and straight down
the path. J. J., meanwhile, had run around the bush, saw the rhino behind
him, and leapt right over the bush to get out of his way. We kept perfectly
still, not moving a muscle, listening to the sound of the crashing branches
disappear into the distance. We had to make sure he did not turn back,
since our best chance was to remain downwind, undetected. Afterwards,
Karin told us that when she realized that the rhino was coming, she did
not know what to do or which way to go. She just stood there, right in the
middle of the rhino's path.

—L. L.

In the modern world, our lives can be complicated, and we are
not always in the right frame of mind to track dangerous animals.

A black rhino comes closer to investigate sounds of an intruder. AL

We sometimes need to balance the need to get our work done and reduce the risks we take. Trying to balance a life that alternates between time in the city and tracking in the bush is not always easy.

We had to find Twalu, a black rhino cow in the Karoo National Park that had not been seen for a while, to make sure she was still in good health. This rhino had a reputation for charging anything that moved, even vehicles, even from a distance. I told J. J. he must look out for me because I had very little sleep and was not concentrating as well as I should. We picked up her tracks and followed them down the valley. Eventually, we could see a dense thicket of acacia karoo in the riverbed up ahead. It was a very windy day and we took care to stay downwind of the tracks as we moved toward the thicket, even though the thicket was still quite a distance away. There were a few small clusters of bushes between us and the dense thicket further ahead, and we assumed that the rhino would be lying up in the shade of the dense bush. For a moment, my mind wandered—I was thinking about a meeting with a potential donor. As we moved carefully around an isolated bush, J. J., who was just in front of me, suddenly spun around then stopped dead in midstride, frozen in his tracks. I froze, too, not even breathing.

The rhino was so close I was looking down at it barely ten feet in front of us. Size and distance seem to be amplified when your mind is suddenly focused. I could see her eyelashes in sharp detail. She was asleep, but her ears were twitching. The texture of her skin, the folds and wrinkles, had a vivid clarity. And as she was lying there in front of us, she was huge. As my mind focused it was as if time stood still. If this rhino woke up, we would be dead. I carefully turned my head to look at J. J., who was still frozen. There was no possibility to communicate with each other—we simply knew what we had to do. The wind was in our favor, so the rhino could not smell us. We were absolutely silent, so she could not hear us. And as long as her eyes were closed she could not see us. Working in a national park, we had no rifles to defend ourselves. We had only one option. We now had to move back very, very slowly. The slightest noise—a scuff of a boot, a crunching dry leaf, a snapping twig—would be fatal. There was simply no room for error. We had to slowly move downwind with complete focus and concentration.

—L. L.

HIPPOPOTAMUSES

Tracking Notes

Senses and Speed: The hippo has good senses of smell, hearing, and eyesight. It can run at speeds up to 22.4 mph.

Warning Signs and Dangers: A territorial bull or cow with calf can be very aggressive in the water and will normally warn the intruder with short charges in their direction. This is sometimes accompanied by snorting and yawning, which exposes the massive teeth. A hippo on dry land will normally not warn an intruder.

Method of Attack: Attacks on boats are common. Hippos surface underneath the boat, tipping it over and then biting the occupants to death. On land, they simply charge, trample, or even bite a human in half. Do not shoot too early, as they sometimes break off the

Hippos. ME

charge. Take note that hippos also charge out of water at intruders and can overturn vehicles parked at the edge of water sources.

Avoiding Conflict and Evasion Techniques: If you are in a boat and encounter a hippo, hug the bank and stay in the shallows, leaving the deeper water for the animal. If the hippo is in the water and you are on the bank, move away to high ground. If a hippo charges you on dry land, get out of its way. Never run down its path, and do not place yourself between it and the water. At night, be very careful not to put a spotlight in the animal's eyes as this will often provoke a charge.

CAPE BUFFALO

It was a cold late-winter morning in the middle of the 1992 drought. We were leading a group of eight guests on the Wolhuter Wilderness Trail in the Kruger National Park. Although the sun was out, a cold wind was pushing hard from the southeast. We were walking on a well-worn rhino path along the base of a high ridge. *The trail, made by many generations of big feet, more or less followed the same contour, making for easy and comfortable walking. We were not trailing any animal in particular, simply using the trail to get into an area we wanted to explore.*

The trail was used by numerous animals during the night to move between water and feeding grounds. We were looking at the obvious signs left by the animals. It was the first morning, and the guests were eager to learn, actively participating in a discussion around a white rhino midden. The waist-high blue thatching grass formed a solid curtain around us, sheltering us from the wind.

An urgent "click, click" from Amos caught my attention. As I rose from a crouch, I saw Amos facing further down the trail, rifle ready. I cocked my rifle and took two steps to reach higher ground and stand next to Amos. The guests stayed put, waiting for instructions.

The old buffalo bull stood only ten yards from us. With his head held high, he stared at Amos through bloodshot eyes. Both his horns were broken off close to his skull, and he looked like a medieval hangman. I shouted at him, but he didn't flinch. Without taking my eyes off him, I ordered the group to slowly stand up and move in a tight group behind a big boulder next to the trail. The bull kept his eyes on Amos, as if the rest of us didn't exist.

After what felt like hours, the bull half-turned and started to walk diagonally away from us down the slope. I shouted at him again and took a few steps in his direction. He disappeared into some bush and looked as though he was moving past us. But when he didn't reappear on the far side of the guarri, both Amos and I felt uneasy. We decided to continue in the direction we were heading but not follow the game path. We chose a contour higher up the slope that offered better visibility.

With the wind in our faces, progress was slow; there was no trail to follow, and the tall grass hid large, loose rocks. I stopped regularly to scan the landscape in search of the bull but he was not to be seen. The guests complained about the difficult terrain, but I still felt uneasy. About three hundred yards from the initial encounter, the guests insisted that we go back down the slope to the path. We stopped, and I asked them to help me and Amos look for the buffalo. We scanned the landscape below but saw nothing. The area was relatively open. The grass was shorter than at the

Buffalo at a wallow. ME

foot of the ridge where the game path was, and there were only a few scat-
tered knob-thorn and marula trees. The only place that was not clear was
where the path went through a belt of tall magic guarri directly below us.
We knew that section well. The path made a sharp S bend within the
bushes.

I asked Amos to take the lead and head down toward the trail. I
wanted to keep an eye out for the buffalo from behind; I was still not con-
vinced that we were out of danger. We hadn't gone thirty yards when a
gust of wind took us by surprise. Hats went flying, and one of the ladies
almost lost her balance. As I turned to the left to face downwind, I caught
a glimpse of black skin inside the guarri thicket. The wind had opened up
the vegetation just enough to offer a glimpse of the buffalo.

We waited five minutes or so before another gust of wind came
through. This time it opened up the guarri more. Inside stood the hang-
man. He had reversed into the blind side of the bend, just off the trail,
waiting for us. He stood there, facing in our direction.

Later, on our return, we walked through the area further down the
slope. We picked up the bull's trail below the guarri belt and backtracking

it, discovered that he had turned back into the wind immediately after he had gone into the drainage line when we lost sight of him. It was as if he had deliberately set an ambush for us.

—*A. L.*

Buffalo are heavy animals, and their feet often leave good sign in soft and medium substrate. On hard surfaces, the saucer-sized hooves of big bulls will usually leave some mark. Buffalo droppings look and smell like cow dung.

Breeding herds can number in the thousands and are made up of family units that stay together on home ranges. The big herds will often break up into these units and disperse during the rainy season (Apps 1992). When you trail breading herds, a lot of time can be wasted if too much attention is paid to the tracks of the old bulls that meander in and out of the herd. Follow the core. You will know when you are getting close to a moving herd because it is noisy: Calves bellow to their mothers, mothers call their calves, dung splatters on the ground, branches break as the animals feed under trees

A buffalo herd at attention. AL

and bushes. In the drier months, you will see a lot of dust rising, especially if the animals are on their way to water.

Young and old bulls leave the big herds and form bachelor herds, or small groups. The very old bulls eventually become solitary. Buffalos are ruminants and bulk grazers, preferring taller grass. They will spend up to eighty-five percent of their time feeding or ruminating. Breeding herds can cover large distances to get enough food, but single bulls or small groups will stay in a small area.

When buffalo are bedded down to sleep and ruminate, the chirping of ox-peckers will often give their position away. It is important for the tracker to learn the call of this little bird that feeds on ticks and other herbivore parasites. When they fly over, pay attention to where they land, as they will often dive down on animals.

Buffalo often feed during the night; they are sensitive to the heat. They drink early in the morning and late in the afternoon, resting under trees during the hottest hours. Bulls tend to wallow to get rid of parasites and cool down. Because they grow up gregarious, they never learn to sleep with "one eye open." It is, therefore, fairly common to stumble across a single bull sleeping in a thicket or wallow.

A single calf is usually born in the afternoon or early evening, when the herd is resting. The cow will leave the herd and give birth in a nearby thicket. She will rejoin the herd a few hours later. Take great care not to wander between the cow and the herd, or the cow and her newborn calf, as she will charge without warning.

Unless you are looking for a specific individual when you're on the trail of a small group of bulls you must simply follow the bulk of the tracks, as the animals will meander in and out of thickets as they feed on the better-quality grass in the shade. A lot of time will be wasted if you work through the trail systematically. The herd will move apart and then recombine as it moves.

Old, solitary bulls are often very elusive, as they tend to hang out in the same area if food, water, and mud are available. You will often have to work through a maze of old and new sign to find the animal. Take care not to walk into the animal at close quarters when it is asleep; you might walk into the attack zone before it wakes up. If the bull becomes aware that he is being trailed, he will most likely run off, but be aware that old bulls sometimes allow you to push them once or twice before they take a stand and fight. Wounded or injured buffalo have a tendency to wait in ambush and will charge you.

If a buffalo has visited a wallow, look for the trail leading away from the water. The buffalo will often simply walk away from the wallow, but if it used a rubbing post, such as a broken tree trunk, look carefully so you don't confuse the sign left by other animals with a buffalo's. You will usually see buffalo tracks quite clearly, and if the animal rubbed against something to get rid of parasites, the rubbing will usually be at a height of two to four feet off the ground.

Tracking Notes

Senses and Speed: Cape buffalo have good senses of smell, hearing, and eyesight. They can run at speeds up to thirty-five mph.

Warning Signs and Dangers: Buffalo, especially in herds, are very inquisitive and often approach a vehicle or even humans on foot if they can't smell them. Once they catch the smell of an intruder, they run off. The danger in this is that they might stampede in any direction. Be very cautious of a cow that has given birth; she will charge without hesitation. A bull will normally walk toward an intruder with its nose up, throwing its head from side to side, sometimes snorting and horning at the ground or trees. The animal will usually bellow as it starts its charge.

Method of Attack: A buffalo encountered at close range will normally turn and run, but if it feels trapped, it will charge. This is not necessarily a vindictive attack but rather a panic run to escape.

If it is a vindictive attack, the animal will charge with its nose up and then at the last moment drop its head either to get its horns into its victim with a sideway sweep or fling the victim over its head. The animal might then turn back to trample and gore its victim. It is not unusual for a buffalo to stay in the area for hours after an attack, and people who escape into trees might be harassed continuously. Wounded buffalo and solitary bulls that have been intruded upon many times often circle back from their tracks and wait to ambush pursuers.

Cape buffalo. AL

Avoiding Conflict and Evasion Techniques: Avoid dense cover around wallows and be on the lookout for ox-peckers. You can normally defuse a panic run by simply getting out of a buffalo's way (and preferably out of its sight), opening the animal's chosen escape route. Climb a tree if one is nearby, but do *not* stand your ground. Buffalo complete the charges they start. If you can't get out of the way, try to avoid the horns. People have saved themselves by either jumping over the animal's head as it lowered its horns or by falling flat on their backs to let the animal run over them.

A Good Day

It was the last morning of the senior tracker evaluation at Singita Lebombo, a private tourist concession in the Kruger National Park. Situated on the boundary with Mozambique in the Central District of the Kruger, this area hosts large herds of plains game and is renowned for its extremely large prides of lions. In the mid-1980s, the late Ross English saw the Sweni Pride totaling fifty-seven members, when a good number of the females had cubs. Today, prides average between twenty and thirty individuals.

Situated at the old Nwanetsi Ranger's Post, the lodge has a stunning view of the Nwanedsi River and, farther out to the east, the rhyolite and granophyre ridges of the Lebombo Mountains. With that view, and the grunts of hippos, calls of the African fish eagle, and roars of distant lions in the early hours of the morning, the modern facility has the ambiance of Old Africa.

With the evaluation finished, we had the morning free, and Louis, Mark, and I decided to track lions. As evaluators, we try and do this as often as possible as a form of peer review. Mark had qualified the previous day as senior tracker and evaluator, and for him it was a bit of a "victory trail."

We drove out to the far north of the concession, where the basalt plains west of the Lebombos are home to large numbers of giraffe, impala, zebra, wildebeest, and other game. Although it was early summer, the intense heat of the previous few days was replaced by a cold wind pushing in low, heavy clouds from Mozambique.

293

A bit of moisture did fall on the fine-grained soil, turning it almost black. Despite this, the strong wind was pushing up little puffs of dust. We picked up the tracks of two lionesses moving to the east into the wind after the moisture had come down. This was a very fresh trail.

Louis started the trail, but after a while we took turns leading in no particular order. We were just happy for the opportunity to trail freely, with no pressure and nothing to prove. The area was relatively flat, with dense stands of knee- to hip-high grass, yellow and gray after the long dry season. In some places, bare patches of soil were visible, and knob-thorns and other trees completed the savanna landscape. Well-worn game paths crisscrossed the area.

The sun had not broken through the clouds, and it soon became obvious that the lionesses were still hunting, their trails splitting up into the wind. At one spot, we saw where one was crouching and then big explosions in the dirt where she was running. And then the tracks were gone. We scanned the area and picked up tracks of zebra running. Then there was a single print of one of the lionesses stepping on the zebra trail. They had missed.

In the broken ground-cover, it would have taken too long to work through the scene systematically so we intuitively moved into the wind and soon picked up the trail of both females walking further, using their noses to sniff potential prey. Their trail was heading east, diagonal to the wind out of the southeast.

We followed further. A big elephant bull was breaking branches off a bush directly ahead of us on the trail. The wet streaks down his temples and strong odor of urine told us that he was in musth. We carefully circled downwind around it and picked up the lionesses' trail on the far side.

Again they hunted—this time a giraffe—and again they had missed. Circling upwind, we found the trail without too much difficulty. The freshness of the tracks indicated that they were still hunting, and that they were moving. We had to move faster if we wanted to catch up to them before they went down to rest.

Without talking about it, we pushed on, helping each other and slowly gaining momentum. Again the lionesses hunted, and again they missed. The warthog got away. We went to the upwind side, but there

Hunting lions pause in cover before their final launch. AL

*were no tracks. They had changed direction. I noticed zebra and wilde-
beest to the southeast of us.*

*"They would have smelled the animals," I whispered. I scanned to
the south across a grassy plain, and saw her about hundred and fifty
yards away. A beautiful lioness was standing upright, looking over the
tall grass from behind a bush at the zebra. She was completely unaware of
us. We watched her for a few minutes, and then she sank into the grass to
continue the stalk.*

*We left without saying much and quietly hiked the three or so miles
back to the vehicle. It was a good day in Africa.*

—A. L.

Two Amazing Trackers

Numerous anecdotes have been sprinkled throughout this book, some our own, and many about other trackers we've observed in the field. Two particular trackers exemplify the skills we discuss. We want to acknowledge the role these exceptional individuals played in developing our own tracking skills.

WILSON MASIA

It was nearly five o'clock in the afternoon, and Louis was evaluating Piet. Piet had been on the trail of a white rhino bull for the last hour or so. A slender Shangaan in his mid-twenties, Piet had worked as a full-time tracker at a lodge for a number of years before he became a field guide. Also in the group were Juan, general manager at Royal Malewane, and Ian, internationally renowned motivational speaker and former field guide—both of them competent trackers in their own right and soon to qualify as senior trackers. And then there was Wilson Masia, master tracker, keeping an eye on the proceedings from the back. My role was to observe and make recommendations on the CyberTracker evaluation process to the Field Guide Association of Southern Africa. I was also keen to learn. Two days later, I was to go through the trailing evaluation myself for the first time.

Piet had picked up the trail where we had seen the rhino walking early that morning. The trail was at least ten hours old, and it was a hot and windy November day. The rhino had walked in an easterly direction,

White rhino. AL

and we followed with the late afternoon sun on our backs. The undulating landscape of the South African Lowveld had had little rain that season, but the dense grass cover from the previous season's cyclones was lying in a thick carpet of dry hay on the ground. The only place the grass was still standing was where it was supported by the sicklebush and other shrubs and small trees growing in open stands. Very little of the coarse granitic soil was visible through this hoof-trampled mosaic of grays and browns. The open woodland and slope were restricting our view in places to about fifty yards.

Piet had lost the trail and, in his search, almost stepped on a black mamba. The eight-foot snake reared up a few yards in front of Piet and Ian, and they froze in their tracks. Although the mamba is seldom aggressive, the fast-acting neurotoxins in its venom can easily be fatal. After a few tense moments, the snake relaxed and moved off. Piet threw his hands in the air, indicating that he needed help. We were all straining our eyes to pick out some sign that might indicate where the rhino had passed. Again Piet looked around, and then Wilson, from behind, signaled for him to continue straight up the rise. Piet walked fifteen or twenty yards further then signaled that he had found the trail again. Louis, Ian, and Juan followed.

I turned and went back to Wilson and asked him to point out what he had seen to indicate where the rhino had moved. Without moving, he signaled me to go forward. Twenty-five yards along the trail he indicated for me to stop and look. I stopped and searched the ground in front of me for signs of the rhino. Nothing. All I could see was the odd sign here and there that we ourselves had made. I turned again and asked Wilson to please point out what I was supposed to see. Walking stick in hand, he limped up the rise with an expression that told me that I still had a long way to go.

"Go right a little bit," he said, pointing with his walking stick. I moved three, four yards and then pulled up my shoulders. Wilson joined me. I still didn't get it.

He looked me square in the eyes and asked, "What time did this rhino walk here?"

"Maybe half past seven this morning," I answered, after quickly calculating the time when we had seen it and the distance from where we started.

"Where was the wind at seven o'clock?" he asked.

Thinking hard, I pointed to the south and said, "It was quite strong that way."

"This grass . . . is it fresh or old?"

He pointed out a blue-gray blade of guinea grass resting on some old brown grass a foot or so above the ground. I stared at the wilted blade and realized it didn't belong there. Everything else was brown, dead, and from the previous season's growth. But this grass was new, just wilted. Where did it come from?

"What did this rhino do over there?" he asked as he pointed back down the trail. Then the penny dropped, and I remembered that the rhino deliberately veered off and walked through a patch of knee-high, fresh, green guinea grass a third of a mile back. I hadn't even noticed that it had taken a few mouthfuls. This piece of grass less than an inch wide and some six inches long had obviously stuck to the rhino's lip before it was blown sideways off the trail by the morning's strong winds.

Signaling to follow the rest of the group up the rise, Wilson simply said, "Okay, let's go."

Amazed with what I'd just witnessed, I realized that he most likely hadn't even been thinking about this as he viewed the group struggling on the trail from behind. He was simply walking on the trail because he had done it a million times before.

That day I understand that Wilson didn't allow himself to get caught up in the process. His intuition came from an intimate knowledge of the animal, landscape, climate, and season. His exceptional ability to observe, using all his senses, came from a huge amount of field experience acquired over a lifetime of tracking.

—A. L.

Wilson Masia was born in October 1951 near the town of Mapu-langwene in Mozambique. He grew up as a cattle herder. As a little boy, whenever he had the day off, he would visit a friend in a nearby village. If he didn't find his friend there, he simply tracked him into town. Part of the life of a cattle herder in those days was fending for oneself by hunting and trapping small game—ideal training for a young tracker.

In those days, there were no fences between Mozambique and South Africa, and the animals of the Kruger National Park moved freely between the protection of the park in South Africa and the general population of rural Africa in Mozambique. To help care for his family, Wilson hunted large game in the area. If an animal were wounded, he would track it down and finish it off as soon as possible, even if this meant crossing the border into South Africa and the park. He was effectively a poacher, although his intent was to end the suffering of an animal.

In the early 1970s, like many of his counterparts, he worked for two short stints in the gold mines near Johannesburg. But his love for the bush and animals pulled him back to the Lowveld, and in the mid-70s, he worked in the Kruger National Park as an antipoaching field ranger. He went back to Mozambique, but by 1985, RENAMO forces brought war very close to his village, and he walked back to South Africa. The crossing involved walking through the national

Wilson Masia, Adriaan Louw, and Louis Liebenberg at Singita, South Africa.
ALAN YEOWART

park at night, a journey of nearly forty miles. He made this trip about ten times for the sake of family and friends, negotiating the wilderness and wildlife and avoiding park staff and South African security forces deployed to prevent these types of crossings.

Wilson settled in the village of Welverdiend just west of the Kruger boundary and began working as a tracker in the ecotourism industry, first in the Timbavati Private Nature Reserve, then in the Thornybush Game Reserve. In 1999, together with Juan Pinto, with whom he had been in a guiding team since 1995, he joined the owners of Royal Malewane, taking charge of the tracking teams.

Although Wilson has incredible humor, his staunch attitude creates respect wherever he goes. He never minces words and keeps everyone honest. During a debrief after a senior tracker evaluation, he praised a successful but cocky youngster for a good performance, and then told him to "come down to where we are or you will play yourself out of tracking forever."

AMOS MHLONGO

*W*e were sitting around the campfire after dinner in the trails camp. Everybody was exhausted after the heat of the day, thankful for the clear night sky and low humidity, which allowed the evening to cool down. The conversation soon died as all of us listened to the chatter from the kitchen hut some ten yards away. None of the guests, all city folk from Johannesburg, could understand a word the two Shangaan men in the hut were saying, but the energy coming out of the little reed building with its corrugated tin roof was contagious. I managed to catch the odd word in Tsonga, but because I had lived the experience Amos was retelling to James, the camp cook, I understood the entire thing.

I had been still training as a wilderness trails ranger in the Kruger National Park. A few days earlier, with a group of guests, we had encountered a rhino that disappeared into a thicket, allowing us just a glimpse of its hindquarters. Amos, who was in the lead with me, was convinced it was a black rhino. I wasn't sure, and Steven, who was walking at the back, was sure it was a white rhino. Amos pointed out its tracks in the soft loose river sand, but Steven was still convinced it was a white rhino. Steven and I wanted to take the group after it, as we hadn't yet seen a rhino on foot with the group. Amos, not wanting to embarrass his seniors in front of the guests, suggested that he and Steven track it to confirm if it was safe to view. I was to stay behind and keep the guests out of trouble.

Well, it was a very big black rhino bull, and it charged Steven and Amos. It first chased Steven around a small thicket a few times and was catching up to him fast when Amos managed to lure it away from Steven, using himself as a decoy. On the rhino's first snort, I ordered the guests to retreat halfway up the opposite riverbank, where a small saddle was formed behind the trunk of a massive sycamore fig. They simply stared at me in disbelief. It was only when Amos appeared in the riverbed a hundred yards upstream with the rhino in hot pursuit that they kicked into action and moved with the speed of light.

Amos managed to dive over a granite boulder and out of sight of the rhino. The beast steamed up the bank, then turned in our direction. It was only then that I realized several guests had not stopped where it was safe but had continued further up the bank.

"Hey, not there. Come back here—the rhino is on its way!" I shouted.

That just spurred them on to try harder to get up the bank. Luckily, the loose soil and the steepness slowed their progress. Again I shouted, but to no avail. Then I realized they were under the impression that they were okay and that I was ordering the others around. Unfortunately, I couldn't remember their names. This left me with only one option, to go after them and hope to get to them before the rhino did. The man slipped again and half-pulled his wife down with him. I was just in time to hold them tight when the rhino raced past our heads like a locomotive atop the bank.

With the rhino gone and no harm done, we could only laugh nervously about it when Steven and Amos rejoined us. We headed straight to the nearest reservoir to cool down and then went back to camp.

During his retelling, Amos's excitement got him so fired up he forgot we had guests in camp. At full voice, he continued telling the story, which was followed by a bit of silence, an "oh" or "ah" from old James, then uncontrollable laughter from them both. This was followed by the next chapter, and more laughter.

Black rhino. AL

Steven, the relief ranger at the time, under whose guidance I was learning the ropes, saw an opportunity to add to the excitement. As the son of the legendary game ranger Ted Whitfield, Steven grew up in the park and could speak the Tsonga language. He stood up from the fire and disappeared into the dark behind the kitchen just as Amos resumed the story. As the chatter continued, Amos was helping James with the dishes and at that point had only the heavy cast-iron pots left.

Amos was busy with the part where the rhino chased him into the riverbed, and, just before the climax of the story, Steven threw himself over the low reed wall of the kitchen directly in front of Amos with an almighty roar, slapping and shaking the wall in the process.

With a loud "huw" from Amos and the clanging of the heavy pots, James took off into the darkness, his progress marked by a "jo, jo, jo" until he slammed the door of his hut behind him. Then there was total and uncontrollable laughter from Amos, and soon we all joined in. A few minutes later, James reappeared with a sheepish smile. For the rest of the evening, everyone had something new to laugh about, and we relived the story over and over.

The next morning, we walked along a section of the Mlambane spruit (a seasonal river) with dense stands of tamboti thickets along its bank and extended stands of raisinbush and red and russet bushwillow further in. The riverbed itself was overgrown with reeds six feet tall. Not long into the walk we came across the tracks of a large black rhino bull. Amos very quickly identified it as the individual responsible for all the excitement over the last few days. Pointing out a long thin line running diagonally across the center of the track of one of the feet he looked up at Steven and said, "It is our friend."

Amos followed the trail a bit to establish the direction the rhino was moving. The animal's trail was heading to where we were planning to walk. Neither Steven or I were keen to bump into the rhino again, so we changed direction and crossed the Mlambane, carefully working our way through the tall reeds, before making our way toward a little hill on the horizon where we could have breakfast. We had only walked about two hundred yards beyond the river when we found ourselves back on our friend's trail. He had been crisscrossing the area during the night as he browsed on the tamboti and raisinbush.

So we crossed back through the reeds and headed off on our original course. Four hundred yards on, we were back on his trail. We crossed the Mlambane again, Amos in front of me. Since he was exceptionally small, I could see right over his head, and had it been necessary, I probably would have been able to shoot over his head as well.

With rifles ready, we carefully pushed through the sixty-yard-wide curtain of reeds. We walked single file on the narrow game trail, with Amos stopping every ten yards or so to listen. Finally, we were through the reeds. The last few feet were less dense, and Amos ran forward to gain a bit of momentum to help him up the steep riverbank. His movement carried him far enough to allow him to see over the edge. A jolt went through his body, his calf muscles popping up like two tennis balls on his thin legs. His face turned to me, and his eyes were as big as saucers.

I could feel the blood draining out of my head. I saw Amos's eyes looking further back to where Steven was—and then he exploded with contagious laughter. He lost his footing and slid down the bank on the seat of his pants. He had just returned the favor of the previous evening!

A week or two later, we were back on the banks of the Mlambane, eating breakfast on the first morning of the very first wilderness trail I was leading. Quite nervous and unsure of myself, I was thankful to be there. I was thankful to be able to live a dream, to be a ranger in the Kruger National Park.

"What is that, Amos?" I asked, as strange growls echoed against the cliffs in the bend of the river.

To me, it sounded like a lion, but Amos didn't look too sure. The noises emanated from a small patch of forest that grew on the bank on the inside of the bend in the river.

I looked at Amos and asked him if we should have a look. He was keen, and off we went with our eight guests in tow. Amos was in front of me as we entered the forest in single file. Every time we approached the noises they seemed to change position, and we had to renegotiate our way through the labyrinth of obstacles in the undergrowth. The sounds were also rapidly changing from almost roaring to grunts, growls, snorts, and squeals. Amos had just jumped over a ditch when a leopard shot out from a thicket directly next to me and disappeared up the ditch. I immediately grabbed the guy behind me by the shoulder-strap of his backpack and jumped over the ditch myself, pulling him closer with the hope that he would at least see the backside of the leopard disappearing. At that moment, a second leopard shot out from the same place, went underneath the arc formed by my arm, and disappeared in the same direction. It was a mating pair of leopards.

A bit shell-shocked, I led the group back to the Wolhuter Trails' Camp. Amos took my rifle to clean it with his, and I took care of the guests during lunch. After a quick bite, I walked toward Amos's hut and found him on his way to see me. We both realized that we almost lost it that morning by walking our guests into potential danger, and that we needed to figure out what went wrong.

I had a hundred percent confidence in his judgment as he was the one with more than twenty years' experience. At the same time, he had a hundred percent confidence in my judgment because I had gone to school and therefore must have all the knowledge. I also learned that he didn't want to embarrass me in front of the guests by showing off his superior knowledge. It was a big wake-up call for both of us. Although we were comfortable going in there alone, we knew it was not the place to take guests.

Both of us decided that we would no longer allow poor judgment and bravado to overrule common sense. Within three months, we had developed a communication system going that enabled me to understand exactly what was happening by simply looking at Amos's face.

If I were kneeling at a rhino midden, explaining the dung-beetle activity, Amos would be on the perimeter, looking for signs of danger. A single click of his tongue would get my attention, and his eyes and posture would tell me to be quiet and get the group off the trail, or that a rhino was on its way but that it was still safe as long as we moved quickly and quietly. This system proved to be very important because that year, 1992, brought the worst drought the Lowveld had ever experienced.

During the forty-nine trails we led that year we had eighty close encounters with dangerous animals that approached the group to within twenty yards or closer. More than half of them charged us. Yet we never shot a single animal, nor were any guests injured.

—A. L.

Adriaan and Amos, 1992, Kruger National Park, South Africa.

Amos Mhlongo (or Amose Chongo, as his South African identity document stated) was born in Mozambique in the 1950s, in the
same area as Wilson. He started work in the Kruger National Park
in 1972 with no formal education. He soon moved up in the ranks
because of his courage, hard work, and eagerness to learn. In 1980,
he transferred to the Wilderness Trails Section as assistant trails
ranger. I started to work with him in 1992 but moved to the north of
Kruger in 1993 to do service on the Nyala Land Trail in the Pafuri
and Punda Maria sections of the park. Amos stayed behind at Wolhuter as it was not too far from his home.

In 1996, Amos contracted malaria that eventually led to kidney
and liver failure. I managed to visit him in the Barberton Hospital on
a Sunday and prayed with him. The next day he asked to be released
into the care of his family. He died in peace at his home that
Wednesday.

Maybe it was because I had very little experience when I started,
or because we shared so many close shaves with dangerous animals

together, but that small man with the big heart will always have a special place in my memories. He was a great friend and mentor. He was full of humor and very humble. He was keen to share his stories and a master in bushcraft.

Amos was an avid bird-watcher. He had learned to read in a semiphonetical way, pronouncing words by the letter, and this enabled him to accurately pronounce the sounds made by birds as they are written in bird guides. If he heard an unfamiliar bird call, he would spend hours looking through his guide, repeating all the calls as they were written. He always got it right.

—A. L.

CyberTracker
Tracker Evaluations

*I*n December 1994, I went to Thornybush Private Game Reserve to conduct the first tracker evaluation. I had only a vague idea of what I was going to do. One of the owners of the reserve, Trevor Jordan, asked me to evaluate his trackers and give them certificates. I decided to issue two types: a tracker certificate for a rating of eighty percent and a senior tracker certificate for a hundred percent. The details of how I was going to rate the trackers I had to figure out as I went along. I just had to follow my gut feeling for what would work; this notion made me nervous.

On my arrival, I was introduced to a group of rangers and trackers who were told that I was going to evaluate them. It was clear they did not think much of the idea; it was something the boss had forced them to undergo. I imagined them thinking: "Who is this guy coming from the city who thinks he can teach them about tracking in their own Bushveld terrain?" Their skepticism was obvious, which made me even more nervous. I gave an introductory talk about how tracker certificates would help trackers get better jobs and negotiate better salaries. I then moved to the next step: a practical test on spoor identification. We went out to the nearest water hole to find some tracks.

Before I could start, one of the Shangaan trackers stopped me. He circled a track in the dust—a faint smudge that looked like nothing. One by one, he asked each of the predominantly white rangers what it was. None of them got it right. Then he asked each one of the Shangaan trackers to tell him what it was, and none of them got it right. Then he turned to me and said, "Tell them what track this is." I've never been so nervous *as I walked over to take a look at what he was pointing to. Looking down, I recognized the larger pattern. I pointed to three other nearby smudges, the four together forming a bounding gait. "It is a hare," I said.*

He looked at me, then said: "Okay, now you can continue."

This Shangaan tracker was Wilson Masia, who subsequently became one of the first three South African trackers to be awarded the master tracker certificate. In some dozen years, he has been the only tracker to receive this certificate in the Lowveld. On my first tracker evaluation, I was myself tested by the best Shangaan tracker I have ever known. If I got the hare track wrong, he would have sent me back to Johannesburg, and the tracker evaluation system would never have been developed. But the moment he called me to identify that track after everyone else got it wrong, I knew that he was the best tracker in the group. I immediately made him part of the evaluation, asking him to help me conduct the assessment. From that day on, Wilson, together with the far-sighted support and encouragement of Juan Pinto (who later became a senior tracker), was part of the tracker evaluation process. Together, we developed and refined it over the next ten years. I often relied on Wilson's local knowledge of the area and especially his phenomenal lion-tracking skills. It took me years to develop my own lion-tracking skills to the point where I could conduct a senior tracker evaluation without Wilson backing me up. In the Kalahari, I developed a similar relationship with master tracker Karel Kleinman (Vet Piet). The success of the tracker evaluation process does not depend on any one individual; it depends on the relationships developed within a community of trackers.

Over the years, we refined the evaluation process. I also found that conducting evaluations was the most effective way to develop my own tracking skills. Every time I went to a new nature reserve or national park, I had no idea who I would be evaluating. There is always the chance that the next master tracker could be in the group, so conducting an evaluation kept me on my toes. I had to learn humility to admit my mistakes when one of the trackers challenged me. The important thing to understand about the tracker evaluations is that it is not about how good you are as an individual. It is a critical peer-review process that develops the skills and expertise of all the trackers who participate.

As the initial evaluator, I acted as a catalyst, setting in motion a process that would give recognition to the skills and expertise of trackers. Once this process is running strong, I myself will no longer be needed.

We honor master trackers not because they are the best individual trackers but because of the contribution they have made developing the tracking expertise of others. The first three master tracker certificates were awarded at the same time to avoid the perception that any one tracker might be the best. And sharing our knowledge flows in two directions. During one evaluation in the Lowveld, Wilson and I found a track that neither of us could identify. Then one of the younger trackers, sitting quietly to one side watching what was going on, discovered that the tiny markings in the wet mud at the edge of a puddle were made by the jaws of a wasp collecting mud to build its nest. In this way, the tracker-evaluation process helps us all to discover more about tracking. Tracking can be infinitely complex in its subtlety and refinement. You can never learn everything there is to know about tracking. In this sense, no matter how many years you have been tracking, we are all just beginners.

—*L. L.*

OBJECTIVES

Over the last twenty years, traditional tracking skills in southern Africa have been lost at an alarming rate. The older generation of traditional trackers has grown old without receiving recognition for what they can do. Over the last fifteen years, some of the best trackers have passed away, their knowledge and skills irretrievably lost. Meanwhile, the younger generation has had no incentive to become expert trackers. Among hunter-gatherers, the bow and arrow has been abandoned as the use of dogs and horses was introduced. This has resulted in a sharp decline in tracking skills.

In national parks and the ecotourism industry, there has been a growing need to verify the abilities of rangers and trackers. Rangers are used to gather data for monitoring wildlife, and it is important to validate that the data they gather is accurate. In research projects, it is important to test the observer reliability of wildlife biologists (Evans et al. 2009). The CyberTracker Tracker Evaluation system pro-

Bushman hunters using CyberTracker software to record wildlife tracks and signs. ERIC VANDEVILLE/ROLEX AWARDS

vides a means to do this work, and has also proved to be a very efficient training tool (Wharton 2006).

The art of tracking should be recognized as a specialized profession. Trackers have had and should continue to develop larger roles in research, monitoring, ecotourism, antipoaching, and crime prevention in nature reserves and national parks. Creating employment opportunities for trackers provides economic benefits to local communities. The employment of trackers will also help to retain traditional skills that might otherwise be lost.

Expert trackers can give valuable assistance to researchers studying animal behavior. The employment of trackers in research requires the highest level of expertise in spoor interpretation. Tracker certificates will help validate data collected by trackers by providing an objective test of observer reliability.

In order to develop the art of tracking as a modern profession, very high standards need be maintained. Trackers are graded during an evaluation in order to determine their level of expertise so they can be promoted according to different salary scales. This provides an incentive for trackers to develop their skills.

An intensive evaluation covers the fundamental principles of tracking as well as the finer details and sophisticated aspects of tracking. This is done on an individual basis, depending on the level of each candidate. The evaluation is in the form of a practical field test. Rather than pointing out details, each individual is first asked to give his or her own interpretation. Mistakes are corrected and explained continuously during the evaluation. This process identifies the strengths and weaknesses of each candidate in order to develop the potential of each individual in accordance to his or her level of skill.

The apprentice tracker is given a percentage rating for the evaluation. The progress a tracker makes depends in large part on his or her incentive to practice. Someone who is not able to develop his or her own skills will never become an expert tracker. The evaluation is therefore intended to teach trackers how to teach themselves.

EVALUATION MODULES

When a tracker has developed the required level of expertise, he or she will be awarded a certificate. The tracker evaluation consists of two parallel modules: track and sign interpretation and trailing.

The following levels can be achieved via the outcome of an assessment. In the lower band: track and sign levels I, II, III, and IV; trailing levels I, II, III, and IV; and tracker levels I, II, III, and IV. In the upper band: track and sign specialist, trailing specialist, and senior tracker. For these levels, certificates are issued once the candidate has proved through an evaluation that he or she has the relevant expertise.

Track and Sign Interpretation Evaluation

In the track and sign interpretation evaluation, the candidate is awarded one (+) point for the correct interpretation of an easy spoor (a so-called "one-pointer") or three (xxx) points for a mistake on easy spoor. Two (++) points are awarded for the correct interpretation of a difficult spoor (a "two-pointer") or two (xx) points for a mistake.

Trackers circle up to discuss footprints during a tracker evaluation at Timbavati, South Africa. WILLIAM DOYLE

Three (+++) points are awarded for the correct interpretation of very difficult spoor (a "three-pointer") or one (x) point for a mistake. The total number of correct (+) points is then divided by the sum of all the correct (+) and wrong (x) points and expressed as a percentage.

"Easy spoor" are defined as spoor of a medium to large species that are clearly defined and therefore unmistakable. "Difficult spoor" include spoor of small species and spoor that are partially obliterated or indistinct due to soft sand or hard substrate. Difficult spoor require an ability to interpret the way the spoor were formed in difficult substrate and are therefore not easy to identify. "Very difficult spoor" include fractions of footprints and very indistinct spoor that require considerable experience to identify or are those of very rare animals in the area.

Some of the best trackers often get the very first question in an evaluation wrong because of nervousness, which is not a reflection on their knowledge. To give trackers the opportunity to gain confidence, the first three questions of an evaluation can be ignored.

Track and Sign I Certificate: The track and sign I candidate must be able to interpret the spoor of small to large animals and have a fair knowledge of animal behavior. To qualify for the track and sign I certificate, the candidate must score at least seventy percent on the track and sign interpretation evaluation for at least thirty-five spoor. The candidate will most likely not achieve this level without at least one year of experience in the field.

Track and Sign II Certificate: The track and sign II candidate must be able to interpret the spoor of small to large animals and have a good knowledge of animal behavior. To qualify for the track and sign II certificate, the candidate must score at least eighty percent on the track and sign interpretation evaluation for at least thirty-five signs. The candidate will most likely not achieve this level without at least two years' experience in the field.

Track and Sign III Certificate: The track and sign III candidate must be able to interpret the spoor of small to large animals and have a very good knowledge of animal behavior. To qualify for the

Evaluator Adriaan Louw explains the nuances of differentiating between antelope species during a Senior Tracking Evaluation in the Thornybush Game Reserve. ME

track and sign III certificate, the candidate must score ninety percent on the track and sign interpretation evaluation for at least thirty-five signs. The candidate will most likely not achieve this level without at least three years' experience in the field.

Track and Sign IV Certificate: The track and sign IV candidate must be able to interpret the spoor of small to large animals and have an excellent knowledge of animal behavior. To qualify for the track and sign IV certificate, the candidate must score one hundred percent on the track and sign interpretation evaluation for at least thirty-five signs. The candidate will most likely not achieve this level without at least four years' experience in the field. A track and sign IV certificate qualifies a candidate for a track and sign specialist evaluation and to train other trackers in track and sign interpretation.

Track and Sign Specialist Evaluation

The process during the track and sign specialist evaluation is identical to the described evaluations, except in the following ways: At least fifty very difficult spoor will be asked, with not more than ten difficult spoor. No easy spoor will be asked. In addition, seven extremely difficult spoor will be asked. No penalty is awarded for an incorrect answer on an extremely difficult spoor (a "3+ question"), but three correctly answered extremely difficult spoor will cancel the penalty of one incorrect spoor.

The track and sign specialist evaluation must be conducted by an evaluator and an external evaluator.

Track and Sign Specialist Certificate: The track and sign specialist must be able to interpret the spoor of all animals, including small species, and distinguish the spoor of male and female animals for larger species. He or she must have a very good knowledge of animal behavior. He or she must be able to make hypothetical-deductive interpretations of spoor. The track and sign specialist must score one hundred percent on the track and sign specialist evaluation for at least fifty very difficult signs. The track and sign interpretation evaluation for track and sign specialist should not only be more rigorous but also place greater emphasis on the interpretation of animal behavior from tracks and signs.

Trailing Evaluation

The trailing evaluation is done in varying terrain (easy, difficult, very difficult) on a human spoor (for trailing I) or an animal that is not easy to follow (such as a hoofed animal, rhino, lion, bear, or cougar). The minimum duration of a trail for evaluation purposes is thirty minutes but may extend several hours. Five aspects are evaluated.

Spoor Recognition: Spoor recognition is the ability of the tracker to recognize and follow spoor at a reasonably good rate. Indicators may include:

- Not looking down in front of feet but looking for signs five to ten yards ahead.
- Moving at a steady rate, not in stop-start manner.
- Recognizing signs in grass or hard substrate.
- Recognizing when there are no signs when no longer on trail.
- Ability to recognize signs after losing spoor.

Spoor Anticipation: Spoor anticipation is the ability of the tracker to anticipate where the animal was going and therefore where he or she will find the spoor further ahead. Indicators may include:

- Looking well ahead and reading the terrain to look for the most probable route.
- Interpreting behavior from tracks.
- Using knowledge of the terrain (water, dongas, clearings) to predict movements of an animal.
- Not overly cautious (too slow) or too confident (too fast).
- Anticipating where to find tracks after losing spoor.

Anticipation of Dangerous Situations: Anticipating dangerous situations is the ability of the tracker to read the terrain and be able to anticipate situations that may be dangerous. Indicators may include:

- Awareness of wind direction.
- Knowledge of behavior, e.g. animals resting at mid-day.
- Animal behavior indicating danger.
- Avoiding danger by leaving the spoor and picking it up further ahead.

- Determining the position of dangerous animals without putting himself or herself at risk.

Alertness: Alertness is the ability of the tracker to spot animals before they spot him or her. Indicators may include:

- Looking well ahead for signs of danger.
- Stopping to listen when necessary.
- Recognizing warning signs, alarm calls, and smells.
- Recognizing signs of other animals.
- Seeing the animal before it sees the tracker.

Stealth: Stealth is the ability to approach animals without being detected by them or being a disturbance in the bush. Indicators may include:

- Minimizing noise levels (walking, talking vs. hand signals, and so on).
- Low impact on other animals.
- Using cover to approach an animal and exiting.
- Appropriate proximity to animal (close enough to observe but not too close).
- Animal unaware of tracker.

In each of these aspects, the tracker will be given points from 0 to 10: Not Yet Competent (0 to 6 points); Fair (7 points); Good (8 points); Very Good (9 points); Excellent (10 points). The total number of points scored is expressed as a percentage for trailing. Depending on circumstances, some indicators may not be applicable. The total score would be divided by the number of aspects scored multiplied by ten to obtain a percentage.

It is easier to obtain realistic scores by deducting points for mistakes rather than awarding points for level of skill. Points deducted would give candidates an indication of how to improve their tracking skills.

Trailing I Certificate: The trailing I candidate must be a fair systematic tracker and be able to track humans or large animals. He or she must have a fair ability to judge the age of spoor. To qualify for the trailing I certificate, the candidate must score seventy percent on the trailing of a human or large mammal spoor. The candidate will most likely not achieve this level without at least one year of experience in the field.

Trailing II Certificate: The trailing II candidate must be a good systematic tracker and be able to track large animals. He or she must have a fair ability to judge the age of spoor. To qualify for the trailing II certificate, the candidate must score eighty percent on the trailing of a large mammal spoor. The candidate will most likely not achieve this level without at least two years' experience in the field.

Trailing III Certificate: The trailing III candidate must be a good systematic tracker and be able to track medium or large animals. He or she must have a fair ability to judge the age of spoor. To qualify for the trailing III certificate, the candidate must score ninety percent on the trailing of a medium or large mammal spoor. The candidate will most likely not achieve this level without at least three years' experience in the field.

Trailing IV Certificate: The trailing IV candidate must be a good systematic tracker and be able to track medium or large animals. He or she must have a fair ability to judge the age of spoor. To qualify for the trailing IV certificate, the candidate must obtain one hundred percent on the trailing of a medium or large mammal spoor. The candidate will most likely not achieve this level without at least four years' experience in the field. A trailing IV certificate qualifies a candidate to attend a trailing specialist evaluation and train other trackers on trailing.

Trailing Specialist Evaluation

The trailing specialist evaluation is done in varying terrain (easy, difficult, very difficult) on an animal that is difficult to follow (such as a leopard or lion in Africa or a bear or cougar in the U.S.). The same five aspects are evaluated as for the lower band.

The trailing specialist evaluation must be conducted by an evaluator and an external evaluator.

Trailing Specialist Certificate: The trailing specialist must be a good speculative tracker. This includes the ability to predict where spoor will be found beyond the immediate area—beyond the range of spoor anticipation in the immediate vicinity ahead of the tracker.

The candidate must be good at judging the age of spoor and able to detect signs of stress or the location of carcasses from spoor. The trailing specialist must score one hundred percent on the trailing of a difficult animal spoor (such as a leopard, lion, or black bear spoor in moderate to difficult terrain or a hoofed animal in extremely difficult terrain).

Tracker Certificates

To qualify for tracker level I, the candidate must have both track and sign level I and trailing level I. To qualify for tracker level II, the candidate must have both track and sign level II and trailing level II. To qualify for tracker level III, the candidate must have both track and sign level III and trailing level III. To qualify for tracker level IV, the candidate must have both track and sign level IV and trailing level IV. To qualify for senior tracker, the candidate must have both track and

Kirrie Tieties is awarded a tracker I certificate in the Kgalagadi Transfrontier Park, South Africa, in 2003. She was the first woman to participate in the process; since then, dozens of women have been certified in both North America and Africa. ME

sign specialist and trailing specialist. For example, if the candidate has track and sign level III and trailing level I, he or she would qualify for tracker level I.

The tracker I must be able to interpret the spoor of small to large animals and have a fair knowledge of animal behavior. He or she must be a fair systematic tracker and be able to track humans or large mammals. He or she must have a fair ability to judge the age of spoor. The tracker I will be qualified to be employed in ecotourism and antipoaching activities.

The tracker II must be able to interpret the spoor of small to large animals and have a fair knowledge of animal behavior. He or she must be able to make empirical inductive-deductive interpretation of spoor and be a good systematic tracker. He or she must be able to track large animals. He or she must have a fair ability to judge the age of spoor. The tracker will be qualified to be employed in eco-tourism and antipoaching activities.

The tracker III must be able to interpret the spoor of small to large animals and have a fair knowledge of animal behavior. He or she must be able to make empirical inductive-deductive interpretation of spoor and be a good systematic tracker. He or she must be able to track medium to large animals. He or she must have a fair ability to judge the age of spoor. The tracker will be qualified to be employed in ecotourism, antipoaching, and wildlife research activities.

The tracker IV would be strongly encouraged to attend a senior tracker evaluation. His or her skill set will be similar to that of a senior tracker, but he or she will need to take the more rigorous field test to be sure.

The Senior Tracker

The senior tracker certificate is the highest certificate that can be earned by means of a practical evaluation. The qualities that characterize the senior tracker are well-defined and testable. The senior tracker evaluation aims to test practical skills to their limit. Tracks and signs tested include a wide range of species, and the individual tracks might be very subtle and difficult to interpret. As a practical evaluation, it places the candidate in a real-world situation that cannot be tested in a classroom on the basis of bookwork.

The senior tracker evaluation is very rigorous, testing not only skill and knowledge but also concentration, which is important in tracking in difficult circumstances. Because so much is at stake with each and every question, with little room for error, candidates often

_____

has been evaluated in

The Art of Tracking

at

_____

Senior Tracker

Evaluator _____

External Evaluator _____ Date _____

According to standards set by

CyberTracker Conservation and Louis Liebenberg

www.cybertracker.org
www.wildlifetrackers.com

Senior tracker certificate.

find it quite intimidating; some literally shake with nerves. The psychological pressure, however, tests the ability to deal with the most difficult situations trackers can find themselves in. Things do not always go according to plan. When tracking lion and something goes wrong, the tracker must have the presence of mind to deal with the situation.

The senior evaluation also offers the best trackers an opportunity to test and improve their skills through peer review. When working in isolation, it is difficult to get an objective measure of whether or not your skills are improving. Interacting with other trackers and engaging in critical debate are vital in developing the higher levels of tracking.

Evaluators also benefit from interaction with those they test, since they expose themselves to criticism if they make mistakes. Because the evaluator works with a group of trackers, it increases the chances that one of them will point out a mistake. Being tested helps you maintain perspective and humility. Conducting tracker evaluations may well be among the best ways to improve tracking skills. Conducting senior evaluations on a regular basis exposes the evaluator to the best trackers, thereby improving and refining the skills of the evaluator as well.

SAFETY

If the candidate does anything that endangers his or her own life or the life of someone else, the evaluator will terminate the evaluation and fail the tracker without further scoring, irrespective of the tracker's earlier performance.

I arrived late in the evening at Phinda Private Game Reserve. After a five-star meal and hot shower, I went to bed, exhausted after the long trip. I woke early the next morning with the dawn chorus all around me. The rooms at Forest Lodge are spacious wood-and-glass structures inside the forest. It was late September, and spring was in the air. Some of the bird calls were familiar, but most of them were completely new to my ears.

Phinda is situated in northern Zulu Land and provides protection to some of the last patches of dry sand forest remaining in South Africa.

Seth Vorster met me for coffee on the deck of the lodge. Growing up in an English home in KwaZulu Natal, with a great love for wildlife, he learned to speak Zulu fluently. He was the resident trainer at the lodge.

We met the group of trackers, climbed onto the game-drive vehicle, and headed out with me in the tracker seat. I wanted to get away from the activity at the lodge before we did the pre-evaluation brief. As we drove deeper into the forest, I couldn't help wondering when and how they would test me. Although Zulus are very friendly people, they are not quick to accept strangers.

I signaled to Seth to pull over, dropped off the vehicle, and positioned myself so I could see all of the trackers where they were sitting on the game viewer. I asked if they all could understand English, and two or three of them indicated that they were not fluent. I asked who they wanted as an interpreter, and Seth was nominated. I told them that although I could understand a bit of Zulu, I was not capable of holding a conversation in it. As this was the first CyberTracker evaluation ever in Zulu Land, I explained a bit of the history of the process, how it would be structured, and what we were going to do over the next few days. I explained to them that it was not an English language test but a tracking test, so that if they were not sure of the English name of an animal, they should use the Zulu name.

I gave them the opportunity to ask questions. A big man with a deep voice in the last row of seats spoke in Zulu. Seth looked up at Mandlakayise with surprise. He translated:

"So tell me, if you cannot speak Zulu how can we give you the answers in Zulu?"

"If I am not sure of the Zulu word you give me, I will make sure I get it translated into English," I replied.

The answer seemed to have satisfied Mandlakayise, or at least for the time being. Mandlakayise Jobe, also known as Petros, was a tall, well-built man with a big untidy beard and a very intense intimidating stare. When he spoke, there was silence among the other trackers.

We started with the track and sign interpretation component. The sixth or seventh question of the morning was the track of a slender mongoose. Most of the trackers gave the correct answer, but a few, including Petros, called it a genet. It was his first mistake of the morning.

As I knelt down to explain the differences between the two species, I noted that Petros was not huddling around the track like the others. He was standing half behind me, with an intense look on his face. I had circled the perfectly preserved front and hind foot tracks of the animal; it was a straightforward discussion and all were happy. Petros spoke only Zulu. During the rest of the morning, he made two more mistakes.

We headed back to the lodge for lunch. Groups of people were sitting in the staff canteen, some talking shop, but most just enjoying the break. Seth and I were sitting outside when another tall Zulu walked past and with a very loud and deep voice asked Petros something. Everybody in the canteen went quiet. All the eyes were fixed on Petros. His reply, also in Zulu, was quieter. Some laughed, but the conversation in general was more subdued after that. I realized that every now and then eyes were staring at me. I asked Seth about it, and he replied that he would explain it later.

We carried on with the evaluation during the afternoon. Petros made another mistake or two. As we arrived back to the lodge at last light, Petros climbed off the vehicle and walked straight to me. He shook my hand and in perfect English said, "Thank you, sir, I learned a lot today. Sleep well, and I'll see you tomorrow."

Genet tracks, front and hind. ME

The other trackers did the same. I was a little surprised but figured this was a Zulu custom. But I noticed that Seth had a surprised look on his face.

"Is this the normal Zulu way of doing things?" I asked.

"No. I have never seen that before," he replied.

He then explained that the man who had asked Petros the question in the canteen was the other opinion leader among the trackers. He was to be evaluated with the next group. Apparently, he asked Petros, "Are you giving this white man a lesson or two in tracking? I hope you are giving him plenty of stick." Petros had responded, "No. Every time I think I'm going to, I am wrong and he is right. The tracks don't lie."

I was amazed. The trackers at Phinda had accepted me and the CyberTracker process. I realized that was the test, and I had passed it. I was also humbled, as it was not me but the evaluation process that had passed. It is a system that is open, fair, and not intended to catch people out. It offers the opportunity to look into a mirror and reflect on what we know and what we might still need to practice to become better trackers.

—A. L.

Senior Tracker Specialist Certificate: The senior tracker specialist can specialize in a particular species. For example, a tracker might develop a highly specialized knowledge of leopard or rhino behavior but might not necessarily have the same level of knowledge of other species. He or she may, for example, be awarded a certificate as a senior tracker rhino specialist. The senior tracker specialist would be the ideal candidate for employment to collect scientific data on that particular animal.

The senior tracker specialist certificate can be awarded to a nominee who is a senior tracker by and at the discretion of the Cyber Tracker Evaluations Standards Committee. Only trackers who have made a particular meritorious contribution to the understanding of the behavior or ecology of a particular species, applying tracking skills, can be nominated. Nominations are made by the Evaluations Standards Committee, an evaluator, or external evaluator.

The Master Tracker

While the senior tracker must attain a high level of skill and refinement, the master tracker is the exceptional individual who represents the best qualities a tracker can develop over an extensive period of experience. The master tracker certificate is not something that can be earned by means of an evaluation. It is an honorary award that gives recognition for a lifetime of exceptional work. The qualities of the master tracker have been inspired by the best traditional hunters, who until recently hunted with the poison bow and arrow.

The master tracker must have an excellent knowledge of animal behavior and be capable of a highly refined interpretation of spoor in difficult terrain. He or she must have originality and creative insight and well-developed intuitive abilities. Qualities of the master tracker include exceptional skill, extensive knowledge and experience, wisdom, humility, creativity, insight, intuition, curiosity, and the ability to make an original contribution to our understanding of tracking and/or knowledge of animal behavior.

In traditional hunter-gatherer communities, the best hunters were expected to show humility. Individuals who boasted about their skills or achievements were quickly put in their place. This helped avoid jealousy in small communities that depended on social harmony. Humility in tracking is more than a social necessity. The master tracker has acquired the wisdom to know that even the best trackers can sometimes be wrong and make mistakes. Scientific understanding is fundamentally fallible. This is why Karl Popper (1959) proposed that falsifiability should be the criteria for whether a hypothesis is scientific or not. Master trackers are quick to admit their own mistakes or if they do not know something and recognize when someone else is right. A lack of humility results in an inability to recognize mistakes. Genuine humility means that the true master tracker would not expect to be awarded the master tracker certificate. Conversely, trackers who expect to be awarded the master tracker certificate have not acquired the wisdom and humility that is characteristic of the deserving honoree.

One of the characteristic qualities of the master tracker is an innate curiosity about the smallest details in nature:

*N**am!kabe once stopped me and pointed to a little bee: "This little bee feeds on that little flower," making a species-specific connection between an insect and a plant. One day, we found a concentration of fresh jackal tracks converging to a point, usually an indication that there is a carcass nearby. !Nate, Kayate, and Boroh//xao started looking for the carcass, hoping to get some meat, while !Nam!kabe stood to one side, silently watching the younger trackers scouring the area. After a while, when they found nothing and could not explain what had happened, !Nam!kabe pointed to some fresh dung. He explained that the jackals were feeding on dung beetles in the dung. Since they ate all the dung beetles, there was no evidence of what the jackals were feeding on.*

—L. L.

*W**ilson Masia would not only be familiar with the smallest animals found in the Thornybush Game Reserve but also animals whose tracks are hardly ever seen. One day he pointed out the indistinct tracks of the Burchell's coucal in coarse riverbed sand. This coucal is a bird that rarely comes down to the ground and so its tracks are rarely seen. But he knew them when he saw them. When conducting tracker evaluations, Vet Piet would point out faint half-moon shapes in the sand, the sign of a grasshopper buried beneath the soft sand that took flight, leaving behind wing-marks. These trackers' intimate knowledge of animal behavior allowed them to visualize what the animal was doing and predict its movements.*

Even when there are no apparent tracks to be seen, such as in thickly matted dry grass, Wilson Masia would read the terrain and, based on the movements of the lions we'd be tracking, point in the general direction where he predicted we would find more tracks. Often, when prompted, he would admit when he did not know where they were and was quick to concede when he had lost them. But usually his intuition would get us back to the trail, sometimes a considerable distance from the last known footprints. When tracking in difficult terrain, the master tracker relies extensively on his knowledge of the behavior of the animals within the context of the local terrain, making predictions that may seem uncanny to someone who does not understand speculative tracking.

Wilson Masia. ME

Vet Piet would glance at some lion tracks going up the side of a dune and immediately could see that a male lion got up, ran up the dune at a trot, stood still to listen to something in the distance, and then trotted off at a steady pace in a specific direction. He explained that the lion had heard a female in the distance, got up, and trotted higher up on the dune, where he stood still to listen, and then trotted off to go and find the female. Vet Piet then got into the vehicle and drove around some high dunes to where he predicted the lion had been going. He picked up the tracks and followed them to a spot where the lion had encountered two other lions, a male and a female. The tracks indicated that the two males had been fighting over the female, after which one of the males went off with the female. The original set of tracks indicated only a male lion that got up, stopped, and continued at a trot. But the way it moved showed that it was not hunting, since it was not trying to move stealthily. Rather, it stopped to listen to something at a distance that it found attractive and then moved off at a steady pace. The way it moved indicated that it was attracted to a female.

—L. L.

The master tracker also has an understanding of ecological processes in the landscape over a period of time. When I first started working with Karel (Pokkie) Benadie, he pointed out that you cannot, as one rhino specialist did, come to the Karoo National Park for only ten days in the year to study their feeding behavior. The black rhino feeds on different plants at different times of the year, depending on the availability during different seasons. His observation was subsequently put to the test when he and James (J. J.) Minye became the first trackers to use the CyberTracker Software to monitor rhino feeding behavior in Karoo. Their results were published in the journal *Pachyderm,* making them the first nonliterate trackers to coauthor a paper published in an academic journal based on data they gathered independently (Liebenberg et al. 1999).

The master tracker has a curiosity about nature that far exceeds practical needs. Perhaps the most striking example of knowledge for the sake of knowledge among /Gwi trackers is found in their detailed knowledge of ants. This knowledge far exceeds their practical hunting requirements. I interviewed Karoha, /Uase, and !Nate of Lone Tree in the central Kalaharui.

The /Gwi have eleven names for ants, including the velvet ant (a wingless wasp), and termites. In addition, some ants referred to by the generic name for ants are clearly recognized as different species and may be described as the "small red ants," the "small ants that live in trees," or "the red ant that bites you." Some ant names are arbitrary; other names describe a distinctive feature. !Gom means "to kneel," because when these ants sting, the poison is strong and acts quickly—and is so painful that one has to sit down on one's knees when stung. I A I aana means "your body shakes," because the poi-

son is so strong. !Uje I e I e means "to carry all things back to their home," because they are both predators and scavengers. I Ham means "sticky," because they have soft bodies.

Some ants are edible. I Da is described as "old people's rice," because it is a food reserved for old people. !Ole is used as a "salt" and is eaten with a plant food.

Much of the knowledge of ants is gained in a tracking context. This is illustrated by *Vet Piet.* ME

the /Gwi's detailed knowledge of the !uri ǀxam. In one instance, we noticed that for quite a large distance there were no tracks of steenbok or duiker. I then noticed large black ants swarming all over the ground, biting the trackers' feet. !Nate told me that this is why we have not seen any steenbok or duiker tracks. The ǀxam ants persist in biting them, forcing them to avoid the area. A short distance further, !Nate pointed at sign where a steenbok had been lying down, showing signs of agitation as it got up and turned around in circles, before eventually leaving the area. They further explained that during the rainy season, the ǀxam cut grass that they drag down their holes to store for the dry season. The ǀxam only eat grass and soft plants. During this period, they do not want any other animals to come near their holes. If a steenbok comes too near, they become aggressive and bite it. When they bite an animal, they cover the bite with a "liquid from the abdomen." They will attack steenbok, duiker, jackals, aardwolves, foxes, hares, spring hares, mongooses, and ground squirrels. The trackers also say that the spring hare eats too much grass, which is why the ants attack them. But they maintain that the aardvark does not eat the ǀxam ant.

A master tracker certificate can be awarded to a nominee who is a senior tracker by and at the discretion of the CyberTracker Evaluations Standards Committee. Only senior trackers who have made a particular meritorious contribution to the understanding of the art of tracking, or its sustainability, or the behavior, ecology or conservation of a particular species, applying tracking skills, can be nominated by members of the committee, an evaluator, or external evaluator. Under normal circumstances, a tracker cannot be nominated unless he or she has at least fifteen years' experience, including at least ten years as a senior tracker, unless he or she achieved the senior tracker certificate on the first try. In recognition of their traditional knowledge, exceptions may be made for traditional trackers in recent hunter-gatherer communities.

For more information on CyberTracker Tracker Evaluations, please refer to http://cybertracker.org or http://wildlifetrackers .com.

Acknowledgments

I would like to thank my late father and my mother, who provided me with financial support when I first started to explore tracking. Without their support, my research on tracking would not have been possible. I would also like to thank the Bushmen trackers who played such an important role in my own development: the late !Nam!kabe, !Nate, Kayate, the late Boroh//xao, Karoha and /Uase of Lone Tree in Botswana; /Ui /Ukxa, Dabe Dam, /Kun //Xari, the late !Nani //Kxao, and the late Ou //Ghau of Nyae Nyae in Namibia. In South Africa: Wilson Masia and Juan Pinto of Royal Malewane, who played a critical role in the development of tracker evaluations in South Africa; the late Karel (Vet Piet) Kleinman, formally of the Kgalagadi Transfrontier Park; the late Dawid Bester, formally of the West Coast National Park; Karel (Pokkie) Benadie, of the Karoo National Park; James (J. J.) Minye, of the Table Mountain National Park; Justin Steventon, whose role in developing the Cyber-Tracker software has also contributed to the development of modern tracking; Adriaan Louw, for the important role he has played in the growth of tracker evaluations in South Africa; Mark Elbroch, who initiated tracker evaluations in North America; Del Morris and Jon Young, who introduced me to North American trackers; Paul Rezendes, with whom I enjoyed many philosophical discussions; Jessica Perkins, one of my best tracker friends; and Glynis Humphrey, for her friendship and support.

—L. L.

I would like to thank all the fantastic trackers who have played a role in my development as a tracker and with whom I've shared many great experiences in the bush. I would also like to mention in particular master tracker Wilson Masia and the following senior trackers: Juan Pinto, Ian Thomas, J. J. Minye, Johnson Mhlanga, Ekson Ndlovu, Brian McConnell, Colin Patrick, and Robert Bryden. Also, track and sign specialists Mark Stavrakis and Lee Guteridge and trailing specialist Alan Yeowart. Then there is Amos Mhlongo, who passed away before he could be evaluated; Callie Roos, who shares the OnTrack experience and the trail of Life with me; my wife and soul-mate, Karin, who shares my love for tracking and creation; my parents, Andre and Marietjie Louw, who allowed me to pursue my dreams; and Karin's parents, Gert and Adeline Mare, for their support.

I would also like to thank coauthors Louis Liebenberg, who with his CyberTracker Evaluation process not only aided me in my tracking abilities but also helped shape my career, and Mark Elbroch, for making me part of this project.

—A. L.

First and foremost, I would like to thank Louis Liebenberg, for his invitation to visit Africa, and the opportunities to immerse in the CyberTracker Evaluation system and meet so many amazing people. Louis provided me with shelter, acted as a guide on countless adventures, and continues to provide me with friendship and creative and intellectual discourse. The evaluation process provided me the first honest feedback on my strengths and weaknesses with regards to tracking and has consequently made me a better tracker. Numerous fantastic trackers in Africa have role-modeled competent tracking in the field for me, and so many welcomed me into their homes and communities. They include Alex Van den Heever; Renias Mhlongo and Elmon Mhlongo at Londolozi; Juan Pinto and Wilson Masia at Royal Malewane; Johnson Mhlanga and Ekson Ndlovu at Singita LeBombo; the late Karel (Vet Piet) Kleinman and David Kruiper in the southern Kalahari; !Nate, Karoha, and Kwassi in the central Kalahari; Ian Thomas; and Adriaan Louw.

In North America, numerous people have stimulated my tracking skills. Foremost among them is Paul Rezendes, who supported and encouraged me even when I struggled through the transition from young adult to man. Numerous others support me continuously, and a special thanks to all of them: Fred Vanderbeck, Nancy Birtwell, Andrea and Keith Badger, Kurt and Susie Rinehart, Mike Pewtherer, Jonathan Talbot, Mike Kresky, Jacob Katz, Kendra Johnson, Bjorn Erickson, Lisa, Heiko Wittmer, George Leoniak, Casey McFarland, and Jonah Evans.

A special thanks to Brian McConnell, senior tracker in the U.S., for his contribution to this project, and to Kurt Rinehart for his significant contributions to the Tracking Notes for elk and moose.

—M. E.

References

Apps, P. 1992. *Wild Ways: Field Guide to the Behaviour of Southern African Mammals.* Halfway House, South Africa: Southern Book Publishers (Pty) Ltd, 198 pp.

Bang, P., and P. Dahlstrom. 1972. *Collins Guide to Animal Tracks and Signs,* translated and adapted by G. Vevers, 1974. London: Collins, 240 pp.

Barnum, S., K. Rinehart, and M. Elbroch. 2007. Habitat, Highway Features, and Animal-Vehicle Collision Locations as Indicators of Wildlife Crossing Hotspots. In *Proceedings of the 2007 International Conference on Ecology and Transportation,* edited by C. Leroy Irwin, Debra Nelson, and K. P. McDermott. Raleigh, NC: Center for Transportation and the Environment, North Carolina State University, pp 511–518.

Begg, C. M., K. S. Begg, J. T. Du Toit, and M. G. L. Mills. 2003. Scent-marking behaviour of the honey badger, *Mellivora capensis* (Mustelidae) in the southern Kalahari. *Animal Behaviour* 66:917–929.

Beveridge, W. I. B. 1950. *The Art of Scientific Investigation.* New York: W. W. Norton, 178 pp.

Blurton Jones, N., and M. J. Konner. 1976. !Kung Knowledge of Animal Behaviour. In R. B. Lee and I. DeVore (eds.) *Kalahari Hunter-Gatherers.* Cambridge, MA: Harvard University Press, 431 pp.

Bryden, B. 2005. *A Game Ranger Remembers Jeppestown, South Africa.* Jonathan Ball Publishers (Pty) Ltd, 408 pp.

Elbroch, M. 2003. *Mammal Tracks and Sign: A Guide to North American Species.* Mechanicsburg, PA: Stackpole Books, 792 pp.

Elbroch, M. 2006. *Animal Skulls: A Guide to North American Species.* Mechanicsburg, PA: Stackpole Books, 740 pp.

Elbroch, M. and E. Marks. 2001. *Bird Tracks and Sign: A Guide to North American Species.* Mechanicsburg, PA: Stackpole Books, 464 pp.

Elbroch, M., and K. Rinehart. 2010. *Peterson Reference Guide: Mammal Behavior.* Boston: Houghton-Mifflin.

Estes, R. D. 1992. *The Behavior Guide to African Mammals: Including Hoofed Mammals, Carnivores, Primates.* Berkeley, CA: University of California Press, 660 pp.

Evans, J., C. Wharton, J. Packard, G. Caulkins, and M. Elbroch. 2009. Determining Observer Reliability in Counts of River Otter Tracks. *Journal of Wildlife Management* 73: 426–432.

Furstenburg, D. and W. van Hoven. 1994. Condensed tannin as anti-defoliate agent against browsing by giraffe *(Giraffa camelopardalis)* in the Kruger National Park. *Comparative Biochemistry and Physiology, Part A: Physiology,* Volume 107, Issue 2, February 1994, Pages 425–431.

Grainger, D. H. 1967. *Don't Die in the Bundu.* Cape Town: Howard Timmins, 172 pp.

Hay, L., and W. Van Hoven. 1988. Tannins and digestibility in the steenbok *(Raphicerus campestris). Comparative Biochemistry and Physiology, Part A: Physiology* Volume 91, Issue 3, 1988, Pages 509–511.

Hildebrand, M. and G. Goslow. 2001. *Analysis of Vertebrate Structure.* Wiley Publishers, 660 pp.

Hurry, M., and D. Broadley. 1990. *Fitzsimons' Snakes of Southern Africa Parklands.* South Africa: Jonathan Ball & Ad. Donker Publishers.

Laughlin, W. S. 1968. Hunting: An Integrating Biobehavior System and Its Evolutionary Importance. In R. B. Lee and I. DeVore (eds.) *Man the Hunter.* Chicago: Aldine.

Lee, R. B. 1979. *The !Kung San. Men, Women and Work in a Foraging Society.* Cambridge: Cambridge University Press, 526 pp.

Lees, D., J. Ferguson, and M. Lawrence. 2003. *Tracks and Signs of Birds of Britain and Europe.* Cambridge: A&C Black Publishers, 336 pp.

Lehmkuhl, J. F., C. A. Hansen, and K. Sloan. 1994. Elk Pellet-Group Decomposition and Detectability in Coastal Forests of Washington. *Journal of Wildlife Management:* 664–669.

Liebenberg, L. 1990. *The Art of Tracking: The Origin of Science.* Cape Town: David Philip, 192 pp.

Liebenberg, L., L. Steventon, K. Benadie, and J. Minye. 1999. Rhino Tracking in the Karoo National Park. *Pachyderm* Number 27: 59-61.

Liebenberg, L. 2006. Persistence hunting by modern hunter-gatherers. *Current Anthropology* 47: 1017–1025.

Louw, A. 1992–1996. *Veldwagters Dagboeke Nasionale Krugerwildtuin.* Suid Afrika: (ongepubliseerde interne verslae)

Lyell, D. D. 1929. *The Hunting and Spoor of Central African Game.* Seeley, Service.

Marsh, B. (date unknown) *U 2 Can WRITE A BOOK!* Cape Town: Laser Facilities.

Marshall, L. 1976. *The !Kung of Nyae Nyae.* Cambridge, MA: Harvard University Press, 403 pp.

Massei, G., P. Bacon, and P. V. Genov. 1998. Fallow Deer and Wild Boar Pellet Group Disappearance in a Mediterranean Area. *Journal of Wildlife Management* 62: 1086–1094.

McBride, C. 1977. *The White Lions of Timbavati.* Johannesburg: Ernest Stanton (Publishers), 220 pp.

Palgrave, K. 1983. *Trees of Southern Africa.* Cape Town: C. Struik (Pty) Ltd.

Pienaar, U. de V. 1990. *Neem Uit die Verlede Pretoria.* Suid Afrika: Nasionale Parkeraad.

Popper, K. R. 1959. *The Logic of Scientific Discovery.* London: Hutchinson, 544 pp.

Prugh, L. R., and C. J. Krebs. 2004. Snowshoe Hare Pellet-Decay Rates and Aging in Different Habitats. *Wildlife Society Bulletin* 32: 386–393.

Rezendes, P. 1999. *Tracking and the Art of Seeing: How to Read Animal Tracks and Sign.* New York: Harper Collins Reference, 336 pp.

Robbins, R. 1977. *Mantracking.* California: Distributed by *Search and Rescue* Magazine.

Roderigues, J. 2003. *Die Veldwagters vertel verder: 'n Bundel ware bosverhale wat die hare laat rys Gezina.* Suid Afrika: J. A. Roderigues.

Silberbauer, G. B. 1965. Report to the Government of Bechuanaland on the Bushman Survey. Gaberones: Bechuanaland Government.

Silberbauer, G. B. 1981. *Hunter and Habitat in the Central Kalahari Desert.* Cambridge: Cambridge University Press, 388 pp.

Sinclair, I., P. Hockey, and W. Tarboton. 2002. *Sasol Birds of Southern Africa: The Region's Most Comprehensively Illustrated Guide.* Cape Town: Struik Publishers, 448 pp.

Skinner, J., and R. Smithers. 1990. *The Mammals of the Southern African Subregion.* Pretoria: University of Pretoria, 872 pp.

Smithers, R. H. N. 1983. *The Mammals of the Southern African Subregion.* Pretoria: University of Pretoria, 736 pp.

Stander, P., and Ghau, Tsisaba, Oma and Ui. 1997. Tracking and the interpretation of spoor: a scientifically sound method in ecology. *Journal of Zoology,* London 242:329–341.

Stuart, C., and T. Stuart. 2003. *A Field Guide to the Tracks and Signs of Southern and East African Wildlife.* Johannesburg: Struik Publishers, 310 pp.

Van Hoven, W. 1984. Tannins and digestibility in greater kudu. *Canadian Journal of Animal Science* 64: 177–178

Van Hoven, W. 1985. The tree's secret weapon. *South African Panorama* 30(3), 34–37.

Van Hoven, W. 1991. Mortalities in Kudu *(Tragelaphus strepsiceros)* populations related to chemical defence of trees. *Revue de Zoologie Africaine* 105, 141–145.

Van Oudtshoorn, F. 1991. *Gids tot Grasse van Suid Afrika.* Arcadia, Suid Afrika: Briza Publikasies Bk.

van Vliet, N., R. Nasi, and J. P. Lumaret. 2009. Factors influencing duiker dung decay in north-east Gabon: are dung beetles hiding duikers? *African Journal of Ecology* 47: 40–47

Wharton, C. A. 2006. Are We Gathering Reliable Data? The Need for Measuring Observer Skill in Wildlife Monitoring. Texas A&M University: MS Thesis, 52 pp.

Williams, R. 1976. The Art of Tracking. In *Wild Rhodesia,* No. 10 and 11.

Wynne-Jones, A. 1980. *Hunting.* Johannesburg: Macmillan South Africa, 180 pp.

Young, J., and T. Morgan. 2007. *Animal Tracking Basics.* Mechanicsburg, PA: Stackpole Books, 298 pp.

Zuercher, G. L., P. S. Gipson, and G. C. Stewart. 2003. Identification of Carnivore Feces by Local Peoples and Molecular Analyses. *Wildlife Society Bulletin,* Vol. 31, No. 4: 961–970

Index

About the Authors

Louis Liebenberg is the managing director of CyberTracker Conservation, an associate of the Anthropology Department at Harvard University, and author of *The Art of Tracking: The Origin of Science* and *A Field Guide to the Animal Tracks of South Africa.* His work, including field research with !Xo and /Gwi trackers of the central Kalahari and published papers in *Current Anthropology* and *The Journal of Human Evolution,* has earned him the aureate 1998 Rolex Award for Enterprise. An honorary member of the Field Guides Association of Southern Africa, he inititated tracker evaluations there in 1994.

Adriaan Louw is one of the leading trainers of ecotourism guides in South Africa. He began his career in nature conservation in 1989 in the Kruger National Park, first as a researcher, later as a wilderness trails ranger. In 2003, he qualified as a CyberTracker senior tracker and evaluator and earned the title Scout from the Field Guides Association of Southern Africa, which he has chaired. He is also a professional member of the Game Rangers' Association of Africa and the International Society of Professional Trackers. He cofacilitates leadership development in corporate groups using tracking as a metaphor.

Mark Elbroch was awarded a senior tracker evaluator certificate in 2005 and is the initial evaluator for CyberTracker tracking evaluations in North America. He is the author of *Animal Skulls: A Guide to North American Species* and *Mammal Tracks and Sign: A Guide to North*

American Species and coauthor of *Bird Tracks and Sign: A Guide to North American Species, Peterson's Field Guide to Animal Tracks: Third Edition,* and *Peterson's Reference Guide to Mammal Behavior.* He is currently studying cougars in northern California and southern Chile and working toward a doctorate in ecology at the University of California, Davis.